Introduction to Music

About the Author

Hugh M. Miller received his B.A. from the University of Oregon and his M.A. and Ph.D. from Harvard University. From 1947 to 1973, he was Professor of Music, and from 1947 to 1957 he was Chairman of the Department of Music, at the University of New Mexico. During 1958, he was Fulbright Lecturer at Auckland University, New Zealand, and during the academic year 1965–66 he was exchange professor of music at the University of Hawaii. In addition to having many articles published and belonging to a number of professional associations, Dr. Miller is a popular lecturer on music. He is the author also of *History of Music,* a companion Barnes & Noble Outline.

INTRODUCTION TO

MUSIC

A Guide to Good Listening

SECOND EDITION

by Hugh M. Miller

Professor Emeritus of Music
University of New Mexico

BARNES & NOBLE BOOKS
A DIVISION OF HARPER & ROW, PUBLISHERS
New York, Cambridge, Philadelphia,
San Francisco, London, Mexico City,
São Paulo, Sydney

Second edition, published 1978
ISBN: 0-06-460177-3

87 88 89 90   20 19 18 17 16 15 14 13 12 11

To Louise, Marilyn, and Peggy

Contents

Part One: Introduction

Appreciation of Music. Agents of Musical Art: Human
Agents, Mechanical Agents. Types of Listening: Passive
Listening, Sensuous Listening, Emotional Listening,
Perceptive Listening, Attitudes Combined. How to De-
velop Perception in Listening: Attention, Repetition,
Familiarity, Background Knowledge, Participation,
Auditory and Visual Approaches. Obstacles to Appre-
ciation: Auditory Difficulties, Time Element, Prefer-
ences and Prejudices. *Recommended Listening.*

Part Two: The Basic Materials and Properties of Music

Properties of Tone: Pitch, Duration, Intensity, Quality.
Properties Combined. *Recommended Listening.*
Tempo: Degrees of Speed, Beats, Ritardando and Ac-
celerando. Meter. Rhythm: Accent, Duration, Character
of Rhythm. Time Elements Combined. *Recommended
Listening.*

Part Four: Principles of Musical Structure

Part Five: Categories of Music Literature

Preface to the Second Edition

Since this *Introduction to Music* was first published twenty years ago, its usefulness has been attested to by the impressive number of textbook adoptions it has had and by the number of copies sold, presently approaching the 350,000 mark.

This second edition retains the same basic approaches to the subject, and its objectives are the same. The organization is such that chapters may be studied in any order. Like the first edition, it adheres to clear and concise presentation of subject matter. The lists of recommended listening at the ends of chapters are retained, as is the index guide to music, to which new titles have been added.

In accordance with increasing interest in twentieth-century trends, some contemporary practices are included and explained: electronic mediums, serialism, and aleatory music. A new chapter on jazz has been added (Chapter 21). The chapter on folk music and nationalism (Chapter 23) has been expanded to include a related section on ethnic music. Although most books on music appreciation neglect the subject of humor in music, the author believes that it is an essential consideration in any study of music literature, and Chapter 26 is devoted to it.

The author wishes gratefully to acknowledge the many valuable suggestions made by students, other readers, and his editor. Over the years, their contributions to the effectiveness of this Outline have been significant.

It is the author's hope that this Outline will continue to inform, interest, and stimulate the musical public.

Preface

There is at the present time a widespread interest in listening to good music, and this interest continues to grow. Of even more significance is the current emphasis in the direction of intelligent, perceptive listening, as opposed to the idea, prevalent only a few years ago, that a popularized sugar-coating was the best method of presenting serious music. Today, students and amateur listeners are seeking something more from music than passive entertainment. They want not only a wider acquaintance with music, but also a deeper understanding of what they hear. The purpose of this Outline is to make these objectives more easily attainable.

This Outline is a summary of the subject material found in the most important textbooks. All recognized approaches to the subject are discussed. History and biography are fully explained in terms of their significance to the understanding of music literature, but these chapters contain little actual history and no biography, for those areas are given more adequate treatment in readily available sources other than books on appreciation.

To treat every composition discussed in all major textbooks is also beyond the scope of this Outline. For the purpose of illustration a few analyses are presented in the text, but the principles explained will be helpful in the study of any musical work.

The Outline is organized in five parts, comprising the major areas of music appreciation, so planned that they can be studied in any order. This method of organization also applies to individual chapters. Thus, one could begin with dance music (Part Four, Chapter 20), with mediums (Part Two, Chapters 9 and 10), or with elements of music (Part One, Chapters 2–7 in any order).

Considerable attention has been given to the listening lists at the end of every chapter, which are subdivided according to the topics discussed within the chapter. These lists are extensive, providing suggestions for representative materials to be selected from both large and small record libraries. They include almost all masterpieces mentioned in the standard texts, and more than are listed in any one text. An Index-Guide to Music indicates all chapters in which each item is listed. In this way a single composition may be heard from several points of view. For example, Bach's *Passacaglia and Fugue in C Minor* is referred to at the end of twelve separate chapters, and can be studied in terms of melody, rhythm, texture, medium, form, and other ways.

An added feature of the record listing in this Outline is "Twenty-five Basic Compositions" which are designated by asterisks in the chapter lists and by bold-faced type in the Index Guide to Music (see page 235). These twenty-five compositions, representing every major category of music literature and every approach to music appreciation, can be used as the core of the study. Every one of the twenty-five is a masterpiece in its own right. Most of them are familiar compositions. Each chapter contains several of these compositions, and each composition is listed in numerous chapters. The "Twenty-five Basic Compositions" are not selected with the intention of implying that these pieces are the greatest in all music literature to the exclusion of other works. A number of comparable lists can be compiled from the Index; many readers will undoubtedly wish to do this.

It is hoped that, being a synthesis of the best current books in this field and at the same time advancing certain original methods, this Outline will in many ways contribute to the true enjoyment of a great art by readers of all backgrounds and interests.

The author wishes to express his gratitude to those of his colleagues who have offered numerous helpful suggestions. Special thanks go to Professors Donald McRae and John Batcheller, both members of the University of New Mexico faculty, who read the entire manuscript and generously gave advice and friendly criticism. Mrs. Exine Anderson Bailey of the University of Oregon School of Music faculty helped to compile a list of songs and arias. There is no way of assessing the total contribution which the author's students have made over a period of years, but the guiding principle in the development of this Outline has evolved from working with them.

Twenty-five Basic Compositions

The following twenty-five basic compositions will be found in the chapter lists, indicated by asterisks, and in the Index-Guide to Music (pages 235–260), indicated by bold-faced type. They constitute a fundamental, representative music selection.

1. Bach. *Cantata No. 140; Wachet auf, ruft uns die Stimme*
2. Bach. *Passacaglia and Fugue in C Minor* (organ)
3. Bach. *Suite No. 3 in D Major for Orchestra*
4. Bartók. *Quartet No. 5* (strings)
5. Beethoven. *Symphony No. 5 in C Minor*
6. Bizet. *Carmen* (opera)
7. Brahms. *Symphony No. 3 in F Major*
8. Chopin. *Sonata No. 2 in B Flat Minor,* Op. 35 (piano)
9. Copland. *Music for the Theatre* (orchestra)
10. Debussy. *Prélude à l'Après-midi d'un Faune (Prelude to the Afternoon of a Faun,* symphonic poem)
11. Handel. *Messiah* (oratorio)
12. Haydn. *Quartet in E Flat Major,* Op. 33, No. 2 (strings)
13. Hindemith. *Sonata No. 3 for Piano*
14. Mendelssohn. *Concerto in E Minor for Violin and Orchestra*
15. Mozart. *Don Giovanni* (opera)
16. Mozart. *Symphony No. 40 in G Minor,* K. 550
17. Palestrina. *Missa Brevis (a cappella* choir)
18. Puccini. *La Bohème* (opera)
19. Ravel. *Boléro* (orchestra)
20. Schubert. *Die Winterreise (The Winter Journey,* a song cycle)
21. Schumann. *Fantasiestücke (Fantasy Pieces,* piano)
22. R. Strauss. *Till Eulenspiegel* (symphonic poem)
23. Stravinsky. *Petrouchka* (ballet suite for orchestra)
24. Tchaikovsky. *Nutcracker Suite* (orchestra)
25. Wagner. *Tristan and Isolde* (opera)

PART ONE

Introduction

1. Introduction

Give a moment of reflection to the idea that your life is made up of many kinds of experiences. Some experiences have been agreeable, others unpleasant; some have been profound, others have left little imprint; some have been valuable while others have contributed no enrichment. Human experience is, of course, infinitely diversified, and no two people have exactly the same experience. Yet there are many kinds of experience which people have in common. Music is one of these. The fact that musical experience is inevitable and immediately accessible suggests the possibility that music is a valuable source of numerous benefits for all mankind.

If you realize the potential significance of music in your life, you will be eager to make that experience more meaningful. This chapter lays the groundwork so that we can start from the same point and proceed toward the same goal.

APPRECIATION OF MUSIC

The appreciation of music may be defined as *the acquired ability to listen to music intelligently*. Although people have different aptitudes in their musical perceptiveness, no one is born with this ability; it is acquired. Conscious effort is at all times necessary in the exercise of intelligent listening. We will be concerned, therefore, with the means by which you can acquire the ability to listen intelligently.

Enjoyment and appreciation are related terms, but they are not synonymous. It is quite possible to enjoy music—that is, to receive pleasure from it—without understanding it or really appreciating it. It is also possible to understand the technicalities of a musical composition without full enjoyment. However, remember that to obtain the greatest enjoyment from music you must have some understanding of it, and that no matter how sublime an experience a musical performance proves to be for you, any additional understanding which you can bring to the music will enhance your ultimate pleasure.

AGENTS OF MUSICAL ART

Before continuing our general discussion of music appreciation, it might be well to describe the human and mechanical agents that make music possible in the first place.

Human Agents. Three categories of participants are essential to the existence of music. These are: (1) the composer, (2) the performer, and (3) the listener.

COMPOSER. To use an analogy, we may liken the composer to the manufacturer. From the basic materials of music—those elements which we will consider in the main body of this book—the composer produces, by means of his creative impulse, his tonal imagination, and knowledge of his craft, the compositions which we hear.

PERFORMER. Extending the analogy, the performer is the merchant. The musical ideas which a composer writes down constitute a mere record of his creation. The music comes to life only when it is translated from musical symbols on paper to physical sound through the artistry of the performer.

LISTENER. The listener, of course, is the consumer. It is apparent that neither the composer nor the performer can exist without the listener; the art of the composer and the performer mean nothing without an audience. It is with you, the listener, that we are primarily concerned in this book.

Mechanical Agents. In addition to the human participants described above, there are certain other agents necessary to the production of music. Although human beings are involved here also, they play secondary roles in these cases.

MEDIUM. All music is performed by a mechanical or physical agent called *medium*. That is, it is played on an instrument or it is sung by the human voice. Mediums will be fully considered in Part Three of the present volume.

PUBLICATION. The publishing of music is an important step in the total process of musical production. It consists in printing and distributing the product of the composer.

Transmission. A relatively recent but exceedingly important agent of music, namely, the *transmission* of sound over vast areas by means of radio and television, has made music available to huge audiences immediately upon its performance. The phonograph (through disc, tape, and wire recording) and the movie sound track are mechanical agents by which music is made indirectly available to a large listening public; they are indirect

THE AGENTS OF MUSICAL ART

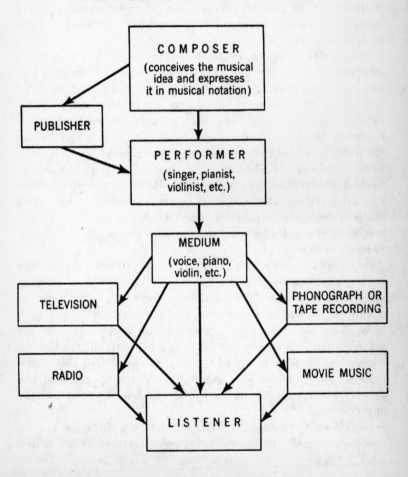

because there is a lapse of time between the original performance and the audience's reception of it.

This discussion of the agents of musical art should help you to realize the twofold importance of the position which you as a listener fill in the total picture of music. Not only is your position of appreciator important to your own cultural experience but it is vital to the total advancement of the art as well.

TYPES OF LISTENING

The extent to which you can attain true appreciation of music depends largely upon your attitudes as a listener. Four types of listening can be distinguished in musical experience (1) passive listening, (2) sensuous listening, (3) emotional listening, and (4) perceptive listening.

Passive Listening. In certain situations music is not intended to claim the full attention of the listener. Dinner music is performed not as concert music but as "background music" intended to enhance the pleasure of dining and conversation. A good share of the music on the movie sound track is intended merely to reinforce the moods of the visual scene. The marching band on the football field is more of a show than a concert. In such situations, the listener's relationship to music is a passive one. He *hears* the music but does not actually *listen* to it, and therefore real appreciation does not exist in such conditions. But when music is being performed for its own sake, the listener should realize that something more than a passive attitude is essential to its enjoyment.

Sensuous Listening. A greater degree of attention is required for sensuous listening. Here the listener obtains pleasure from an awareness of the sheer beauty of the sound. The clear tones of a flute or distant bells, the sonority of a cathedral organ or a large choir, the richness of a symphony orchestra—all these are sounds which can be enjoyed for themselves without the listener having any understanding of the music. The pleasurable sensations of musical tone have some value to the appreciator, but they do not constitute the sum total of what is meant by true appreciation.

Emotional Listening. With this attitude toward music the listener is concerned mainly with his own reactions to the music, with the emotions and moods which the music arouses. This is by no means an undesirable attitude. Music is capable of producing sublime experience in the listener. Emotional listening, however, is an inherent attitude toward music, and therefore it does not require intense concentration or training.

Perceptive Listening. Perceptive listening—as opposed to passive, sensuous, and emotional listening—requires concentration on the music itself and a sharp awareness of what is going on musically. It is this type of listening, more than any other, that brings true appreciation. Music appreciation in this sense means knowing what to listen for, understanding what is heard, and thereby having an objective basis for experiencing musical art.

Attitudes Combined. It is probably true that no one of these four attitudes toward music exists in a pure form with any individual. Certainly no one's total musical experience is exclusively passive, sensuous, emotional, or perceptive. It is likely that in hearing a long composition your attitude will shift from one to another type of listening. Of the four attitudes, however, it is perceptive listening which requires the most effort on the part of the listener, and it is this attitude by which your own capacity to appreciate music in the fullest sense of the word grows through experience.

HOW TO DEVELOP PERCEPTION IN LISTENING

The following paragraphs summarize certain prerequisites to the development of perceptive listening.

Attention. The first prerequisite to intelligent listening is attention. It is imperative that you learn to concentrate on the music. Because of previously acquired attitudes it is not easy to develop the habit of concentration. The sedative character of music, its emotional "pull," and the natural inclination of the listener to let the mind wander, are barriers to be overcome on the road to appreciation. Above all, avoid talking or listening to someone else talk while music you want to hear is being played.

Repetition. No one can hope to grasp in one hearing all that goes on in a piece of music. We do not retain auditory impressions as readily as visual impressions. Therefore, it is necessary for you to hear over and over a piece of music which you wish to understand. (This is a distinct advantage of recorded music.) There is virtually no limit to the benefits gained by repeated hearing; there is always something new to be heard in a given composition.

Familiarity. Repeated hearing of a piece of music leads to familiarity. One is naturally attracted to old friends and familiar faces. So it is in music. You naturally prefer, and perhaps get more out of, music that is familiar. But you should not rely entirely on familiar compositions to acquire appreciation, for that would deprive you of the satisfaction derived from exploring new music and broadening your musical horizons.

Background Knowledge. No small part of achieving an appreciation of music is that of acquiring a musical background. This means not only a general familiarity with a quantity of musical literature but also knowledge about that music. In this sense musical background can be divided into two types: (1) general background and (2) specific background.

GENERAL BACKGROUND. The sum total of your musical experience constitutes the general musical background. This includes such musical activities as going to concerts, listening to broadcasts and recordings, singing in choral groups, and playing in orchestras or bands. It also includes any formal study: music lessons, reading musical biography and history, and books about music theory (the mechanics of musical construction: harmony, counterpoint, form, orchestration).

SPECIFIC BACKGROUND. One builds an appreciation also by the study of individual works. What one is able to learn about a particular composition creates a specific background for that composition, and the background, in turn, enhances the appreciation of the music itself. This background information includes such items as the form of the composition, the outstanding characteristics of the music (its style), information about the composer, and pertinent information about the composition (when it was written, under what circumstances, for what purpose or function, and what ideas the composer had in mind). Some of this background is acquired through astute listening to the music, and some of it is acquired through reading about the music in various types of books about music.

Participation. Although active participation in the production or creation of music undoubtedly contributes to appreciation, it is not essential. You do not have to play in a symphony, sing in an opera, or conduct a chorus to appreciate symphonic, operatic, and choral music. Furthermore, the amateur is usually so preoccupied with the mechanics and technical difficulties of reading the score that he is hardly in a position to listen to the music itself.

Auditory and Visual Approaches. Two additional approaches contribute to the development of an appreciation of music: (1) the auditory approach and (2) the visual approach.

AUDITORY APPROACH. The auditory approach simply means studying music by listening to it. Because music is essentially an auditory art, i.e., one which exists in time through the medium of sound, the auditory approach is by far the more important in acquiring an appreciation of music.

VISUAL APPROACH. You can greatly increase your perceptiveness by developing the ability to follow a musical score while the music is being played. You will soon develop the ability to "see" things in the music which your ear did not catch.

A more common aspect of the visual approach is of less value. This is a natural inclination to watch the performer. (This applies, of course, only to concert and television; in radio performances and phonograph recording, the listener is not visually distracted by the performer.) The solo performer does not convey by his appearance and mannerisms much of the essence of the music. People enjoy watching the conductor of a symphony orchestra and the various actions of the musicians under his direction. But here also, little clue as to the real musical content is provided. Watching the performer is actually a visual distraction from the sound of the music.

OBSTACLES TO APPRECIATION

Facility in a discipline and mastery of a technique—and appreciation depends upon both of these—are not acquired easily. Although the difficulties encountered on the road to music appreciation are often overemphasized, it is well to be fully aware of them in advance.

Auditory Difficulties. As previously pointed out, we are less perceptive in our auditory sense than in our visual sense. Hence, perception of an art that is based on physical sound and its reception requires a special effort. Habits of passive listening must be overcome.

Even the simplest music presents to the ear a complex auditory stimulus. Intelligent, perceptive listening enables you to unravel the complex arrangements of the musical elements, to evaluate them in terms of context, and thus to understand the whole.

Time Element. Another aspect of auditory difficulty lies in the fact that music moves in time rather than in space. Any moment in music must be grasped "as it goes by" and must be related to all that has gone before and what is yet to come. When the performance of a piece is finished, one must see the whole composition in retrospect. In examining a picture, a piece of sculpture, or a building, you can stop to examine any detail, and you can see whole sections of the creation at a time. This is not possible in music. Thus, the development of musical memory is essential to appreciation.

Preferences and Prejudices. Perhaps the most serious obstacles to true appreciation are preferences and prejudices. We are all too prone to let our likes and dislikes determine or affect our musical experiences. We may like this composer and not that one; we may like piano music but not voice, symphonic music but not opera; we may prefer nineteenth-century music to "modern" music. If preferences and prejudices dominate the selection of music literature, or if prejudices against certain classes of music are allowed to affect our listening, then our appreciation of music can only be an exceedingly narrow one. True appreciation is actually not based on likes and dislikes. Its solid foundation is the intellectual acumen which can be brought to bear on a piece of music. And so, if you can abolish your aversions completely, you will be amazed at how much more music you can enjoy through understanding.

Recommended Listening*

Begin your development of perception by selecting from the following list of compositions a piece of music already familiar to you. Attain additional specific background by learning what you can about the composer and the composition beforehand. Develop your familiarity further by paying close attention to the music and by hearing it over again (if it is one of the shorter compositions). Study your own listening habits according to the categories discussed in this chapter. Also, see how many of the components of musical art you can identify. Do the same with two compositions you have not heard previously. Compare them; see in how many respects they differ. You will, of

---

* All compositions designated by asterisks in this and subsequent lists at ends of chapters are included in the "Twenty-five Basic Compositions" (see pp. xvi, xvii).

course, not be able to go as far with perception now as you will later on, but
you can make a beginning.

*Bach. *Cantata No. 140; Wachet auf, ruft uns die Stimme:* "Wachet auf"
(opening chorus); "Wachet auf" (final chorale, chorus)

*———. *Passacaglia and Fugue in C Minor* (organ)

*———. *Suite No. 3 in D Major for Orchestra:* "Air"

Barber. *Adagio for Strings*

*Bartók. *Quartet No. 5* (strings): any movement

Beethoven. *Sonata No. 23 in F Minor* (piano, "Appassionata")

*———. *Symphony No. 5 in C Minor:* any movement

*Bizet. *Carmen:* "Séguidille" ("Près des remparts")

Brahms. *Wiegenlied* (*Lullaby*)

Britten. *The Young Person's Guide to the Orchestra*

Byrd. *The Carman's Whistle* (harpsichord)

———. *Ergo Sum Panis Vivus* (motet for *a cappella* choir; No. 25 in *Masterpieces of Music before 1750*)

Chopin. *Nocturne in E Flat Major,* Op. 9, No. 2 (piano)

———. *Polonaise No. 6 in A Flat Major,* Op. 53 (piano)

———. *Prelude No. 1 in C Major* (piano)

———. *Waltz in D Flat Major,* Op. 64, No. 1 (piano, "Minute")

Copland. *Billy the Kid* (ballet, orchestral suite)

*———. *Music for the Theatre:* II ("Dance")

*Debussy. *Prélude à l'Après-midi d'un Faune* (*Prelude to the Afternoon of a
Faun,* symphonic poem)

Delibes. *Lakmé* (opera): "Bell Song"

Gabrieli. *Canzonas* (for brass choirs)

Grieg. *Peer Gynt Suite No. 1* (orchestra)

*Handel. *Messiah* (oratorio): "Hallelujah Chorus"

———. *Sonata No. 4 in D Major for Violin and Harpsichord* (or piano),
Op. 1 No. 13

*Haydn. *Quartet in E Flat Major,* Op. 33, No. 2 (strings): any movement

———.*Symphony No. 94 in G Major* ("Surprise"): II

Hindemith. *Mathis der Maler* (orchestra): any movement

*———. *Sonata No. 3 for Piano:* I

Mendelssohn. *A Midsummer Night's Dream* (orchestra): *Scherzo*

———. *Sonatina for Clarinet and Piano*

Mozart. *Concerto in E Flat Major for Piano and Orchestra,* K. 271: I

———. *Eine Kleine Nachtmusik* (*Serenade,* for small orchestra), K. 525

*———. *Symphony No. 40 in G Minor,* K. 550: any movement

*Puccini. *La Bohème* (opera): "Mi chiamano Mimi"

Rachmaninoff. *Isle of the Dead* (symphonic poem)

*Ravel. *Boléro* (orchestra)

Scarlatti, D. *Sonata in D Major* (harpsichord)

Schubert. *Der Erlkönig* (*The Erlking,* a song)

———. *Heidenröslein* (*Hedge Rose,* a song)

*———. *Die Winterreise* (*The Winter Journey*): any song from the cycle

*Schumann. *Fantasiestücke* (*Fantasy Pieces*), Op. 12 (piano): "Warum"
("Why"); "Grillen" ("Whims")

———. *Kinderscenen* (*Scenes of Childhood,* piano): No. 7, "Traumerei"
("Reverie")

Sibelius. *The Swan of Tuonela* (tone poem for orchestra)

*Strauss, R. *Till Eulenspiegel* (symphonic poem)

Stravinsky. *Apollon Musagète* (ballet, string orchestra)

————. *L'Histoire du Soldat* (*The Soldier's Tale*, ballet for narrator and 7 instruments)

*————. *Petrouchka* (ballet suite for orchestra)

*Tchaikovsky. *Nutcracker Suite* (orchestra): "Waltz of the Flowers"

————. *Symphony No. 5 in E Minor:* II

Vaughan Williams. *Fantasia on a Theme of Thomas Tallis* (string orchestra)

Verdi. *Aida* (opera): "Celeste Aida"; "Triumphal March"

*Wagner. *Tristan and Isolde* (opera): *Prelude to Act I*

PART TWO

The Basic Materials and Properties of Music

2. Tone

The appreciation of any art depends in part upon familiarity with the materials which the artist uses. The architect's plans call for the use of certain structural materials such as stone, wood, steel, glass, and concrete. The painter may employ such mediums as water color, oil, and pastel. The composer uses only one basic material, *tone,* which is the physical property of all music. Tone, as distinguished from common noise, is a sound produced by regular vibrations of air. Sounds made by wind, traffic, clapping hands, or breaking glass are merely noise because the vibrations thus set up are irregular. Sounds produced by whistling, humming, singing, plucking a taut string, or blowing into a brass or reed instrument are tones because the vibrations are regular.

Properties of Tone. All musical tone consists of four properties: (1) pitch, (2) duration, (3) intensity, and (4) quality.

PITCH. The term *pitch* refers to the highness or the lowness of a tonal sound. It is a physical principle that the faster the vibrations are, the higher the pitch will be, and the slower the vibrations, the lower the pitch. The human ear can detect pitches as low as 16 vibrations per second and as high as 20,000 vibrations per second. The tones of the piano, an instrument which includes almost all the pitches found in music, range from 30 to 4,000 vibrations per second.

DURATION. All musical tones are subject to variability in *duration;* that is, a tone may be sustained for varying lengths of time. This property of tone becomes one of the bases of *rhythm.* (See Chapter 3.)

INTENSITY. Tones may vary in their degree of loudness and soft-

15

ness. This property of tone is called *intensity*. Intensity is fundamental to musical rhythm (as *accent*), and it provides the basis for a separate musical element (*dynamics*). (See Chapter 7.)

QUALITY. All musical tone possesses characteristic *quality*. This property enables one to distinguish between the sound of a violin and, for example, that of a flute, piano, organ, or human voice. The quality of a tone is referred to as *timbre, tone quality,* or *tone color*.

Whereas every musical instrument has its own peculiar timbre, the human voice can produce a variety of tone qualities. These qualities are evident in the different vowel sounds of a song. Furthermore, each human voice has its own characteristic quality, so that it is easy to distinguish between the voices of different singers even when they sing at the same pitch. The property of timbre is fundamental to the study of musical mediums. (See Part Three.)

Properties Combined. The four properties of tone and the variety within each property combine to produce infinite possibilities in musical art. To summarize, musical tones may range from high to low, from long to short, from loud to soft, and they may possess different qualities or colors.

Recommended Listening

While listening to the tones of the melody in the following compositions, identify the different properties separately. Notice that some tones are higher than others (pitch), that some are longer than others (duration), that some are louder than others (intensity, accent), and that some differ from others in quality, especially in the orchestral pieces.

Albéniz. *Tango in D Major* (piano)
*Bach. *Cantata No. 140; Wachet auf ruft uns die Stimme:* "Zion hört die Wachter" (chorale, tenors in unison)
*————. *Suite No. 3 in D Major for Orchestra: Air*
Beethoven. *Concerto No. 5 in E Flat Major for Piano and Orchestra* ("Emperor"): I
*Bizet. *Carmen* (opera): "Séguidille" ("Près des remparts"); "Habanera" ("L'amour est un oiseau rebelle")
Brahms. *An die Nachtigal (To the Nightingale)*
————. *Dein blaues Auge (Thy Blue Eyes)*
*————. *Symphony No. 3 in F Major:* III
————. *Variations on a Theme by Haydn,* Op. 56a (orchestra): theme
————. *Ein Wanderer (A Wanderer)*
————. *Wiegenlied (Lullaby)*
Britten. *The Young Person's Guide to the Orchestra*
Chávez. *Sinfonia India* (orchestra): first theme
Chopin. *Waltz in C Sharp Minor* (piano)

*Debussy. *Prélude à l'Après-midi d'un Faune* (*Prelude to the Afternoon of a Faun;* symphonic poem)

Fauré. *Après un rêve* (*After a Dream*)

Handel. *Largo* (*Ombra mai fù,* from the opera *Xerxes*)

*————. *Messiah* (oratorio): "I know that my Redeemer liveth"

Kreisler. *Rondino on a Theme by Beethoven* (violin and piano)

Massenet. *Thaïs* (opera): "Méditation"

*Mendelssohn. *Concerto in E Minor for Violin and Orchestra:* II

Mozart. *Sonata in A Major,* K. 331 (piano): I (theme)

————. *Das Veilchen* (*The Violet*), K. 476

Prokofiev. *Concerto No. 2 in G Minor for Violin and Orchestra:* II

Puccini. *Madame Butterfly* (opera): "Un bel dì vedremo" ("One fine day")

*Ravel. *Boléro* (orchestra)

————. *Pavane pour une Infante Défunte* (*Pavane for a Dead Princess,* for piano or orchestra)

Saint–Saëns. *Carnival of the Animals* (orchestra or two pianos): "The Swan"

Schubert. *Heidenröslein* (*Hedge Rose,* a song)

————. *Die Schöne Müllerin* (*The Miller's Daughter,* a song cycle): "Das Wandern" ("The Wanderer")

————. "Serenade" ("Ständchen," from the song cycle *Swan Song;* No. 4)

*————. *Die Winterreise* (*The Winter Journey,* a song cycle): No. 1, "Good Night"

Schumann. *Dichterliebe* (song cycle): No. 7, "Ich grolle nicht" ("I shall not complain")

*————. *Fantasietücke* (*Fantasy Pieces*), Op. 12 (piano): No. 2, "Aufschwung" ("Soaring"); No. 3, "Warum" ("Why"); No. 4, "Grillen" ("Whims")

————. *Kinderscenen* (*Scenes of Childhood,* piano): No. 7, "Traumerei" ("Reverie")

Sibelius. *Valse Triste* (orchestra)

Strauss, J. *Blue Danube Waltz* (orchestra)

Tchaikovsky. *Concerto No. 1 in B Flat Minor for Piano and Orchestra:* I

Verdi. *Rigoletto* (opera): Quartet, "La donna è mobile"

Wagner. *Die Meistersinger* (opera): "Prize Song" (Morgenlicht leuchtend")

————. *Tannhäuser* (opera): "Song to the Evening Star" (O du mein holder Abendstern")

3. Time Elements

Music is an art which exists in time; its medium is physical sound, which is not stationary but moves within a span of time. Therefore, the time element is fundamental to music. In music this element is divided into three factors: (1) tempo, (2) meter, and (3) rhythm.

TEMPO

Tempo, an Italian word which literally means time, refers in music to speed. Music may move at a fast, moderate, or slow speed, and in varying degrees among these.

Degrees of Speed. Formerly it was customary to indicate tempo only by such general terms as *presto* (very fast), *allegro* (fast), *vivace* (lively), *moderato* (moderate speed), *andante* (moderately slow), *adagio* (slower than *andante*), *lento* (slow), *largo* (very slow), and so on. These terms are still employed,* but tempo is now more accurately indicated in musical scores by metronome designations, which show the number of beats per minute.

Beats. If we conceive of music as consisting of a series of regularly spaced *beats* or *pulses*, then the faster the tempo becomes, the more frequently the pulses occur; and the slower the tempo, the longer the time between the beats or pulses. This can be represented diagrammatically:

Fast tempo: ● ● ● ● ● ● ● ● ● ● ● ● ● ● ●
Slow tempo: ●　　　●　　　●　　　●　　　●

---

*To find the meaning of other tempo terms, consult a music dictionary such as *Harper's Dictionary of Music* or the *Pronouncing Pocket-Manual of Musical Terms.*

Ritardando and Accelerando. Music does not always move along at an even, regular pace. It may slow down or speed up. Gradual decrease of tempo is called *ritardando;* gradual increase of speed is called *accelerando.* When tempo becomes faster, the music is in general more tense and exciting; when the music slows down, relaxation usually takes place. A *ritardando* is often employed in the concluding measures of a composition.

METER ⇒ BEAT

If we listen to a series of regular pulses, as in the ticking of a clock, and think of them as being grouped in twos, threes, or fours, we are in this way measuring the pulses. This grouping in music is called *meter.* Meter can be represented diagrammatically:

Groups of 2
Groups of 3
Groups of 4
Groups of 6

In the written score, meter is indicated by *time signatures* which show the number of beats to a measure. Measures are indicated by means of vertical lines drawn through the staff (see p. 229 in Appendix I). In most music there is the same number of beats to each measure. We hear the meter of music because the first beat of each measure is given stress, or accent. We can distinguish a waltz from a march because we hear the grouping of three beats in the former and the grouping of four beats in the latter. The waltz beats are counted ONE–two–three, ONE–two–three; the beats of the march are counted ONE–two–three–four, ONE–two–three–four.

The most common meters are those with two beats to a measure (duple meter); three beats to a measure (triple meter); four beats to a measure (quadruple or common meter); and two or more groups of three to a measure (compound meters: ,   ,

Composers sometimes employ irregular metric schemes with five beats to a measure (e.g., the second movement of Tchaikovsky's *Sixth Symphony*), or with seven or ten beats to a measure. In the twentieth century, composers have experimented with metric effects in which the time signature is changed every few measures (e.g., in Stravinsky's *L'Histoire du Soldat*), and they have even combined several different meters simultaneously. These devices result in complex time factors in the music, which produce vastly interesting effects.

Some music, e.g., plainsong (see page 175), is nonmetric. This means that it has no fixed grouping of beats, no time signature, no measure bars. Some composers in the twentieth century have written music without time signatures or bar lines (e.g., in Charles Ives's *Concord Sonata*). One of the most pronounced characteristics of contemporary electronic music is that, with few exceptions, it is devoid of any metric scheme (see page 64).

The gestures which a symphony orchestra conductor makes with his baton indicate the beats of a measure. It will be noticed that the first beat of every measure is indicated by a downward motion of the conductor's right arm. This is the "downbeat," or the count of ONE in each measure, as in the waltz and march, previously mentioned.

RHYTHM

Rhythm is one of the most difficult musical concepts to define. There are various definitions for this term, but for our purposes we may consider rhythm to be the time element in music produced by two factors: (1) accent and (2) duration.

Accent. Stress or emphasis on a note to make it sound louder is called *accent*. Accent may conform to the metric plan by being placed on the first beat of each measure. Accent may also appear on other beats of a measure. Appearing on any note in a series of regularly recurring beats, it produces rhythm.

Duration. As already mentioned, musical tones vary in the length of time they are sustained. Any combination of notes of different durations produces rhythm: e.g., alternating long and short notes, two short notes and a long one, or a long note and several short ones. Thus, the Bach *Passacaglia in C Minor* is based on a theme consisting of alternating long and short notes (in triple meter). The "Butterfly Étude" of Chopin consists of a rhythmic pattern of one long and two short notes (in duple meter).

Since either accent or duration by itself can produce rhythm, it is axiomatic that both may be combined to produce rhythm. The following diagram of the first two measures of "Home on

the Range" illustrates the meter and both rhythmic factors: accent (heavy dots) and duration (spacing of dots).

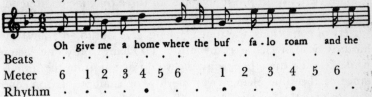

		Oh	give	me	a	home	where	the	buf	-	fa	-	lo	roam		and the
Beats		·	·	·	·		·		·		·		·	·		·
Meter	6	1	2	3	4	5	6		1	2		3		4	5	6
Rhythm	·	·	·	·		·		·		·		·		·		·

Character of Rhythm. Music has many rhythmic characteristics. Rhythm may be strong or weak. It may be very regular when
its patterns of accent and duration are repeated, or it may be
irregular when the accents and/or the duration are constantly
changing. Rhythm may be simple when these patterns consist
only of a few note values, or it may be complex when accent and
duration are highly diverse or when several rhythmic patterns
exist simultaneously.

A special kind of rhythm called *syncopation* occurs in relation
to meter when a note on a weak beat of a measure is accented
and held over into a strong beat (examples *a, b,* and *c* below).
Syncopation also occurs when a tone beginning after a beat is carried over into the next beat (example *d*). In these examples of
syncopated patterns, the underlined are normally strong beats.

TIME ELEMENTS COMBINED

Since virtually all music includes all three time factors (tempo, meter, and rhythm), and since each factor itself is subject to a variety of conditions, the time elements give rise to an almost infinite variety of character in music. To change only one factor while keeping the others constant would demonstrate the importance of the time elements to music. For example, if someone were to play the famous Chopin "Funeral March" at a fast tempo (while keeping the meter and rhythm the same), the very nature of the music would be destroyed. Or again, if one were to change the note values and accents which make up the rhythm of any well–known tune while retaining the same meter and tempo, the character of the music would be altered.

Recommended Listening

Each of the following compositions is selected for some special emphasis on one or more of the time elements. For each piece you listen to you should describe *all* the time factors by answering the following questions: is the tempo fast or slow; do you hear any *ritardando* or *accelerando;* is the meter duple, trible, quadruple, or compound; can you count the beats of every measure; is the rhythm strong or weak, regular or irregular, simple or complex? All the music, of course, can be enjoyed for its total effect, but you should concentrate primarily on the time elements in order to develop your perception of those particular elements in this assignment. It will not be necessary to hear every composition all the way through. Listen for a *ritardando* at the conclusion of a composition.

Tempo

Comparison of tempos:

*Chopin. *Sonata No. 2 in B Flat Minor,* Op. 35 (piano): III ("Funeral March"), IV

Mendelssohn. *A Midsummer Night's Dream* (orchestra): *Nocturne, Scherzo, Wedding March* (Also compare meters.)

*Mozart, *Don Giovanni* (opera): *Overture* (andante, molto allegro)

*———. *Symphony No. 40 in G Minor,* K. 550 (Compare tempos and meters of the four movements.)

Accelerando, ritardando:

Chopin. *Waltz in C Sharp Minor,* Op. 64, No. 2 (piano)

———. *Waltz in D Flat Major,* Op. 64, No. 1 (piano, "Minute")

Grieg. *Peer Gynt Suite No. 1* (orchestra): *In the Hall of the Mountain King*

Honegger. *Pacific 231* (orchestra)

Rossini. *The Barber of Seville* (opera): *Overture,* final section

*Tchaikovsky. *Nutcracker Suite* (orchestra): "Miniature Overture," "Waltz of the Flowers" (final section)

———. *Symphony No. 6 in B Minor* ("Pathétique"): I

Meter

Duple and quadruple:

Albéniz. *Tango in D Major* (piano)

Prokofiev. *Classical Symphony in D Major:* III (Gavotte)
———. *March*, from *Love of Three Oranges* (orchestra)
*Tchaikovsky. *Nutcracker Suite* (orchestra): "Chinese Dance," "Dance of the Reed Flutes," "Dance of the Sugar-Plum Fairy," "March," "Overture," "Russian Dance"

Triple:
*Bach. *Passacaglia and Fugue in C Minor* (organ): theme
Beethoven. *Sonata No. 12 in A Flat Major* (piano): I (theme), II
*Bizet. *Carmen* (opera): "Séguidille" ("Près des remparts")
Brahms. *Wiegenlied (Lullaby)*
Chopin. *Mazurka in A Flat Major*, Op. 59, No. 2 (piano)
———. *Waltz in D Flat Major*, Op. 64, No. 1 (piano, "Minute")
*Tchaikovsky. *Nutcracker Suite* (orchestra): "Arabian Dance," "Waltz of the Flowers"

Compound:
Bach. *Brandenburg Concerto No. 5 in D Major* (concerto grosso): III
———. *Partita No. 5 in G Major* (harpsichord or piano): *Gigue*
*Hindemith. *Sonata No. 3 for Piano:* I
Home on the Range
Rossini. *La Danza (Tarantella Napolitana)*

Irregular:
*Bartók. *Quartet No. 5* (strings): I, III
Chávez. *Sinfonia India* (orchestra)
*Copland. *Music for the Theatre* (orchestra): II (*Dance*)
Stravinsky. *L'Histoire du Soldat* (*The Soldier's Tale*, ballet for narrator and 7 instruments)
Tchaikovsky. *Symphony No. 6 in B Minor* ("Pathétique"): II (5/4 meter)
No meter: any example of Gregorian Chant (See list under this heading in Index-Guide to Music, page 245); also, electronic music listed on page 73.

Rhythm

Strong:
Bach. *Brandenburg Concerto No. 5 in D Major:* I, III
Dukas. *The Sorcerer's Apprentice* (orchestra)
Morley. *Now Is the Month of Maying* (madrigal, *a cappella*)

Weak:
*Debussy. *Prélude à l'Après-midi d'un faune* (*Prelude to the Afternoon of a Faun*, symphonic poem)
*Palestrina. *Missa Brevis* (*a cappella* choir): "Kyrie"
Victoria. *O Magnum Mysterium* (motet, *a cappella* choir)
———. *O Quam Gloriosum* (motet, *a cappella* choir)
*Wagner. *Tristan and Isolde* (opera): *Prelude to Act I*

Regular patterns:
Bach. *The Well-Tempered Clavier* (harpsichord or piano): Vol. I; *Prelude in C Major*
Chopin. *Étude in G Flat Major*, Op. 25, No. 9 ("Butterfly" Étude)
———. *Préludes*, Op. 28 (piano): *No. 1 in C Major; No 4 in E Minor; No. 7 in A Major, No. 12 in G Sharp Minor; No. 20 in C Minor*
Franck. *Symphony in D Minor:* II
*Ravel. *Boléro* (orchestra)

Irregular, complex:
*Bartók. *Quartet No. 5* (strings): III

*Copland. *Music for the Theatre* (orchestra): I, (*Prologue*); II (*Dance*)
Stravinsky. *L'Histoire du Soldat* (*The Soldier's Tale;* ballet for narrator and 7 instruments)
————. *Le Sacre du Printemps* (*The Rite of Spring,* a ballet)
Varèse. *Ionization* (percussion ensemble)

Syncopation:
Boccherini. *Quintet in E:* III (*Minuet*)
*Copland. *Music for the Theatre* (orchestra): I (*Prologue*); II (*Dance*)
Debussy. *Children's Corner Suite* (piano): *Golliwog's Cake-walk*
Gershwin. *Preludes* (3, piano)
Haydn. *Quartet in D Major,* Op. 20, No. 4 (strings): III
Milhaud. *Le Boeuf sur le Toit* (comic ballet): first theme
*Mozart. *Don Giovanni* (opera): *Overture* (first theme)
*————. *Symphony No. 40 in G Minor,* K. 550: III (first theme)
Saint-Saëns. *Introduction and Rondo Capriccioso* (violin and orchestra): first theme of the rondo
*Schumann. *Fantasiestücke* (*Fantasy Pieces*), Op. 12 (piano): No. 2, "Aufschwung" ("Soaring"); No. 4, "Grillen" ("Whims")
Stravinsky. *L'Histoire du Soldat* (*The Soldier's Tale*): final section

4. Melody

With a few minor exceptions, all music has melody. It is the element which we most easily and naturally remember in a composition.

Definition. Melody is a series of consecutive tones usually varying in pitch and duration. This basic definition is necessarily broad because of great diversity in the character of melodies. It should be added that, like words in a sentence, the tones of a melody form a complete musical idea. To grasp the idea of a sentence, you need to remember the words in their consecutive order; to perceive a melody, you need to remember the tones in *their* consecutive order.

You will frequently come across other terms that are used to indicate melody: *tune, air, theme,* and *melodic line.*

Properties. Melody has a number of properties which give it infinite variety. An understanding of these properties will help you listen perceptively to melody.

RHYTHM. As indicated in the preceding chapter, rhythm is one of the time elements. Whereas rhythm can exist without melody (as in drum beats, tapping a pencil on a desk, or clapping hands), melody cannot exist without rhythm. All melody has rhythm which affects its character, and melody is subject to all the properties discussed in Chapter 3.

DIMENSIONS. Melody has two dimensions: (1) *length* and (2) *range*. Some melodies are characterized by being short and fragmentary. Such melodic fragments are called *motives*. Other melodies are long and extended. Many melodies are not particularly outstanding in respect to length, being neither extremely short nor unusually long. The *range* of a melody is the pitch distance from its lowest to its highest tone. Some melodies are characteristically wide in range; other melodies may be narrow in range; and many melodies have only a moderate range.

REGISTER. Register is the relative highness or lowness of the aggregate tones of a melody. A melody may occupy a high, medium, or low register. In a given composition the same melody may shift from one register to another. In any case, register affects the quality of a melody.

DIRECTION. Melody moves in two directions of pitch: (1) upwards and (2) downwards. Either direction may predominate in a melody. Moreover, a melody may move rapidly or gradually in either direction: rapidly ascending, rapidly descending, gradually ascending, or gradually descending. A melody which remains at a given pitch level, moving neither up nor down any appreciable distance, is called a static melody. Usually a melodic line moves toward a high point which is the climax of the melody. A melodic climax may appear near the beginning, in the middle, or at the end of the line. Observation of melodic contours will greatly increase your perception and enjoyment of the world's great melodies.

PROGRESSION. Melodic progression refers to the intervals (pitch distance) between the tones as a melody moves from one tone to the next. A melody may move mostly stepwise; that is, it progresses to adjacent notes of the scale or adjacent keys of the piano (as in "America"). This is called *conjunct progression*. On the other hand, a melody may contain numerous prominent skips (as in "The Star–Spangled Banner"), in which case it is said to have *disjunct progression*. A melody often contains both conjunct and disjunct progression.

Properties Combined. The character of a given melody is the result of the combination of these properties. To see how they are at work in a given tune, let us examine the theme of Bach's *Passacaglia in C Minor.*

The rhythm consists of regular alternation between short and long notes. The range from the lowest tone (last note of the melody) to the highest tone (A♭, the sixth note of the melody)

is a distance of an octave and a sixth, a wide range. The length of the melody is eight measures, a moderate length. The register of the melody is generally low. (But if you listen to the *Passacaglia* all the way through, you will hear the theme appearing in an upper register.) The direction of the melody is upwards to the high note which is the climax of the melodic line in the third full measure; then it descends gradually to the low note at the end. The progression of the melody can be described as disjunct because of the numerous prominent skips. But notice that from the third to the sixth tones the melody moves in conjunct progression.

Function of Melody. Melody is usually thought of as the basis of musical composition. It is the musical idea around which a composition is constructed. This melodic idea or basic tune of the composition is called a *theme*. The theme is of paramount importance to a composition, and it provides one of the most important approaches to intelligent listening. The ability to recognize one or more themes when they recur in a composition is a big step toward full appreciation. The various ways in which a theme may be employed in a composition will be taken up later in the study of musical structure (Part Three).

Recommended Listening

The following music has been selected for diversity of melodic styles and for the prominence of one or more melodic traits. In each case listen to the melody several times, and focus your attention on the different melodic properties separately. Do not be distracted by harmony, accompaniments, tone color, or other musical elements. Make a check list of melodic properties to be observed, and determine for each melody which of the properties seem to be more prominent.

Length

Bach. *Italian Concerto* (harpsichord or piano): II (long line)
*———. *Suite No. 3 in D Major for Orchestra: Air* (long line)
———. *The Well-Tempered Clavier* (harpsichord or piano): Vol. I; *Fugue No. 1 in C Major:* theme (short line)
Handel. *Largo* (*Ombra mai fù*, from the opera *Xerxes*) (long line)
Schubert. "Liebesbotschaft" ("Love's Message"); No. 1 in song cycle *Schwanengesang* (*Swan Song*) (short lines)
*———. *Die Winterreise* (*The Winter Journey,* a song cycle): No. 24, "The Organ Grinder" (short lines)
*Strauss, R. *Till Eulenspiegel* (symphonic poem): theme of Till (short line)

Range

Wide:
*Beethoven. *Symphony No. 5 in C Minor:* III (*Scherzo*); first theme
Schumann. *Kinderscenen* (*Scenes of Childhood*): No. 7; **"Traumerei"** ("Reverie")

Strauss, R. *Ein Heldenleben* (*A Hero's Life,* symphonic poem): first theme
*Stravinsky. *Petrouchka* (ballet suite for orchestra): "Russian Dance," first theme
Narrow:
Gregorian Chant. *Antiphon: Miserere*
————. *Hymn: Virgo Dei Genetrix*
Sibelius. *Finlandia* (tone poem for orchestra): main theme

Register

*Haydn. *Quartet in E Flat Major,* Op. 33, No. 2 (strings): IV, opening theme (high register)
Hindemith. *Sonata for Two Flutes* (canonic): I (high)
*Mendelssohn. *Concerto in E Minor for Violin and Orchestra:* I, first theme (high register)
Stravinsky. *Firebird Suite* (orchestra): opening theme (low)
Tchaikovsky. *Symphony No. 6 in B Minor:* I, introduction (low)

Direction (at beginning)

*Bach. *Passacaglia and Fugue in C Minor* (organ) (up, then down; see page 24)
*Beethoven. *Symphony No. 5 in C Minor:* III, first theme (up)
Brahms. *Symphony No. 1 in C Minor:* I, introduction (up)
Chopin. *Ballade No. 3 in A Flat Major,* Op. 47 (piano): opening theme (up)
*Copland. *Music for the Theatre* (orchestra): IV (*Burlesque*), first theme (down)
*Puccini. *La Bohème* (opera): "Mi chiamano Mimi" (up); "Quando m'en vo'" (down)
————. *Madame Butterfly* (opera): "Un bel dì vedremo" ("One fine day") (down)
*Schubert. *Die Winterreise* (*The Winter Journey,* a song cycle): No. 1 (Good Night") (down)
*Stravinsky. *Petrouchka* (ballet suite for orchestra): "Charlatan's Solo" (flute) (up–down)
Tchaikovsky. *Symphony No. 6 in B Minor:* II, first theme (up)
Wagner. *Die Meistersinger* (opera): "Prize Song" ("Morgenlicht leuchtend") (down)

Progression

Bach. *Cantata No. 4, Christ lag in Todesbanden* (chorale) (conjunct)
*————. *Passacaglia and Fugue in C Minor* (organ): theme (disjunct)
Beethoven. *Sonata No. 7 in D Major* (piano): III (Trio of the Minuet) (disjunct)
*Brahms. *Symphony No. 3 in F Major:* I, opening theme (disjunct); IV, opening theme (conjunct)
Chopin. *Ballad No. 3 in A Flat Major,* Op. 47 (piano): first theme (conjunct); second theme (disjunct)
*Debussy. *Prélude à l'Après-midi d'un Faune* (*Prelude to the Afternoon of a Faun,* symphonic poem): opening theme (chromatic, conjunct)
Gregorian Chant. *Antiphon: Miserere* (conjunct)
————. *Hymn: Virgo Dei Genetrix* (conjunct)
*Mozart. *Symphony No. 40 in G Minor,* K. 550: I (see page 99) (themes *a* and *e* are mostly conjunct; themes *b* and *c* disjunct)
Ravel. *Le Tombeau de Couperin:* "Forlane," first theme (disjunct)
Schubert. *Der Erlkönig* (*The Erlking,* a song) (conjunct)

————. *Die Schöne Müllerin* (*The Miller's Daughter,* a song cycle): No. 1, "Das Wandern" ("The Wandered") (disjunct)

*Stravinsky. *Petrouchka* (ballet suite for orchestra) "Charlatan's Solo" (flute) (disjunct)

Wagner. *Die Meistersinger* (opera): "Prize Song" ("Morgenlicht leuchtend") (conjunct)

Webern. *Concerto for Nine Instruments* (disjunct)

5. Harmony and Tonality

Harmony and *tonality* are two of the most complex elements encountered in the study of music.

HARMONY

The professional student of music devotes at least two years to developing a knowledge of the basic principles of conventional harmony. A technical knowledge of harmony is not an absolute prerequisite to the enjoyment of music, but the amateur listener should be aware of harmony as an element and should be cognizant of certain basic principles, properties, and uses of this element.

Harmony as an element is more sophisticated than rhythm and melody. It is virtually nonexistent in primitive cultures. Moreover, it is an element which appeared comparatively late in the history of music (around the ninth century A.D.), and which was developed primarily in Western civilization.

Definition. Harmony is a musical element based on the simultaneous combination of tones, as distinguished from the consecutive tones of melody. Whereas melody is a horizontal concept, harmony is a vertical concept. This is illustrated in this harmonization of *Home on the Range,* in which the "horizontal" melody in the upper staff is accompanied by "vertical" groups of tones in the lower staff.

Chords. A group of three or more tones sounding together is called a chord. The underlying principles of harmony are (1) chord construction and (2) chord progression.

CHORD CONSTRUCTION. A few rudimentary principles will help you to understand the nature of conventional chord construc-

tion. The simplest chord is a *triad*, which consists of three tones. We can build a triad by selecting any tone and by adding two more tones above it on alternate degrees of the scale (on alternate white keys on the piano, on adjacent lines or adjacent spaces of the staff). For example, if we start with the tone C as *do,* the first scale degree, we get the triad *do–mi–sol,* 1–3–5, or using letter names C–E–G, as shown in the following example:

The principal triads are built on the first degree of the scale (I, called *tonic*), fourth scale degree (IV, called *subdominant*), and fifth scale degree (V, called *dominant*). As with many folk songs, *Home on the Range* (page 31) is harmonized entirely by these three chords. The addition of other triads (II, *supertonic,* III, *mediant;* VI, *submediant;* and VII, *leading tone*) makes a more interesting harmony.

Chords consisting of four different tones are called *seventh chords* (see the next to last chord in the harmonization of *Home on the Range,* page 31). Chords built with five different tones are called *ninth chords.*

The tones of any chord may be arranged in different orders, and they may be duplicated an octave above or below without changing the essential nature of the chord:

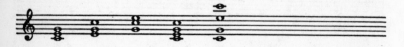

Building chords in thirds (i.e., on alternate scale degrees as described above) was the basis of all conventional harmony from about 1700 to 1900. In the twentieth century, composers have expanded chord vocabulary by additional means of construction for the sake of more colorful and complex effects.

CHORD PROGRESSION. Chords not only are constructed in an infinite variety of ways, but they also progress from one to another according to many different plans. The scheme by which chords change is called *chord progression*. The simple chord progression in the harmonization of *Home on the Range* (see page 31) is I–IV–I–V–I–IV, and so on.

Harmony, like melody, has rhythm. Chord changes may come at regular or irregular intervals of time, thus producing a *harmonic rhythm*. Harmonic rhythm may be independent of melodic rhythm. The harmonic rhythm of *Home on the Range* is one chord to a measure (except the 7th and 15th measures), whereas the melodic rhythm moves in faster and more varied note values. Harmonic rhythm is static when a given chord is maintained for a number of measures (as in Wagner's *Prelude to Das Rheingold*), or chord changes may come frequently, producing a more energetic and exciting effect (as in the conclusion of the first movement of Beethoven's *Sonata for Piano*, Op. 2, No. 1).

Consonance and Dissonance. One of the chief properties of harmony which relates both to chord construction and to chord progression involves the distinction between consonance and dissonance.

CONSONANCE. Certain combinations of tones produce a quality of repose or relaxation, which is called *consonance*. Conventionally, a composition ends with a consonant chord. (The final chord of *Home on the Range*, page 31, is a consonant chord.)

DISSONANCE. Certain other combinations of tones produce a quality of unrest or tension which is called *dissonance*. Since tension is normally followed by relaxation, dissonance normally resolves to consonance. (The next to last chord in *Home on the Range* is a dissonant chord which resolves to the final consonance.)

A more technical explanation of consonance and dissonance is that combinations of tones consisting entirely of consonant intervals are consonant chords; combinations which contain one or more dissonant intervals are dissonant chords. The larger the number of dissonant intervals a chord contains, the more dissonant is its quality. On page 34 is a list of consonant and dissonant intervals. (The letter "D" refers to dissonant intervals; "C" refers to consonant intervals.)

2nd	3rd	4th	5th	6th	7th	Octave	9th
D	C	C	C	C	D	C	D

Using this list of intervals, we can analyze any chord to determine its consonant or dissonant character.

The first chord, a triad, consists entirely of consonant intervals (two thirds and a fifth) and is therefore a consonant chord. The second chord contains one dissonant interval (a seventh) and is therefore a dissonant chord. The third chord contains three dissonant intervals (a second, a seventh, and a ninth) and is therefore a very dissonant chord. In varying degrees all seventh and ninth chords are dissonant.

General Harmonic Qualities. You may wish to pursue the study of harmony further in order to obtain a more comprehensive grasp of this element (see theory books listed on page 224). But even without acquiring a technical knowledge of harmonic functions, you can develop an awareness of certain general harmonic qualities which affect the overall style of music.

SIMPLE AND COMPLEX HARMONY. A simple harmony is one in which chords consist of few tones (simple harmonic construction) and few chord changes (simple harmonic progression). The harmonization of *Home on the Range* used in this chapter illustrates a simple harmony. A complex harmony consists of a large number of chord tones together with unconventional progressions. Rich musical sounds are frequently produced by means of a complex harmony. The harmony of the nineteenth century and especially of the twentieth century is characteristically complex.

In fact, the whole history of music shows an evolution from simple to more complex harmony.

CONSONANT AND DISSONANT HARMONY. A harmonic style may be predominantly dissonant (e.g., Schoenberg's *Quartet No. 4* for strings) or comparatively consonant (e.g., Haydn's *Quartet in C Major* for strings, Op. 76, No. 3, Second Movement). In general, the use of dissonance has increased gradually from earliest times to the present.

DIATONIC AND CHROMATIC HARMONY. Somewhat related to simple and complex harmony are the attributes of *diatonic* and *chromatic* harmony. A diatonic harmony is one in which there are very few altered tones (i.e., sharps, flats, and natural signs). *Home on the Range* has a diatonic harmony. A chromatic harmony is one in which there are numerous altered tones (e.g., Wagner's *Prelude* to *Tristan and Isolde*).

TONALITY

One of the properties of music which is closely related to and dependent upon harmony is tonality. It is an element which is elusive and difficult to define. At the same time it is an element which should be generally understood for a clear insight into music.

Definition. For our purposes we shall define tonality as a musical property which creates a sense of gravitation toward a key center. Most music is written in a key. That means all its harmony is related to a single tone known as the *tonic*. When the tonic is the tone C, the key is C, when the tonic is F, the key is F, and so forth. Thus we find compositions labeled "Sonata in D Major," "Symphony in E Minor," "Mass in B Minor," and so forth. Such music, whether in a major or a minor key, is tonal music.

Key Schemes. Compositions consisting of several large sections or movements usually have one or more of these movements in contrasting keys. Yet the composition as a whole conveys a strong sense of key feeling. Even with shorter pieces other keys may be introduced without disturbing the effect of the main key of the composition.

Modality. Music before about 1600 is based mainly upon scale systems known as modes. This music is called modal music. Since it, too, conveys some feeling of key center it is tonal music in the broad sense of the word. Modal harmonic effects have been employed by modern composers (e.g., Debussy's *La Cathédrale Engloutie,* Vaughan Williams' *Fantasy on a Theme of Thomas Tallis*).

Tonal Obscurity. In the nineteenth century composers began to experiment with tonal effects by using remotely related keys and prolonged modulations. (*Modulation* is the harmonic progression which changes the key feeling from one tonic to another.) The result of this experimentation was to obscure key feeling; it became harder to hear what key the music was in. Finally, in the twentieth century, some composers have arrived at an almost completely obscured tonality or have done away with key feeling altogether. These results are achieved in a number of ways.

POLYTONALITY. Music in which two or more keys are combined simultaneously in a single composition is *polytonal.*

MULTITONALITY. Another practice of the twentieth century is referred to as *multitonality* or *displaced tonality.* Here the composer rapidly shifts from one key center to another so that the entire key feeling is disturbed.

MICROTONALITY. Absence or obscurity of key feeling may be produced by dividing the octave into more than the customary twelve different tones. This is called *microtonality.* The use of microtones is a marked characteristic of much non-Western music (see page 170) and electronic music (see page 63 ff).

ATONALITY. The most pervasive trend in twentieth-century tonality is *atonality,* defined as the absence of key feeling or tonal center. The most important system in atonal music is called *dodecaphonic* or *twelve-tone.* Originated by Arnold Schoenberg in the 1920s, dodecaphonic music is based on a *tone row* created by arranging the twelve tones within an octave so as to avoid any implication of a tonic or key center. Melodic and harmonic factors are derived from the tone row, which can be manipulated in numerous ways with each repetition.

Attitude toward Tonality. Because our musical experience normally gives us more familiarity with tonal music than with atonal, polytonal, multitonal, or microtonal music, we are likely to react with less satisfaction to the latter kinds. Nevertheless, a flexible attitude toward tonality makes possible a clearer insight into, and apperception of, this "less–tonal" music and, hence, more enjoyment of it.

Recommended Listening

The following compositions have been selected to illustrate various harmonic styles and various types of tonality. With each composition that you listen to, you should concentrate on the particular characteristic which it illustrates.

Harmony

Diatonic:

Morley. *My Bonny Lass* (madrigal, *a cappella*)
————. *Now Is the Month of Maying* (madrigal, *a cappella*)
Mozart. *Sonata in A Major,* K. 331 (piano): I (theme)
*Palestrina. *Missa Brevis* (*a cappella* choir): "Kyrie"
Ravel. *Concerto in G Major for Piano and Orchestra:* II
————. *Pavane pour une Infante Défunte* (*Pavane for a Dead Princess,* for piano or orchestra)
Schubert. *Die Schöne Müllerin* (*The Miller's Daughter,* a song cycle): "Das Wandern" ("The Wanderer"); "Heidenröslein" ("Hedge Rose")

Chromatic:

Bach. *Mass in B Minor:* second "Kyrie," "Crucifixus"
Chopin. *Prélude No. 4 in E Minor,* Op. 28
Franck. *Symphonic Variations* (piano and orchestra)
Reger. *Chorale Preludes,* Op. 67 (organ)
*Wagner. *Tristan and Isolde* (opera): *Prelude to Act I*

Simple harmony:

Brahms. *Symphony No. 1 in C Minor:* IV, first theme (after introduction)
Haydn. *Quartet in C Major,* Op. 76, No. 3 ("Emperor," for strings): II (theme)
Ravel. See compositions listed under *Diatonic*
Schubert. See compositions listed under *Diatonic*

Complex harmony:

Franck. *Symphonic Variations* (piano and orchestra) (also chromatic)
Ravel. *La Valse* (orchestra)
*Stravinsky. *Petrouchka* (ballet suite for orchestra)
————. *Le Sacre du Printemps* (*The Rite of Spring,* a ballet)

Consonant harmony:

Morley. See madrigals listed under *Diatonic*
*Palestrina. *Missa Brevis* (*a cappella* choir): "Kyrie"
————. *Improperia* (motet, *a cappella*)

Dissonant harmony:

*Bartók. *Quartet No. 5* (strings)
*Copland. *Music for the Theatre* (orchestra)
Křenek. *Pieces for Piano*
Schoenberg. *Drei Klavierstücke* (Three Piano Pieces), Op. 11
————. *Quartet No. 4* (strings), Op. 37
Webern. *Concerto for Nine Instruments*

Harmonic rhythm:

Bach. *The Well-Tempered Clavier* (harpsichord or piano); Vol. I: *Prelude No. 1 in C Major* (regular, one harmony to a measure)

Beethoven. *Sonata No. 18 in E Flat Major* (piano): III (irregular, frequent changes)

Chopin. *Étude in G Flat Major,* Op. 25, No. 9 ("Butterfly" Étude; regular)

———. *Mazurka in A Flat Major,* Op. 59, No. 2 (irregular, frequent changes)

Wagner. *Das Rheingold* (opera): *Prelude to Act I* (static harmony)

Tonality

Key schemes:

Beethoven. *Sonata No. 20 in G Major* (piano): II (The keys are G, D, G, C, and G, all major keys.)

*Chopin. *Sonata No. 2 in B Flat Minor,* Op. 35 (piano): III ("Funeral March") (The principal keys are B Flat Minor, D Flat Major, and B Flat Minor.)

Haydn. *Quartet in C Major,* Op. 76, No. 3 ("Emperor," for strings): III (The minuet is in C Major, the trio in A Minor and A Major, and the minuet returns in C Major.)

*Schubert. *Die Winterreise* (*The Winter Journey,* a song cycle): No 7 ("On the Stream") (The keys are E Minor, E Major, E Minor.)

*Schumann. *Fantasiestücke* (*Fantasy Pieces*): No. 2, "Aufschwung" ("Soaring") (The keys are F Minor, A Flat Major, D Flat Major, F Minor, B Flat Major, F Minor, A Flat Major, and F Minor.)

Modern modality:

Debussy. *La Cathédrale Engloutie* (*The Sunken Cathedral,* piano)

Satie. *Gymnopédies,* Nos. 1, 2, 3 (piano)

Vaughan Williams. *Fantasia on a Theme of Thomas Tallis* (string orchestra)

Polytonality:

Casella. *Five Pieces for String Quartet:* III (*Valse Ridicule*)

*Copland. *Music for the Theatre* (orchestra)

Ives. *Sixty-Seventh Psalm* (8-part chorus, bitonal)

Milhaud. *Le Boeuf sur le Toit* (comic ballet)

———. *Saudades do Brazil* (suite for piano, arr. orchestra): No. 7, "Corcovado"

———. *Suite Provençale* (orchestra; beginning in Keys B Flat and F)

Prokofiev. *Lieutenant Kije Suite* (orchestra): Kije's Wedding, second theme

*Stravinsky. *Petrouchka* (ballet suite for orchestra): second theme ("Chez Petrouchka") (C Major and F Sharp Major chords appear simultaneously.)

Microtonality:

Hába. *Duo for Two Violins* (in *Columbia History of Music,* Vol. 5)

Atonality:

Berg. *Wozzeck* (atonal opera; also illustrates extreme dissonance)

Casella. *Five Pieces for String Quartet:* IV (*Notturna*)

Ruggles. *Men and Mountains* (orchestra)

Schoenberg. See compositions listed under *Dissonant harmony.*

Multitonality:

Prokofiev. *Concerto No. 3 in C Major for Piano and Orchestra:* II (Note the sudden shift of tonality between the theme stated by the orchestra and the first variation stated by the piano alone.)

———. *Lieutenant Kije Suite* (orchestra): "Kije's Wedding," first theme

6. Texture

In the weaving of fabrics the characteristic disposition or connection of threads is called *texture*. This term is now commonly borrowed in musical usage to refer to an important property of music. An analogy does exist between the warp and woof of fabrics and the vertical (harmonic) and horizontal (melodic) elements in music.

Definition. Musical texture is the characteristic disposition and relationship of melodic and harmonic factors in music.

Types of Texture. The relations between melodic and harmonic factors give rise to four distinct types of texture: (1) monophonic texture, (2) homophonic texture, (3) polyphonic texture, and (4) nonmelodic texture. In addition, certain aspects of harmony and timbre make possible another kind of texture called *sonority*.

MONOPHONIC TEXTURE. When music exists solely as a single melody with no accompaniment, the texture is *monophonic*. This term means literally a single sound, i.e., a single melodic line. Plainsong constitutes the largest body of monophonic music. Any instrument or voice performing a melody without an accompaniment is effecting a monophonic texture.

HOMOPHONIC TEXTURE. When a single melody is accompanied by subordinate harmonic material (i.e., chords) the texture is *homophonic*. The harmonization of *Home on the Range* (page 31) is a clear example of a homophonic texture. A folk song with guitar accompaniment is homophonic music. An operatic recitative in which the supporting material consists of a few isolated chords is purely homophonic.

POLYPHONIC TEXTURE. When two or more melodies of more or

less equal prominence are sounded simultaneously, the resulting texture is said to be *polyphonic*. The terms "polyphonic" and "contrapuntal" are nearly synonymous, as are the corresponding nouns "polyphony" and "counterpoint."

A number of musical forms are based on a polyphonic (or contrapuntal) texture: fugue, canon, motet, madrigal, chorale prelude, etc. (These forms will be taken up in Chapter 15.)

The three kinds of texture—monophonic, homophonic, and polyphonic—are illustrated in the examples below, in which the same melody is used successively in three kinds of texture.

NONMELODIC TEXTURE. Some music is constructed for special effects in which harmonic sounds obscure or partly exclude melodic content. This is a *nonmelodic texture*. It is not found in a great many musical compositions. Honegger's *Pacific 231,* Mossolov's *Iron Foundry,* and Varèse's *Ionization* are examples of almost entirely nonmelodic texture; in them, there is virtually no melodic content. Electronic music (see page 63 ff), which characteristically emphasizes sonorities above other considerations, is usually nonmelodic, or at least has minimal melodic content.

Sonority. Another attribute of texture, one which is based more on harmonic than melodic considerations, is its quality of richness or thinness. This quality, referred to as *sonority,* is determined by a number of factors.

Number of Parts. A polyphonic composition that consists of six or eight parts (i.e., separate simultaneous melodies) has a far richer sonority than one consisting of only two parts. Likewise, a homophonic composition with an elaborate accompaniment of full chords and many tones has a richer sound than one having an accompaniment of only a few tones. Because of the number of instruments which may be sounding simultaneously in different registers, the symphony orchestra has a richer sonority than the string quartet, which consists of only four instruments.

Spacing of Tones. When voice parts or the tones of a chord are closely spaced, the result is apt to be a thick texture; when tones are widely spaced, the texture is apt to be thin.

Register of Tones. A thin sonority is likely to result from music in which a high register predominates, and a thick sonority from music in which a bass register predominates.

Timbre. Tone quality, or *timbre,* also affects sonority. A quartet of flutes has a thinner sound than four horns playing exactly the same tones. An extreme contrast of textural sonority can be observed in comparing a flute solo with a full symphony orchestra sounding a complex chord. In the flute solo, we hear only a thin sound; in the symphonic chord, we hear a rich sound resulting from multiple timbres, a large number of tones, high and low registers, and a close spacing of tones throughout the entire orchestral register.

Combination of Textures. The two categories of texture—(1) its classification into monophonic, homophonic, polyphonic, and nonmelodic and (2) its sonority—operate independently of each other. That is to say, heavy and rich textures may be found in homophonic, polyphonic, and nonmelodic music (but not in monophonic music, which is always thin in texture); and light, thin textures exist in homophonic, polyphonic, and nonmelodic music (as well as in monophonic music).

A single composition does not necessarily remain consistently in only one kind of texture. The texture may shift from a rich, heavy sonority to a thin, clear one; moreover, it may change in any sequential order, from monophonic to homophonic, polyphonic, and nonmelodic. A good example is the last movement of Mozart's *String Quartet in G Major*, K. 387, which begins contrapuntally and with thin texture, but, in the 17th measure, abruptly becomes homophonic. Throughout the movement the textures and sonorities change frequently.

Recommended Listening

Monophonic texture:

Bach. *Partita No. 2 in D Minor for Unaccompanied Violin:* Gigue

*Debussy. *Prélude à l'Après-midi d'un Faune* (*Prelude to the Afternoon of a Faun*, symphonic poem): opening flute solo (followed by homophonic texture)

Gregorian Chant. (See listings under this title in the Index-Guide to Music, page 239.)

Sibelius. *Symphony No. 1 in E Minor: I* (introduction, clarinet solo)

*Stravinsky. *Petrouchka* (ballet suite for orchestra): "Charlatan's Solo" (flute unaccompanied)

Polyphonic texture:

Bach. *The Art of Fugue* (*Die Kunst der Fuge*)

*———. *Cantata No. 140; Wachet auf, ruft uns die Stimme:* "Wachet auf" (opening chorus); "Wenn kommst du" (duet for soprano and bass)

———. *Mass in B Minor:* "Dona Nobis Pacem," "Kyrie"

———. *Oregelbüchlein* (*Little Organ Book*, a set of chorale preludes)

*———. *Passacaglia and Fugue in C Minor* (organ)

———. *The Well-Tempered Clavier* (harpsichord or piano): any of the 48 fugues in Vol. I or II

———. *Two-Part Inventions* (harpsichord or piano)

Byrd. *Ergo Sum Panis Vivus* (motet for *a cappella* choir; No. 25 in *Masterpieces of Music before 1750*)

*Handel. *Messiah* (oratorio): "For unto us a Child," "And with His stripes"

Hindemith. *Sonata for Two Flutes* (canonic), Op. 21, No. 3

*———. *Sonata No. 3 for Piano:* IV

Lasso. *Tristis Est Anima Mea* (*Sad Is My Soul*, motet for *a cappella* choir; No. 23 in *Masterpieces of Music before 1750*)

*Palestrina. *Missa Brevis* (*a cappella* choir)

———. *Missa Papae Marcelli* (*a cappella* choir)

Victoria. *O Magnum Mysterium* (motet, *a cappella* choir)

———. *O Quam Gloriosum* (motet, *a cappella* choir)

Homophonic texture:

Chopin. *Nocturne in E Flat Major*, Op. 9, No. 2 (piano)

———. *Prélude in E Minor*, Op. 28, No. 4 (piano)

*———. *Sonata No. 2 in B Flat Minor*, Op. 35 (piano): III

Handel. *Largo* (*Ombra mai fù,* from the opera *Xerxes*)

Haydn. *Quartet in F Major,* Op. 3, No. 5 (strings): II

*Mendelssohn. *Concerto in E Minor for Violin and Orchestra:* II

Monteverdi. *Orfeo* (opera): Recitative: "Tu se' morta" (No. 31 in *Masterpieces of Music before 1750*)

*Puccini. *La Bohème* (opera): "Mi chiamano Mimi"

Saint–Saëns. *Carnival of the Animals* (orchestra or two pianos): "The Swan"

Satie. *Gymnopédies,* Nos. 1, 2, 3 (piano or orchestra)

Schubert. *Heidenröslein* (*Hedge Rose,* a song)

———. *Die Winterreise* (*The Winter Journey,* a song cycle): No. 1 ("Good Night")

*Schumann. *Fantasiestücke* (*Fantasy Pieces*), Op. 12 (piano): No. 2, "Aufschwung" ("Soaring")

*Tchaikovsky. *Nutcracker Suite* (orchestra): "Waltz of the Flowers"

Nonmelodic texture (or minimum melodic content):

Bach. *The Well-Tempered Clavier* (harpsichord or piano); Vol. I: *Prelude No. 1 in C Major* (The fugue which follows the prelude is polyphonic.)

Chopin. *Étude in C Major,* Op. 10, No. 1 (piano)

*———. *Sonata No. 2 in B Flat Minor,* Op. 35 (piano): IV

Honegger. *Pacific 231* (orchestra)

Mossolov. *Iron Foundry* (orchestra)

Varèse. *Ionization* (percussion ensemble)

See also list of electronic music, page 73.

Rich, heavy sonority:

Bach. *Mass in B Minor:* "Dona Nobis Pacem," "Sanctus"

———. *St. Matthew Passion:* "Wir setzen uns mit Thränen nieder" (finale for double chorus)

*Brahms. *Symphony No. 3 in F Major:* I (opening theme)

Chopin. *Étude in C Major,* Op. 10, No. 1 (piano)

Gabrieli. *Canzonas* (for brass choirs)

Rachmaininoff. *Isle of the Dead* (symphonic poem)

Vaughan Williams. *Fantasia on a Theme of Thomas Tallis* (string orchestra)

Thin, light sonority:

Bartók. *Duos for Two Violins* (24)

Couperin. *La Galante* (harpsichord; No. 40 in *Masterpieces of Music before 1750*)

Delibes. *Lakmé* (opera): "Bell Song"

Gounod. *Faust* (opera): "Jewel Song" ("Ah! Je ris")

Hindemith. *Sonata for Two Flutes* (*canonic*), Op. 21, No. 3

Landino. *Chi più le vuol sapere* (ballata; No. 14 in *Masterpieces of Music before 1750*)

Scarlatti, D. *Sonata in D Major* (harpsichord

Stravinsky. *L'Histoire du Soldat* (*The Soldier's Tale,* ballet for narrator and 7 instruments)

Variable texture:

Bach. *Toccata and Fugue in D Minor* (organ)

Bartók. *Quartet No. 5* (strings)

*Chopin. *Sonata No. 2 in B Flat Minor,* Op. 35 (piano) (Compare III, which is homophonic with rich sonority, and IV, which is mostly light and has a nonmelodic texture.)

Debussy. *La Mer* (suite for orchestra) (variety of sonorities)

Mozart. *Quartet No. 14 in G Major,* K. 387 (strings): IV (See page 42.)

*Ravel. *Boléro* (orchestra) (changing sonority)

7. Dynamics

Intensity is one of the properties of tone discussed in Chapter 2. When applied to a piece of music, rather than to a single tone, this property is referred to as *dynamics*. The term includes all degrees of loudness and softness and the processes involved in changing from one to the other.

Terminology. Certain Italian words are used to indicate dynamics. The most important are *forte* (loud), *piano* (soft), *fortissimo* (very loud), *pianissimo* (very soft), *mezzo forte* (moderately loud), and *mezzo piano* (moderately soft). The terms which mean a gradual change in the dynamic level are *crescendo* (becoming louder) and *diminuendo* (becoming softer).

Relative Values. Unlike tempo, which can be exactly determined by metronome indications, dynamics are only relative values. There is no absolute level for *piano* or *forte,* for example.

Intensity and Volume. Another term related to dynamics and perhaps more commonly used is *volume*. This term refers not only to the combined intensity of each tone, but also to the degree of loudness or softness produced by the number of separate tones sounding at the same time. For example, greater volume is produced by twenty violins playing the same tone *forte* than by a single violin playing that tone *forte*.

Expression. The element of dynamics is the most salient aspect of musical expression, which also includes nuances in tempo, phrasing, accent, and other factors. Dynamics contribute greatly to tensions in music. Generally, the louder the music is, the greater the tension becomes, and conversely, the softer the music the less the tension. Correspondingly, a *crescendo* causes increasing tension, whereas a *diminuendo* relaxes tension. (See also Chapter 30, under the heading "Dynamics.")

Recommended Listening

In listening to the following compositions, observe the various ways in which dynamics are employed: sometimes for abrupt contrast of loud to soft or soft to loud, sometimes gradually increasing or decreasing the dynamic level to augment or diminish the tension respectively.

Bach. *Brandenburg Concerto No. 5 in D Major* (concerto grosso): I (Note the contrast of volume between the sections for the entire orchestra and those for the solo instruments.)

*Bartók. *Quartet No. 5* (strings)

Beethoven. *Sonata No. 21 in C Major* (piano, "Waldstein"): I

———. *Sonata No. 23 in F Minor* (piano, "Appassionata"): I

Debussy. *Nocturnes* (3 pieces for orchestra): *Fêtes* (*Festivals*)

Franck. *Chorale No. 3 in A Minor* (organ)

Grieg. *Peer Gynt Suite No. 1* (orchestra): *In the Hall of the Mountain King*

*Haydn. *Quartet in E Flat Major,* Op. 33, No. 2 (strings): II

———. *Symphony No. 94 in G major* ("Surprise"): II (The "surprise" for which the symphony is named is a sudden *forte* chord in the second movement after a soft beginning.)

Honegger. *Pacific 231* (orchestra) (increase of volume and dynamics)

*Ravel. *Boléro* (orchestra) (gradual orchestral crescendo from beginning to end)

Rossini. *The Barber of Seville* (opera): *Overture,* closing section

Saint–Saëns. *Danse Macabre* (orchestra)

*Schubert. *Die Winterreise* (*The Winter Journey,* a song cycle): No 1 ("Good Night"); No. 5 ("The Linden Tree")

*Schumann. *Fantasiestücke* (*Fantasy Pieces*), Op. 12 (piano): No. 2, "Aufschwung" ("Soaring") (contrast and gradations of dynamic level)

*Tchaikovsky. *Nutcracker Suite* (orchestra): "Miniature Overture," "Waltz of the Flowers"

Wagner. *Lohengrin* (opera): *Prelude to Act I*

PART THREE

Musical Mediums

8. Definitions

Chapters 2 through 7 have dealt with the essential materials with which a composer creates music. We are now in a position to consider another element of music which is in a somewhat different category. This is *musical medium,* which we mentioned in the Introduction as an agent of musical art. This component is of immediate concern to the performer, but the composer, too, must be thoroughly acquainted with the special nature of the medium for which he is writing. You, as the listener, will derive greater pleasure from music if you become fully aware of the nature of the various mediums.

Medium. Medium in music is the intermediate agent between the composer's ideas on the printed page and their realization in actual musical sound (see chart on page 5). In other words, the performer translates the written symbols into physical tone through the *medium* of one or more instruments. In the case of vocal music, the singer is both performer and medium at the same time.

Medium and Timbre. You will recall that timbre (tone quality) is one of the four properties of tone (see Chapter 2). Every musical medium has its own distinctive quality of tone. You can already identify many of these: the tone quality of a piano, an organ, an orchestra, a band, a voice, a chorus, etc. Now you will be developing further your ability to identify certain timbres with certain mediums, an ability which enhances listening enjoyment.

Solo Mediums. When one performer on an instrument, or a single voice, is the principal medium of a composition, the music is said to be a solo. This is true even when a singer or an instrumentalist is accompanied by one or more performers. When only a single performer is required to play (or sing) a composition, the medium is more correctly referred to as unaccompanied solo.

Ensemble Mediums. When two or more performers are equally engaged in playing or singing a piece of music, the medium is called an *ensemble,* and the music is called *ensemble music.*

Recommended Listening

The music listed here will help to give you a more acute awareness of the difference between solo and ensemble mediums.

Solo mediums:

Bach. *Partita No. 2 in D Minor for Unaccompanied Violin*

————. *Toccata and Fugue in D Minor* (organ)

*Bizet. *Carmen* (opera): "Séguidille" ("Près des remparts")

*Handel. *Messiah* (oratorio): "I know that my Redeemer liveth"

Liszt. *Hungarian Rhapsody No. 2 in C Sharp Minor* (piano)

*Mendelssohn. *Concerto in E Minor for Violin and Orchestra:* II (Although the orchestra itself is an instrumental ensemble, it serves here primarily as an accompaniment to the solo violin.)

Schubert. *Heidenröslein* (*Hedge Rose,* a song)

*————. *Die Winterreise* (*The Winter Journey,* a song cycle): No. 1 ("Good Night")

Ensemble mediums:

Bach. *Mass in B Minor:* "Crucifixus," "Dona Nobis Pacem," "Kyrie"

Trouvère Song ("Or la Truix," unaccompanied)

*Beethoven. *Symphony No. 5 in C Minor*

Brahms. *Trio in E Flat Major* (piano, violin, horn)

Gregorian Chant. (Monophonic music sung in unison by a *chorus* is ensemble music; by a *single voice,* solo medium.)

*Handel. *Messiah* (oratorio): "For unto us a Child is born," "And with His stripes," "Hallelujah Chorus"

Hindemith. *Sonata for Two Flutes* (canonic), Op. 21, No. 3

Morley. *My Bonny Lass* (madrigal, *a cappella*)

————. *Now Is the Month of Maying* (madrigal, *a cappella*)

Mozart. *Quartet No. 14 in G Major* (strings), K. 387

*Palestrina. *Missa Brevis* (*a cappella* choir)

Stravinsky. *L'Histoire du Soldat* (*The Soldier's Tale,* ballet for narrator and 7 instruments)

————. *Octet for Wind Instruments*

9. Vocal Mediums

Vocal mediums comprise solos and ensembles.

Vocal Solo. A large share of the world's great music is composed for the solo singer, either with or without accompaniment. Such musical forms as the *aria, Lied, folk song, troubadour song,* and dramatic recitative are vocal solos.

Vocal Ensemble. When two or more voices are employed, the medium is called a *vocal ensemble.* It may consist of parts for two voices (vocal duet), three voices (trio), four voices (quartet), or more.

When an ensemble is made up of a large number of singers with more than one person taking a part, the medium is referred to as a *chorus.* A body of church singers is called a *choir.* A chorus or a choir may consist of male voices, female voices, or a combination of both (called a *mixed chorus*). When two complete choruses (or choirs) are employed, the medium is referred to as a *double chorus.* (The opening chorus of Bach's *St. Matthew Passion* is for double chorus.) The term *a cappella* refers to a chorus without instrumental accompaniment.

Vocal Registers. Voices differ considerably in range and register. The six classes of vocal register are (1) *soprano* (high-register female voice), (2) *mezzo–soprano* (medium–register female voice), (3) *alto* or *contralto* (low–register female voice), (4) *tenor* (high-register male voice), (5) *baritone* (medium–register male voice), and (6) *bass* (low–register male voice).

Vocal Qualities. In addition to these six vocal registers, voices are also classified according to certain styles of music for which they are specially qualified. The *coloratura soprano* can sing rapid runs, trills, and light ornaments. The *dramatic soprano*

and *dramatic tenor* have heavier voices and are capable of con-
veying intense emotions in dramatic situations. The *lyric soprano*
and *lyric tenor* have voices especially suited to sweet songlike
melody in which beauty of tone is the predominant quality.

Text and Language. Obviously, the greatest difference between
instrumental and vocal mediums is the ability of the latter to
convey ideas through words. Text and music have a close relationship in vocal compositions. The quality of language has a
profound effect upon the sound of vocal music. A song sung in
German sounds different from one sung in Italian.

Recommended Listening

Famous solo and ensemble compositions listed below will serve as a guide
to identification of various types of vocal mediums. They have been selected
from large vocal works (operas, oratorios, cantatas, etc.) rather than from the
literature of single solo songs because in the former the particular medium
remains constant, whereas in the latter the song may be performed by any
voice. For example, the "Bell Song" from *Lakmé* is invariably sung by a
coloratura soprano, whereas Schubert's "Heidenröslein" and Brahms's "Lullaby" are performed by voices of all registers: soprano, alto, tenor, baritone,
bass.

Record catalogues contain lists of albums of arias and songs by famous singers and indicate the voice register of each.

Vocal Solo

Coloratura soprano:
Delibes. *Lakmé* (opera): "Bell Song"
Donizetti. *Lucia di Lammermoor* (opera): "Mad Scene"
Gounod. *Faust* (opera): "Jewel Song" ("Ah! Je ris")
Handel. *Judas Maccabaeus* (oratorio): "Oh shall the lute and harp"
*———. *Messiah* (oratorio): "Rejoice greatly"
Mozart. *The Magic Flute* (opera): "Queen of the Night" aria
Rossini. *The Barber of Seville* (opera): "Una voce poco fa"
Thomas. *Mignon* (opera): "Je suis Titania"
Verdi. *Rigoletto* (opera): "Caro nome"
———. *La Traviata* (opera): "Ah, fors' è lui"

Dramatic soprano:
Gluck. *Alceste* (opera): "Divinités du Styx"
*Handel. *Messiah* (oratorio): "I know that my Redeemer liveth"
Mendelssohn. *Elijah* (oratorio): "Hear ye Israel"
Mozart. *The Marriage of Figaro* (opera): "Dove sono"
Puccini. *Madame Butterfly* (opera): "Un bel dì vedremo" ("One fine day")
Verdi. *Aida* (opera): "O patria mia"
———. *La Forza del Destino* (opera): "Pace, pace"
Wagner. *Götterdämmerung* (*The Twilight of the Gods,* opera): "Brünn-
hilde's Immolation"
———. *Tannhäuser* (opera): "Dich teure Halle"

Lyric soprano:
*Bizet. *Carmen* (opera): "Je dis que rien"

Brahms. *A German Requiem (Ein deutches Requiem)*: "Ye that now are sorrowful" ("Ihr habt nun Traurigkeit")

*Handel. *Messiah* (oratorio): "Come unto Him" (follows alto aria, "He shall feed His flock," same melody)

Haydn. *The Creation* (oratorio): "And God said" (recitative), "With verdure clad" (aria)

*Mozart. *Don Giovanni* (opera): "Non mi dir"

————. *The Magic Flute* (opera): "Ach ich fühl's"

*Puccini. *La Bohème* (opera): "Mi chiamano Mimì," "Quando m'en vo' "

————. *Manon Lescaut* (opera): "In quelle trine morbide"

Villa-Lobos. *Bachianas Brasileiras No. 5* (8 cellos and soprano)

Mezzo-soprano:

*Bizet. *Carmen* (opera): "Habanera" ("L'amour est un oiseau rebelle"), "Séguidille" ("Près des remparts")

Donizetti. *La Favorita* (opera): "O mio Fernando"

Mahler. *Kindertotenlieder (Songs of Children's Death,* a cycle of 5 songs with orchestra)

Mendelssohn. *Elijah* (oratorio): "O rest in the Lord"

Meyerbeer. *Le Prophète* (opera): "Ah, mon fils"

Offenbach. *Tales of Hoffmann* (opera): "Barcarolle" ("Belle Nuit")

Saint–Saëns. *Samson and Dalila* (opera): "Amour viens aider," "Mon coeur s'ouvre à ta voix"

Tchaikovsky. *Jeanne d'Arc* (opera): "Adieu forêts"

Thomas. *Mignon* (opera): "Connais-tu le pays"

Verdi. *Don Carlo* (opera): "O Don fatale"

Alto (contralto)

Bach. *St. Matthew Passion:* "Herzliebster Jesu," "Buss und Reu"

Brahms. *Alto Rhapsody* (alto, male chorus, and orchestra)

Gluck. *Orfeo ed Euridice* (opera): "Che faro senza Euridice"

*Handel. *Messiah* (oratorio): "Then shall the eyes of the blind" (recitative), "He shall feed His flock"

Mozart. *Ombra Felice,* K. 255 (recitative and aria)

Ponchielli. *La Gioconda* (opera): "Voce di donna"

Wagner. *Das Rheingold* (opera): "Weiche Wotan"

Lyric tenor:

*Bizet. *Carmen* (opera): "La fleur que to m'avais jetée"

————. *The Pearl Fishers* (opera): "Je crois entendre"

Donizetti. *L'Elisir d'Amore (The Elixir of Love,* opera in 2 acts): "Una furtiva lagrima" ("A furtive tear")

*Handel. *Messiah* (oratorio): "Comfort ye" (recitative), "Every valley" (aria)

Mozart. *The Magic Flute* (opera): "Dies Bildnis ist bezaubernd schön"

*Puccini. *La Bohème* (opera): "Che gelida manina"

Rimsky-Korsakov. *Sadko* (opera): "Song of India"

Rossini. *The Barber of Seville* (opera): "Ecco ridente"

Dramatic tenor:

Giordano. *Fedora* (opera): "Amour ti vieta"

Leoncavallo. *I Pagliacci* (opera): "Vesti la giubba"

Massenet. *Manon* (opera): "Ah fuyez"

Meyerbeer. *L'Africaine* (opera): "O Paradis"

Puccini. *La Tosca* (opera): "E lucevan le stelle"

Verdi. *Requiem:* "Ingemisco"

———. *Rigoletto* (opera): "La donna è mobile"

Wagner. *Lohengrin* (opera): "In fernem Land"

Baritone:

Bach. *St. Matthew Passion:* "Gerne will ich mich bequenen"

*Bizet. *Carmen* (opera): "Toréador en garde" ("Toreador Song")

Brahms. *A German Requiem (Ein deutsches Requiem):* "Lord make me know the measure of my days"

Fauré. *Requiem:* "Offertoire," "Libera me" (both with chorus)

Gounod. *Faust* (opera): "Avant de quitter ces lieux"

Handel. *Semele* (oratorio): "Where e'er you walk"

Mendelssohn. *Elijah* (oratorio): "It is enough"

Mussorgski. *The Song of the Flea*

Puccini. *La Tosca* (opera): "Se la giurata fede"

Rossini. *The Barber of Seville* (opera): "Largo al factotum"

Verdi. *A Masked Ball* (opera): "Eri tu che macchiavi"

———. *Otello* (opera): "Credo"

———. *La Traviata* (opera): "Di provenza"

Wagner. *Tannhäuser* (opera): "Song to the Evening Star" ("O du mein holder Abendstern")

Bass:

Gounod. *Faust* (opera): "Mephisto's Serenade," "Le Veau d'Or"

*Handel. *Messiah* (oratorio): "The people that walked in darkness," "Thus saith the Lord," "But who shall abide"

Haydn. *The Creation* (oratorio): "Rolling in foaming billows"

*Mozart. *Don Giovanni* (opera): "Madamina" ("Catalogue Song")

———. *The Magic Flute* (opera): "O Isis und Osiris"

———. *The Marriage of Figaro* (opera): "La vendetta"

Mussorgski. *Boris Godounov* (opera): "Farwell of Boris"

Verdi. *Requiem:* "Confutatis"

Wagner. *Lohengrin* (opera): "Landgraf Aria"

Vocal Ensemble*

Duet:

*Bach. *Cantata No. 140, Wachet auf:* "Wenn kommst du, mein Heil," "Mein Freund ist mein" (SB)

———. *Mass in B Minor:* "Et in unnum Deum" (SA), "Domine Deus" (ST)

*Bizet. *Carmen* (opera): "Parle-moi de ma mère" (ST)

*Handel. *Messiah* (oratorio): "O death, where is they sting" (AT)

Massenet. *Thaïs* (opera): "Athanaël and Thaïs at the Oasis" (SB)

Mendelssohn. *Duets for Soprano and Alto*

*Mozart. *Don Giovanni* (opera): "Là ci darem la mano" (SB)

*Puccini. *La Bohème* (opera): "O soave fanciulla" (ST), "Quando m'en vo'" (Musetta's waltz, SB)

Rossini. *Stabat Mater:* "Quis est homo"

Verdi. *Aida* (opera): "O terra addio" (ST)

———. *Otello* (opera): "Now in the thick of night" (ST)

———. *Rigoletto* (opera): "Piangi, fanciulla" (SB)

*Wagner. *Tristan and Isolde* (opera), Act II: "Love Duet" (ST)

* In this list the following letters indicate the voices: S (soprano), mS (mezzo-soprano), A (alto), T (tenor), and B (baritone or bass).

Trio:
* Bizet. *Carmen* (opera): "Mêlons, coupons" (SS mS)
Haydn. *The Creation* (oratorio): "The heavens are telling" (STB with (chorus), "On Thee each living soul awakes" (STB)
Mendelssohn. *Elijah* (oratorio): "Lift thine eyes" (SSA)
* Mozart. *Don Giovanni* (opera): "Ah, soccorso" (BBB: Don Giovanni, Commandatore, Leporello)
————. *The Magic Flute* (opera): "Soll ich dich, teurer" (STB)
————. *The Marriage of Figaro* (opera): "Cosa sento?" (STB)
Saint–Saëns. *Christmas Oratorio:* "My soul doth magnify" (STB)
Verdi. *A Masked Ball* (opera): "Della città all'occaso" (SAT)
————. *Requiem:* "Lux aeterna" (STB), "Quid sum miser" (SST)

Quartet:
Beethoven. *Symphony No. 9 in D Minor* ("Choral"), IV: "Seid umschlungen, Millionen" ("O ye millions"; with chorus)
Gounod. *Faust* (opera): "Seigneur Dieu, que vois-je!" (S mS T B)
* Mozart. *Don Giovanni* (opera): "Non ti fidar" (SSTB)
————. *Requiem:* "Tuba mirum," "Benedictus" (SATB)
* Puccini. *La Bohème* (opera): "Addio dolce svegliare" (SSTB)
Rossini. *Stabat Mater:* "Quando corpus morietur" (S mS T B)
Saint–Saëns. *Christmas Oratorio:* "Alleluia" (SSAB)
Verdi. *Requiem:* "Kyrie," "Pie Jesu" (SSTB and chorus)
————. *Rigoletto* (opera): "Bella figlia dell'amore" (SATB)

Quintet:
* Bizet. *Carmen* (opera): "Nous avons en tête une affaire" (S mS S T T)
Mozart. *The Magic Flute* (opera): "Hm! Hm! Hm!" (SSATB
Saint–Saëns. *Christmas Oratorio:* "Arise now, Daughter of Zion" (SSATB)
Verdi. *A Masked Ball* (opera): "Di che fulgor, che musiche" (SSBBB)
————. *La Traviata* (opera): "Prendi, quest' e l'immagine (SSTBB)

Sextet:
* Bizet. *Carmen* (opera): "Écoute, compagnon" (SSSTTB)
Donizetti. *Lucia di Lammermoor* (opera): "Chi mi frena in tal momento?" (S mS T T BB) (This is the famous "Sextet from Lucia.")
* Mozart. *Don Giovanni* (opera): "Sola, sola in bujo loco" (SSSTBB)

Octet (or double quartet):
Mendelssohn. *Elijah* (oratorio): "For He shall give His angels" (SSAATTBB)
Verdi. *La Traviata* (opera): "Di sprezzo degno si stesso rende" (S mS T T BBBB)

Male chorus:
* Bach. *Cantata No. 140, Wachet auf:* "Zion hört die Wächter" (tenors in unison)
* Bizet. *Carmen* (opera): "Sur la place" (opening chorus, tenors and basses)
Brahms. *Alto Rhapsody* (alto, male chorus, orchestra)
Copland. *In the Beginning* (for soprano solo and male chorus *a cappella*)
Liszt. *A Faust Symphony:* III *(Finale)*
Verdi. *Aida* (opera): "Triumphal Chorus"
————. *Il Trovatore* (opera): "Anvil Chorus"

Female chorus:
Brahms. *Part Songs for Women's Voices,* Op. 17
Debussy. *La Damoiselle Élue (The Blessed Damosel,* cantata)

Debussy. *Nocturnes: Sirènes* (orchestra and female chorus without text)
Pergolesi. *Stabat Mater* (with soprano and alto solos)

A cappella chorus:
Bach. *Singet dem Herrn* (motet)
Byrd. *Ergo Sum Panis Vivus* (motet)
Lasso. *Tristis Est Anima Mea* (motet)
Morley. *My Bonny Lass* (madrigal)
————. *Now Is the Month of Maying* (madrigal)
Palestrina. *Improperia* (motet)
*————. *Missa Brevis*
————. *Missa Papae Marcelli*
Victoria. *O Magnum Mysterium* (motet)
————. *O Quam Gloriosum* (motet)

Mixed chorus:
*Bach. *Cantata No. 140, Wachet auf, ruft uns die Stimme:* "Wachet auf" (opening chorus)
————. *Mass in B Minor:* "Kyrie," "Sanctus," Dona nobis pacem"
————. *St. Matthew Passion:* "Kommt ihr Töchter," "Wir setzen uns mit Thränen nieder" (double choruses)
Beethoven. *Symphony No. 9 in D Minor* ("Choral"): IV
Brahms. *A German Requiem (Ein deutsches Requiem):* "How lovely is Thy dwelling place" ("Wie lieblich sind deine Wohnungen")
————. *Liebeslieder Waltzes*
Britten. *Te Deum in C Major*
Bruckner. *Psalm 112*
Fauré. *Requiem:* "Introit," "Kyrie," "In Paradisum," "Sanctus," "Agnus Dei"
Gilbert and Sullivan. *Iolanthe* (operetta): "Bow, bow, ye lower middle classes"
*Handel. *Messiah* (oratorio): "Hallelujah Chorus," "And the glory of the Lord," "For unto us a Child is born," "And with His stripes we are healed"
Haydn. *The Creation* (oratorio): "Achieved is the glorious work"
Mendelssohn. *Elijah* (oratorio): "Baal, we cry to thee," "He is watching over Israel," "And then shall your light"
Mozart. *Requiem*, K. 626
Mussorgski. *Boris Godounov* (opera): "Coronation Scene"
Verdi. *Requiem:* "Dies Irae," "Sanctus" (double choir)
Wagner. *Tannhäuser* (opera): "Pilgrims' Chorus"

10. Instrumental Mediums

There are four main classes of conventional instruments: (1) *keyboard instruments,* (2) *string instruments,* (3) *wind instruments,* and (4) *percussion instruments.*

KEYBOARD INSTRUMENTS

These instruments are operated by means of a keyboard, which consists of a series of black and white keys. When the performer depresses a key, a tone sounds. Keyboard instruments produce tone in a variety of ways.

Piano. This instrument came into use during the late eighteenth century. The *piano* produces tone by means of a hammer that strikes a string when a key is depressed. The piano is capable of sustaining tone to a limited extent, and it can produce a wide range of dynamics.

Organ. The *organ* has an ancient history dating back to pre-Christian times. Its tone is produced by air passing through a set of pipes of different lengths. The keys control valves which release the air into the pipes. Sets of pipes differing in size, shape, and material give the pipe organ a vast range of pitch and color. An organ is capable of sustaining tone indefinitely.

Harpsichord. An important keyboard instrument of the sixteenth, seventeenth, and eighteenth centuries was the *harpsichord.* It is known by a variety of names: *clavecin* (French), *clavicembalo* (Italian), and *virginal* (a smaller instrument of Elizabethan England). The harpsichord produces tone by means of strings that are plucked mechanically when a key is depressed. The harpsichord is incapable of accent or shaded dynamics. It has a clear, brilliant tone of limited volume and duration.

Clavichord. The *clavichord* was developed in the Middle Ages; its use continued throughout the eighteenth century. Its tone, more delicate than that of the harpsichord, is produced by means of a brass wedge that strikes the string when the key is depressed. It does not have the volume or the variety of tone of the harpsichord, but it can produce subtle gradations of tone and mild accents. Because of its limited volume of tone, the clavichord was designed for use in a small room rather than in a large hall.

Miscellaneous Keyboard Instruments. The principal keyboard instruments have been mentioned. There are a number of other instruments which are played by means of a keyboard. The *piano accordion* has a melody keyboard for the right hand. The *celesta,* usually classified as one of the percussion instruments of the orchestra (see below) rather than as a solo instrument, produces a bell–like tone by means of hammers that strike steel bars. The *harmonium* is a keyboard instrument related to the organ in that its tone is produced by air (bellows operated by the feet) which sets thin strips of metal (reeds) vibrating. Still other keyboard instruments are for the most part related to types already mentioned. (See also Electronic Instruments, page 63.)

STRING INSTRUMENTS

String instruments, also called *stringed instruments,* produce tone by means of the vibrations of a stretched string. (Usually, keyboard instruments such as the piano and harpsichord, which also produce tone through the vibration of strings, are not included in this category.) There are two types of string instruments: (1) *bowed strings* and (2) *plucked strings.*

Bowed Strings. The two families of *bowed strings* are the older viol family (in use principally in the sixteenth and seventeenth centuries) and the more modern violin family. All these instruments produce tone by means of a bow of horsehairs drawn across the strings.

Viols. The *viols* have a more delicate and soft tone than violins. They existed principally in three sizes: *treble viol, tenor viol,* and *viola da gamba.* Although no longer commonly used in the eighteenth century and obsolete in the nineteenth century, these instruments are again used today in authentic performances of the older music. The modern *bass viol* (also called *double bass* and *string bass*) is the only descendant of the old viol family which is still used in the symphony orchestra.

VIOLINS. The *violin* family of instruments came into general use in the seventeenth century. These instruments have more brilliance and versatility of tone than the older viols. The principal instruments in this family are the *violin* (the soprano of the orchestra), *viola* (the alto or tenor of the orchestra), and the *violoncello* or *cello* (the baritone–bass of the orchestra). The instrument for low bass parts is the bass viol which, although it belongs properly to the viol family, is a full-fledged member of the modern string orchestra. In orchestral ensembles it is customary to write two violin parts, called *first violin* and *second violin,* but the instruments which are used to play them are identical.

The violin and other members of the violin family can produce a wide variety of tone qualities and special effects. *Pizzicato* means plucking the string instead of bowing it. *Double stopping* means bowing on two strings simultaneously. A *mute* attached to the bridge produces a muffled, veiled sound. *Tremolo* is produced in two ways: (1) by rapid movement of the bow back and forth in short strokes across the string and (2) by rapid alternation between two tones on one string. Tremolo is used to create tension and excitement. *Harmonics* are high, thin, almost flute-like tones produced on bowed string instruments by lightly touching the string with the fingers of the left hand instead of by pressing the string down firmly on the fingerboard. *Sul ponticello* is a dry metallic tone produced by bowing near the bridge of the violin. *Portamento* is produced by sliding the finger along the string from one pitch to another. *Col legno* means playing with the wood of the bow for a dry, staccato effect. Compositions which illustrate the use of these special effects are listed at the end of this chapter.

Plucked Strings. Although instruments of the bowed-string class can produce tone by the strings being plucked (*pizzicato*), the plucked string instruments produce tone solely by this means. The player plucks the strings either with his fingers or with a plectrum held in his hand.

HARP. The *harp* is one of the most ancient types of instrument still in use. Its musical function is now predominantly in ensembles rather than in solo performance. The harp adds considerable color to the orchestral palette.

LUTE. A variety of plucked string instruments belong under this family classification. *Lutes* have pear-shaped bodies and flat necks. Although the instrument dates far back into pre-Christian times and is now mostly obsolete, music for the lute is an important segment of sixteenth- and seventeenth-century musical literature.

GUITAR. The *guitar* family resembles the lute except that the former has a flat back and a "waist" shaped somewhat like that of a violin. Although the guitar today is associated mostly with dance band instrumentation and popular song accompaniment, its history and literature have made their contributions to music, especially to that of Spain and the sixteenth century.

OTHERS. Other plucked string instruments of lesser importance as musical mediums are the *ukulele* (Hawaiian), the *banjo* (Afro-American), the *mandolin,* and numerous exotic and ancient instruments of the same general type.

WIND INSTRUMENTS

Wind instruments generate tone through a vibrating column of air enclosed in a tube or a pipe. (The pipe organ, which produces tone in the same way, is classed as a keyboard instrument. See above.) The two classes of wind instruments are (1) woodwinds and (2) brass.

Woodwinds. *Woodwinds,* with the exception of the flute, produce vibration by means of a single reed or a double reed.

SINGLE-REED INSTRUMENTS. The principal single-reed instruments are *clarinets* and *saxophones,* both of which are made in various sizes and have correspondingly different registers.

DOUBLE-REED INSTRUMENTS. The principal double-reed instruments are the *oboe,* the *English horn,* the *bassoon,* and the *contra bassoon.*

FLUTE AND PICCOLO. The *flute* and the *piccolo* (the latter is the highest–pitched instrument in the band or orchestra) produce tone by air blown across a mouth hole. In the older type of flute, called a *recorder,* the air is blown from the end into a whistle-like mouthpiece.

Brass Instruments. The tones of *brass instruments* are produced by vibration of the player's lips pressed into a cup–shaped mouthpiece. Change of pitch is effected both by lip pressure and by the manipulation of valves. There are a great many instruments of this class, both ancient and modern. We shall describe here the four principal brass instruments of the orchestra.

HORN. The *horn,* or *French horn* as it is often called, is derived from the seventeenth-century hunting horn. The horn has a wide compass and produces rich, full tones.

TRUMPET. The *trumpet* has a brilliant tone. The *cornet,* which is similar to the trumpet, has a more mellow tone. Both are used in bands and orchestras, and there is an increasing solo literature for these instruments.

TROMBONE. The *trombone* may be regarded as the bass of the trumpet, but it has a more mellow tone than the trumpet. It adds tremendous sonority and power to the brass choir.

TUBA. The *tuba* is the lowest brass instrument of the band and orchestra. Tubas are made in various sizes and shapes.

PERCUSSION INSTRUMENTS

Percussion instruments, which are primarily rhythmic in function, are characterized by the fact that the tone or sound is produced by the performer striking or shaking the instrument. In the present classification, certain keyboard instruments such as the piano are excluded, although they may be grouped with percussion instruments in the orchestral score. Percussion instruments are divided into two groups: (1) instruments of definite pitch and (2) instruments of indefinite pitch.

Definite–Pitch Instruments. The principal percussion instruments of definite pitch are the *kettledrums* (or *timpani*), *bells* (or *glockenspiel*), *xylophone, celesta, marimba,* and *chimes.* In ensembles, they have melodic as well as rhythmic functions.

Indefinite–Pitch Instruments. The chief percussion instruments in this class are the *snare drum* (or *side drum*), *bass drum, tambourine, triangle, cymbals, gong* (or *tam–tam*), *castanets,* and *maracas* (*rattle*).

ENSEMBLES

Instrumental ensembles exist in almost infinite combinations. There are two main classes: (1) chamber ensembles and (2) large ensembles (orchestra, band).

Chamber Ensembles. Chamber music, a medium which calls for only a few performers, is usually played with one performer to a part. The most common chamber music ensembles are listed below.

SOLO SONATAS. Music written for a solo instrument (violin, cello, flute, oboe, horn, etc.), with an accompaniment for such instruments as the piano or the harpsichord, belongs in the category of chamber music ensemble. Such combinations as these are most commonly in the form of a sonata or suite. (These forms will be discussed in Chapter 17.)

STRING QUARTET. Perhaps the most common medium of chamber music is the *string quartet*. It consists of two violins, a viola, and a cello. When the piano replaces one of the four instruments, the ensemble is called a *piano quartet*.

DUOS, TRIOS, QUINTETS, AND OTHERS. Music in which two instruments have equal importance is called a duo; music for three instruments is a *trio;* for five, a *quintet;* for six, a *sextet;* for seven, a *septet;* for eight, an *octet;* for nine, a *nonet*. These ensembles may consist of any combination of instruments, including strings, woodwinds, brass, keyboard, and percussion instruments.

Chamber Orchestra. The term *chamber orchestra* is applied to small instrumental ensembles in which there are only a few performers for a part. Chamber orchestras are in a category of ensemble which belongs between chamber ensemble and the full orchestra.

Large Ensembles. Large ensembles are classified according to two main types: (1) orchestra and (2) band.

ORCHESTRA. An *orchestra* is any sizable group of instrumental performers. In the orchestral ensemble, several instruments of the same kind usually play a given part. This is particularly true of the strings. An orchestra may vary in size from a relatively small group (see *chamber orchestra* above) to an ensemble of a hundred or more players.

The *symphony orchestra* consists of the following standard groups of instruments: woodwinds, brass, percussion, and strings. A string orchestra consists only of strings.

The *concerto* is a form written for orchestra and usually one solo instrument (piano, violin, etc.) which is given a prominent role in the music.

The *concerto grosso,* a common orchestral medium of the Baroque period (1600–1750), employs an orchestra consisting mainly of strings, with a group of several solo instruments (called the *concertino*) which plays in opposition to the whole orchestra (called *ripieno* or *tutti*).

BAND. A band is an instrumental ensemble consisting mainly or exclusively of wind and percussion instruments. Although the band is closely associated with outdoor events (parades, football games, etc.), it is also used as a concert ensemble, for which there is a limited literature of high caliber.

Mixed Ensembles. A considerable literature of music exists for large mixed ensembles which include instruments and voices. Such musical types as opera, oratorio, cantata, Mass, Requiem Mass, and even symphonies (e.g., Beethoven's *Ninth*) may employ vocal soloists, chorus, and orchestra. Mixed chamber ensembles have made their appearance in the twentieth century (e.g., Vaughan Williams' *On Wenlock Edge* and Schoenberg's *Pierrot Lunaire*).

ELECTRONIC MEDIUMS

The twentieth century has witnessed numerous innovations in mediums. Not only have conventional instruments been used in unconventional ways (e.g., John Cage's music for "prepared piano"), but new sound-producing mediums have been introduced (cow bells, steel plates, whistles, brake drums, etc.). Electronic technology has provided virtually unlimited means for creating entirely new effects.

Electronic Instruments. Under this heading are included musical instruments that produce tones by oscillation through vacuum tubes as opposed to mechanical tone generators (piano, strings, winds, etc.). Instruments of this class, most of them keyboard operated, include the Elektrochord, Ondes Martinot, Orgatron, Hammond Organ, Baldwin Electronic Organ, Novachord, Solovox, Trautonium, and Theremin. Some of these are now obsolete. In addition, conventional instruments can be electronically amplified in such a way as to produce new effects.

Tape Recorder. Shortly before 1950, the *tape recorder* became a means of creating music. Tape-recorder music (also called *tape music* and *musique concrète*) employs several techniques. Conventional media, both vocal and instrumental, as well as unconventional media and natural sounds, can be recorded on electromagnetic tape and then distorted by reversing the direction of the tape, altering the speed (thus changing the entire pitch level), splicing sections of tape, and combining different recordings simultaneously. The composer creates his compositions directly onto the tape. Tape-recorder technique is now combined with synthesizer and computer techniques.

Synthesizer. Audio-electronic technology created the *synthesizer*. This is a complex instrument that can produce all frequencies (pitches), a wide range of amplitude (dynamics), an infinite spectrum of timbres, and predetermined rhythmic patterns singly and in combinations. It is also able to control tonal impact (attack) and "decay" (dying out of tone). The computer can be programmed to "compose" music utilizing all these possibilities. The result is a complex of new sounds preserved on magnetic tape. The term "electronic music" now includes "tape music," but it excludes music performed on "electronic instruments" listed above under that heading.

Characteristics of Electronic Music. Electronic music requires of the listener a new esthetic approach to the concept of music; in it conventional ideas of melody, harmony, tonality, timbre, and form are virtually abandoned. Since the creator of electronic "happenings" is at once composer and performer, there is no latitude for interpretation; and phonograph recordings rather than concerts are the principal means of dissemination.

Recommended Listening

A modern high-fidelity performance of a composition in which several different instruments are prominent can be a source of delight to the listener who wishes to develop his ability to identify the tone quality of mediums. The following list is classified according to the various categories discussed in this chapter. If you are unfamiliar with the timbre of any particular medium, it is best to start with a composition in which that medium is given prominence above all others, as in the solo sonata. Then you should progress to compositions in which a few different instruments are used, as in various chamber and orchestral ensembles. Ultimately, you may be able to distinguish the various tone colors in complex orchestral ensembles. Sometimes record jackets and concert guides (see page 220) are helpful for identifying instruments in a particular composition.

Keyboard Instruments

Piano:
Beethoven. *Sonata No. 12 in A Flat Major*
———. *Sonata No. 23 in F Minor* ("Appassionata")
Chopin. *Étude in C Major*, Op. 10, No. 1
———. *Polonaise No. 6 in A Flat Major*, Op. 53
*———. *Sonata No. 2 in B Flat Minor*, Op. 35
Debussy. *La Cathédrale Engloutie* ("The Sunken Cathedral")

————. *Children's Corner Suite* (piano): *Golliwog's Cake–walk*
Griffes. *The White Peacock* (piano)
*Hindemith. *Sonata No. 3 for Piano*
Křenek. *Pieces for Piano*
Liszt. *La Campanella*
————. *Hungarian Rhapsody, No. 2 in C Sharp Minor* (piano)
Ravel. *Le Tombeau de Couperin* (piano)
Schoenberg. *Drei Klaierstücke* (*Three Piano Pieces*), Op. 11
*Schumann. *Fantasietücke* (*Fantasy Pieces;* piano): No. 2, "Aufschwung" ("Soaring"); No. 3, "Warum" ("Why"); No. 4, "Grillen" ("Whims")

Organ:
Bach. *Orgelbüchlein* (*Little Organ Book,* a set of chorale preludes)
*————. *Passacaglia and Fugue in C Minor*
————. *Toccata and Fugue in D Minor*
Dupré. *Variations sur un Vieux Noël*
Franck. *Chorale No. 3 in A Minor*
————. *Pièce Héroïque*
Hindemith. *Sonatas for Organ* (3)
Reger. *Chorale Preludes,* Op. 67
Sowerby. *Symphony in G Major for Organ*

Harpsichord:
  Note. Most of these pieces are played and recorded on the modern piano as well as on the harpsichord for which they were originally written.
Bach. *English Suites* (6)
————. *French Suites* (6)
————. *Partita No. 5 in G Major*
————. *The Well-Tempered Clavier*
Couperin. *La Galante* (No. 40 in *Masterpieces of Music before 1750*)
Falla. *Concerto for Harpsichord and Orchestra*
Farnaby. *Virginal Music* (album)
Martin. *Concerto for Harpsichord and Small Orchestra*
Scarlatti, D. *Harpsichord Sonatas* (See albums by Kirpatrick, Marlowe, Valenti.)

Strings (Bowed)

Viols:
Jenkins. *Pavan for Four Viols*
Locke. *Consort of Four Parts* (contrapuntal fantasies for small string ensemble)

Violin:
Bach. *Partita No. 2 in D Minor for Unaccompanied Violin*
Bartók. *Sonata for Unaccompanied Violin*
Handel. *Sonata No. 4 in D Major for Violin and Harpsichord,* Op. 1, No. 13
Lalo. *Symphonie Espagnole* (violin and orchestra)
*Mendelssohn. *Concerto in E Minor for Violin and Orchestra*
Paganini. *Caprice No. 24,* Op. 1, No. 24 (unaccompanied violin)
Saint–Saëns. *Introduction and Rondo Capriccioso* (violin and orchestra)
Serly. *Sonata for Solo Violin*
Tartini. *Sonata in G Minor* ("Devil's Trill")

Viola:
Bartók. *Concerto for Viola and Orchestra*
Bloch. *Jewish Pieces for Viola and Piano*

Hindemith. *Trauermusik (Funeral Music,* for viola and orchestra)

Walton. *Concerto for Viola and Orchestra*

Cello:

Bach. *Suite No. 5 in C Minor for Unaccompanied Cello*

Barber. *Concerto for Cello and Orchestra*

Beethoven. *Sonata No. 3 in A Major* (cello and piano)

Bloch. *Schelomo* (cello and orchestra)

Elgar. *Concerto in E Minor for Cello and Orchestra*

Fauré. *Élégie for Cello and Orchestra*

Kabalevsky. *Concerto for Cello and Orchestra*

Saint–Saëns. *Concerto in A Minor for Cello and Orchestra*

Shostakovitch. *Sonata for Cello and Piano*

Strauss, R. *Don Quixote* (orchestra and cello solo)

Bass viol:

*Beethoven. *Symphony No. 5 in C Minor,* III (trio of the *Scherzo*)

Dragonetti. *Concerto for Double Bass with Piano*

Saint–Saëns. *Carnival of the Animals* (orchestra): "The Elephant"

Note. The double bass can be heard in most orchestral compositions providing the rich foundation of the music. It is rarely heard in melodic solo passages and is usually doubled with the cellos an octave higher.

Special effects on string instruments:

Bach. *Partita No. 2 in D Minor for Unaccompanied Violin:* Sarabande, Chaconne, Gigue (double and triple stopping)

*Bartók. *Quartet No. 5* (strings): IV (*portamento*)

Britten. *Passacaglia,* from *Peter Grimes* (col legno)

Debussy. *Rhapsody for Saxophone and Orchestra* (viola and cello harmonics at beginning)

———. *Rondes de Printemps* (sul ponticello)

Dvořák. *Symphony No. 5 in E Minor* ("New World"): II (*Largo;* mute)

Grieg. *Peer Gynt Suite No. 1:* "Anitra's Dance" (*pizzicato*)

Holst. *The Planets:* "Mars, the Bringer of War" (*col legno*)

Paganini. *Caprice No. 24,* Op. 1, No. 24 (several special devices and techniques employed)

Prokofiev. *Concerto No. 1 in D Major for Violin and Orchestra* (*sul ponticello*)

Ravel. *Ma Mère l'Oye (Mother Goose Suite):* "Hop o' My Thumb," "Fairy Garden" (harmonics)

Sibelius.*The Swan of Tuonela* (col legno and *tremolo*)

*Tchaikovsky. *Nutcracker Suite:* "Arabian Dance" (mutes)

———. *Symphony No. 4 in F Minor:* III (*pizzicato*)

Wagner. *Lohengrin* (opera): *Prelude to Act I* (solo violins, harmonics)

Note. For sounds of strings combined, see also the music listed under "string quartet" and "string orchestra" below.

Strings (Plucked)

Harp:

Casella. *Sonata for Harp*

*Debussy. *Prélude à l'Après-midi d'un Faune (Prelude to the Afternoon of a Faun,* symphonic poem)

Dello Joio. *Concerto in A Major for Harp and Chamber Orchestra*

Ditters von Dittersdorf. *Concerto in A Major for Harp and Orchestra*

Fauré. *Impromptu for Harp Solo*

Glière. *Concerto for Harp and Orchestra*

Ravel. *Introduction and Allegro for Harp and Strings*
*Tchaikovsky. *Nutcracker Suite:* "Waltz of the Flowers"

Lute:
  Note. Record catalogues list a number of albums of lute music in the section "Classical, Miscellaneous." See especially *Music in Shakespeare's Time* and *Renaissance Music* (Suzan Bloch, lutanist).

Guitar:
Castelnuovo–Tedesco. *Concerto for Guitar and Orchestra*
Ibert. *Entr'acte for Flute and Guitar*
See also albums of guitar music played by Andres Segovia.

Woodwinds

Flute:
Bach. *Sonata in A Minor for Unaccompanied Flute*
*Debussy. *Prélude à l'Après-midi d'un Faune* (*Prelude to the Afternoon of a Faun,* symphonic poem): opening solo
Griffes. *Poem for Flute and Orchestra*
Handel. *Sonata in F Major for Flute and Continuo,* Op. 1, No. 11
———. *Sonatas* (4, for recorder and continuo)
Haydn. *Sonata in G Major for Flute and Piano*
Hindemith. *Sonata for Flute and Piano*
———. *Sonata for Two Flutes* (canonic)
Leclair. *Sonatas* (8, for flute and continuo)
Loeillet. *Sonata in F Major for Flute and Harpsichord*
———. *Sonata in G Minor for Recorder and Harpsichord*
Martinu. *Sonata for Flute and Piano*
Milhaud. *Sonatine for Flute and Piano*
Saint–Saëns. *Carnival of the Animals* (orchestra): "Birds"
*Tchaikovsky. *Nutcracker Suite* (orchestra): "Chinese Dance," "Dance of the Mirlitons"

Piccolo:
Ippolitov–Ivanov. *Caucasian Sketches: March of the Sardar*
Milhaud. *Symphony No. 2:* I
Prokofiev. *Lieutenant Kije Suite:* "*The Birth of Kije,*" opening movement
Sousa. *Stars and Stripes Forever* (band)

Clarinet:
Bartók. *Contrasts for Violin, Clarinet and Piano*
Berg. *Four Pieces for Clarinet and Piano*
Copland. *Concerto for Clarinet with Strings, Harp, and Piano*
Debussy. *Rhapsodie No. 1 for Clarinet and Piano*
Hindemith. *Sonata for Clarinet and Piano*
Milhaud. *Sonatina for Clarinet and Piano*
Mozart. *Concerto in A Major for Clarinet and Orchestra,* K. 662
Saint–Saëns. *Carnival of the Animals* (orchestra): "Fossils"
Sibelius. *Symphony No. 1 in E Minor:* I, introduction

Saxophone:
Creston. *Sonata for Saxophone and Orchestra*
Debussy. *Rhapsodie for Saxophone and Orchestra*
Ibert. *Concertino da Camera for Saxophone*
Webern. *Quartet for Saxophone, Clarinet, Violin and Piano*

Oboe:
Brahms. *Symphony No. 2 in D Major:* III
Britten. *Phantasy Quartet for Oboe and Strings*

Donovan. *Suite for String Orchestra and Oboe*
Handel. *Sonata in B Flat Major for Flute, Oboe, and Continuo*
Ravel. *Le Tombeau de Couperin* (orchestra): "Prélude"

English horn:
Copland. *Quiet City* (trumpet, English horn, and strings)
Dvořák. *Symphony No. 5 in E Minor* ("New World"): II (Largo), first theme
Franck. *Symphony in D Minor:* II, first theme
Honegger. *Concerto da Camera for Flute and English Horn*
Sibelius. *The Swan of Tuonela* (tone poem for orchestra)

Bassoon:
Dukas. *The Sorcerer's Apprentice* (orchestra)
Hindemith. *Sonata for Bassoon and Piano*
Mozart. *Concerto in B Flat Major for Bassoon and Orchestra,* K. 191
——. *Sonata in B Flat Major for Bassoon and Cello,* K. 292
*Tchaikovsky. *Nutcracker Suite* (orchestra): "Chinese Dance"

Contrabassoon:
Ravel. *Ma Mère l'Oye* (*Mother Goose Suite;* orchestra): "Beauty and the Beast"

Bass clarinet:
*Tchaikovsky. *Nutcracker Suite* (orchestra): "Dance of the Sugar-Plum Fairy"
Wagner. *Siegfried* (opera): "Forest Murmurs"

Brass

Trumpet:
Bach. *Brandenburg Concerto No. 2 in F Major* (solo instruments: high trumpet, flute, oboe, violin)
Hindemith. *Sonata for Trumpet and Piano*
Jolivet. *Concerto for Trumpet, Piano, and Strings*
Kaufman. *Music for Trumpet and Strings*
Torelli. *Concerto in D Major for Trumpet and String Orchestra*
Verdi. *Aida* (opera): "Triumphal March"

Horn:
*Brahms. *Symphony No. 3 in F Major:* III
——. *Trio in E Flat Major* (piano, violin, horn)
Glière. *Concerto for Horn and Orchestra*
Mendelssohn. *A Midsummer Night's Dream: Nocturne*
Mozart. *Concerto in D Major for Horn and Orchestra,* K. 412
Schubert. *Symphony No. 7 in C Major:* I, opening solo
*Strauss, R. *Till Eulenspiegel* (symphonic poem)
Tchaikovsky. *Symphony No. 5 in E Minor:* II, first theme
Weber. *Oberon Overture,* opening theme

Trombone:
Hindemith. *Sonata for Trombone and Piano*
Poulenc. *Sonata for Trumpet, Trombone, and Horn*
Wagner. *Tannhäuser* (opera): Overture

Tuba:
Berlioz. *Symphonie Fantastique* (*Fantastic Symphony*); V, "Dies Irae"
Mussorgski. *Pictures at an Exhibition* (symphonic suite, transcribed from piano by Maurice Ravel): "The Ox Cart"
*Stravinsky. *Petrouchka:* fourth tableau, "The Bear"
Wagner. *Siegfried* (opera): "Fafner" (the dragon)

Percussion

Note. The compositions listed under this heading are not classified according to individual percussion instruments. Some of the pieces feature one instrument, others include several.

Antheil. *Ballet Mécanique*

Bartók. *Sonata for Two Pianos and Percussion*

Chávez. *Toccata for Percussion*

Delibes. *Lakmé* (opera): "Bell Song" (bells)

Farberman. *Evolution*

Fauré. *Requiem:* "In Paradisum" (celeste)

Glanville–Hicks. *Sonata for Piano and Percussion*

Hindemith. *Symphonic Metamorphoses:* "Turandot"

*Ravel. *Boléro* (orchestra): opening snare drum solo

———. *Ma Mère l'Oye* (*Mother Goose Suite;* orchestra): "Laideronette (cymbals, celeste, gong, xylophone)

Saint–Saëns. *Carnival of the Animals* (orchestra): "Fossils" (xylophone)

———. *Danse Macabre* (xylophone)

Sibelius. *Symphony No. 1 in E Minor:* III (timpani)

Stravinsky. *Symphony of Psalms: finale* (timpani)

*Tchaikovsky. *Nutcracker Suite* (orchestra): "Dance of the Sugar-Plum Fairy" (celeste)

———. *Overture, 1812* (chimes)

Varèse. *Ionization* (percussion ensemble)

Chamber Ensembles

String orchestra:

Barber. *Adagio for Strings*

Britten. *Simple Symphony for Strings*

Corelli. *Concerto Grosso No. 8 in G Minor,* Op. 6 ("Christmas")

Dvořák. *Nocturne in B Major for Strings*

Hindemith. *The Four Temperaments* (piano and string orchestra)

Janáček. *Suite for String Orchestra*

Martinu. *Partita for String Orchestra*

Mennini. *Arioso for Strings*

Stravinsky. *Apollon Musagète* (ballet)

Vaughan Willams. *Fantasia on a Theme by Thomas Tallis*

Wind ensembles:

Dittersdorf. *Three Partitas for Wind Quintet*

Donovan. *Quartet for Wood Winds*

Fine. *Partita for Woodwind Quintet*

Françaix. *Quintet for Winds*

Gabrieli. *Canzonas for Brass Choirs*

Glanville–Hicks. *Concertino da Camera for Piano, Flute, Clarinet, and Bassoon*

Goeb. *Quintet for Woodwinds*

Lockwood. *Concerto for Organ and Brasses*

Persichetti. *Pastoral for Winds*

Pezel. *Music for Brasses*

Poulenc. *Sonata for Trumpet, Trombone, and Horn*

Stravinsky. *Ocete for Wind Instruments*

———. *Symphonies of Wind Instruments*

Varèse. *Octandre*

String quartets:
*Bartók. *Quartet No. 5* (strings)
Beethoven. *Quartet No. 2 in G Major*
————. *Quartet No. 7 in F Major*
————. *Quartet No. 12 in E Flat Major*
Bloch. *Quartet No. 2*
Brahms. *Quartet No. 2 in A Minor*
Casella. *Five Pieces for String Quartet*
Debussy. *Quartet in G Minor*
Dvořák. *Quartet in F Major* ("American")
Haydn. *Quartet in F Major*, Op. 3, No. 5
*————. *Quartet in E Flat Major*, Op. 33, No. 2
————. *Quartet in C Major*, Op. 76, No. 3 ("Emperor")
Hindemith. *Quartet in E Flat Major* (1943)
Mozart. *Quartet No. 14 in G Major*, K. 387
Prokofiev. *Quartet No. 1*
Riegger. *Quartet No. 2*
Roussel. *Quartet in D Major*
Schoenberg. *Quartet No. 4*
Schubert. *Quartet No. 14 in D Minor* (strings; "Death and the Maiden")
Schumann. *Quartet in A Major* (strings)
Stravinsky. *Three Pieces for String Quartet*
Tchaikovsky. *Quartet No. 1 in D Major* (strings)
Walton. *Quartet in A Minor* (strings)
Wolf. *Italian Serenade*

Solo sonatas: See lists under individual string and wind instruments above.

Miscellaneous chamber ensembles:
Bach. *Musical Offering* (*Das Musicalisches Opfer;* different instrumental combinations)
————. *Trio Sonata in D Minor for Flute, Oboe, and Harpsichord*)
Bartók. *Music for Strings, Percussion, and Celesta*
Beethoven. *Septet in E Flat Major* (strings and wind)
————. *Trio No. 7 in B Flat Major* ("Archduke"; piano, violin, cello)
Brahms. *Quintet in B Minor* (clarinet and strings)
Diabelli. *Trio for Flute, Viola, and Guitar*
Handel. *Duet in D Major for Violin and Cello*
D'Indy. *Suite for Trumpet, Two Flutes, and Strings*
Kodály. *Duo for Violin and Cello*
Loeillet. *Sonata for Flute, Oboe, and Continuo*
Marais. *Suites for Flute, Viola, and Harpsichord*
Martinu. *Duo for Violin and Cello*
Milhaud. *Pastorale for Oboe, Clarinet, and Bassoon*
————. *Sonata for Flute, Oboe, Clarinet, and Piano*
————. *Suite for Violin, Clarinet, and Piano*
Mozart. *Quintet in A Major for Clarinet and String Quartet*, K. 581
————. *Quintet in E Flat* (Piano, oboe, clarinet, horn, bassoon), K. 452
Poulenc. *Sextet for Piano and Winds*
————. *Sonata for Clarinet and Bassoon*
————. *Trio for Piano, Oboe, and Bassoon*
Prokofiev. *Sonata for Two Violins*
Ratner. *Serenade for Oboe, Horn, and String Quartet*
Ravel. *Sonata for Violin and Cello*

Riisager. *Sonata for Two Violins*

Schoenberg. *Pierrot Lunaire* (voice and chamber ensemble)

Schubert. *Quintet in A Major,* Op. 114 ("Trout," for piano and string quartet)

Schumann. *Quintet in E Flat Major* (piano and strings)

Stravinsky. *L'Histoire du Soldat* (*The Soldier's Tale,* ballet for narrator and 7 instruments)

Telemann. *Trio Sonata in E Minor for Flute, Oboe, and Continuo*

Villa-Lobos. *Bachianas Brasileiras No. 1* (eight cellos)

Orchestral Ensembles

Orchestral compositions helpful for identification of instrumental timbres:

Britten. *The Young Person's Guide to the Orchestra*

Prokofiev. *Peter and the Wolf* (narrator and orchestra)

Saint–Saëns. *Carnival of the Animals* (orchestra)

*Tchaikovsky. *Nutcracker Suite* (orchestra)

The Complete Orchestra (an album of five long-playing records demonstrating 33 instruments, first as solo, then with orchestral background)

Symphony orchestra:

*Bach. *Suite No. 3 in D Major for Orchestra* (oboes, trumpets, strings)

*Beethoven. *Symphony No. 5 in C Minor*

———. *Symphony No. 6 in F Major* ("Pastorale")

Berlioz. *Symphonie Fantastique* (*Fantastic Symphony*)

Brahms. *Academic Festival Overture*

———. *Symphony No. 1 in C Minor*

———. *Symphony No. 2 in D Major*

*———. *Symphony No. 3 in F Major*

———. *Symphony No. 4 in E Minor*

———. *Variations on a Theme of Haydn,* Op. 56a (orchestra)

Chávez. *Sinfonia India*

Debussy. *La Mer* (suite for orchestra)

———. *Nocturnes* (3 pieces for orchestra)

*———. *Prélude à l'Après–midi d'un Faune* (*Prelude to the Afternoon of a Faun,* symphonic poem)

Dukas. *The Sorcerer's Apprentice*

Dvořák. *Symphony No. 5 in E Minor* ("New World")

Elgar. *Enigma Variations*

Franck. *Symphony in D Minor*

Grieg. *Peer Gynt Suite No. 1*

Griffes. *The Pleasure-dome of Kubla Khan*

———. *The White Peacock* (orchestra)

Haydn. *Symphony No. 94 in G Major* ("Surprise")

———. *Symphony No. 101 in D Major* ("Clock")

Hindemith. *Mathis der Maler* (orchestra)

Ippolitov–Ivanov. *Caucasian Sketches* (orchestra)

Liszt. *A Faust Symphony* (orchestra, tenor solo, and male chorus)

———. *Les Préludes* (symphonic poem)

Mendelssohn. *A Midsummer Night's Dream* (orchestra)

———. *Symphony No. 4 in A Major* ("Italian")

Milhaud. *Symphony No. 2*

Mozart. *Eine Kleine Nachtmusik* (*Serenade,* for small orchestra), K. 525

*———. *Symphony No. 40 in G Minor,* K. 550

———. *Symphony No. 41 in C Major,* K. 551 ("Jupiter")

Mussorgski. *Night on Bald Mountain*

———. *Pictures at an Exhibition* (symphonic suite, transcribed from piano by Maurice Ravel)

Prokofiev. *Classical Symphony in D Major*

Rachmaninoff. *Isle of the Dead* (symphonic poem)

*Ravel. *Boléro* (orchestra)

———. *Daphnis et Chloé Suite No. 2* (orchestra)

———. *Ma Mère l'Oye* (*Mother Goose Suite,* for orchestra)

———. *La Valse* (orchestra)

Respighi. *The Pines of Rome* (orchestral suite)

Rimsky–Korsakov. *Scheherazade* (orchestral suite)

Saint–Saëns. *Carnival of the Animals* (orchestra)

———. *Danse Macabre* (orchestra)

Schubert. *Symphony No. 7 in C Major*

———. *Symphony No. 8 in B Minor* ("Unfinished")

Schumann. *Symphony No. 3 in E Flat Major* ("Rhenish")

Shostakovitch. *Symphony No. 5*

Sibelius. *Finlandia* (tone poem for orchestra)

———. *The Swan of Tuonela* (tone poem for orchestra)

———. *Symphony No. 1 in E Minor*

———. *Symphony No. 5 in E Flat Major*

Strauss, R. *Don Quixote* (orchestra)

———. *Ein Heldenleben* (*A Hero's Life,* symphonic poem)

*———. *Till Eulenspiegel* (symphonic poem)

Stravinsky. *Firebird Suite* (orchestra)

*———. *Petrouchka* (Ballet suite for orchestra)

———. *Le Sacre du Printemps* (*The Rite of Spring;* a ballet)

———. *Symphony in Three Movements*

Tchaikovsky. *Overture, 1812*

*———. *Nutcracker Suite* (orchestra)

———. *Symphony No. 4 in F Minor*

———. *Symphony No. 5 in E Minor*

———. *Symphony No. 6 in B Minor* ("Pathétique")

Wagner. *Lohengrin* (opera): *Prelude to Act I*

———. *Die Meistersinger* (opera): *Prelude to Act I*

———. *A Siegfried Idyll* (tone poem)

*———. *Tristan and Isolde: Prelude to Act I* and "Liebestod" ("Love-death")

Concerto:

Bach. *Concerto in D Minor for Two Violins and Orchestra*

———. *Concerto No. 2 in E Major for Violin and Orchestra*

Bartók. *Concerto for Violin and Orchestra*

———. *Concerto No. 3 for Piano and Orchestra*

Beethoven. *Concerto in D Major for Violin and Orchestra*

———. *Concerto No. 4 in G Major for Piano and Orchestra*

———. *Concerto No. 5 in E Flat Major for Piano and Orchestra* ("Emperor")

Berg. *Concerto for Violin and Orchestra* ("To the Memory of an Angel")

Brahms. *Concerto in D Major for Violin and Orchestra*

———. *Concerto No. 2 in B Flat Major for Piano and Orchestra*

Bruch. *Concerto No. 1 in G Minor for Violin and Orchestra*

Grieg. *Concerto in A Minor for Piano and Orchestra*

Gruenberg. *Concerto for Violin and Orchestra*

Haydn. *Concerto in D Major for Harpsichord and Orchestra*

Honegger. *Concertino for Piano and Orchestra*

Kabalevsky. *Concerto for Violin and Orchestra*
Khachaturian. *Concerto for Piano and Orchestra*
Lalo. *Symphonie Espagnole* (violin and orchestra)
Leclair. *Concerto in A Minor for Violin and Orchestra*
Liszt. *Concerto No. 1 in E Flat Major for Piano and Orchestra*
MacDowell. *Concerto No. 1 in A Minor for Piano and Orchestra*
*Mendelssohn. *Concerto in E Minor for Violin and Orchestra*
Mozart. *Concerto in D Minor for Piano and Orchestra*, K. 466
———. *Concerto in E Flat Major for Piano and Orchestra*, K. 271
———. *Concerto No. 3 in G Major for Violin and Orchestra*, K. 216
Prokofiev. *Concerto No. 2 in G Minor for Violin and Orchestra*
———. *Concerto No. 3 in C Major for Piano and Orchestra*
Rachmaninoff. *Concerto No. 2 in C Minor for Piano and Orchestra*
Ravel. *Concerto in G Major for Piano and Orchestra*
Rubinstein. *Concerto No. 4 in D Minor for Piano and Orchestra*
Saint–Saëns. *Concerto No. 2 in G Minor for Piano and Orchestra*
Schumann. *Concerto in A Minor for Piano and Orchestra*
Sibelius. *Concerto in D Minor for Violin and Orchestra*
Tchaikovsky. *Concerto in D Major for Violin and Orchestra*
———. *Concerto No. 1 in B Flat Minor for Piano and Orchestra*
Vivaldi. *Concerto No. 6 in C Major for Violin and Orchestra*
  Note. See also the concertos listed under individual instruments above.

Concerto grosso:
Bach. *Brandenburg Concerto No. 2 in F Major* (concerto grosso)
———. *Brandenburg Concerto No. 5 in D Major* (concerto grosso)
Corelli. *Concerto Grosso No. 8 in G Minor* ("Christmas")
Handel. *Concerto Grosso No. 5 in D Major*, Op. 6
Vivaldi. *Concerto Grosso No. 11 in D Minor*, Op. 3

Band:
Barber. *Commando March*
Bennett. *Suite of Old American Dances*
Gould. *Ballad for Band*
Hanson. *Chorale and Alleluia*
Hindemith. *Symphony in B Flat Major*
Holst. *Suite No. 1 in E Flat Major*, Op. 28
Mennin. *Canzona*
Persichetti. *Divertimento for Band*
Piston. *Tunbridge Fair: Intermezzo for Band*
Schuman. *George Washington Bridge: An Impression for Band*
Thomson. *A Solemn Music*
Vaughan Williams. *Toccata Marziale*

Tape-recorder music (musique concrète):
Powell. *Second Electronic Setting*
Ussachevsky. *Of Wood and Brass*
———. *Piece for Tape Recorder*
———. *A Poem in Cycles and Bells*
Xenakis. *Concret P-H II*

Synthesizer:
Babbitt. *Composition for Synthesizer*
Ellis. *Kaleidoscope*, for Orchestra, Synthesizer, and Soprano
Stockhausen. *Hymnen für Elektronische und Konkrete Klänge*

PART FOUR

Principles of Musical Structure

11. General Principles

The plan of organization which a composer follows in assembling his musical materials is called *musical structure* or *musical form*. Certain general principles of structure are at work in a composition—principles which are also found in other arts such as painting, sculpture, and architecture.

THEME

Music is almost always constructed upon one or more musical ideas called *themes*. A theme consists of melodic, rhythmic, and (usually) harmonic elements which combine to give the musical idea a distinct character or individuality. The importance of theme to music can be realized from the fact that most compositions are recognized or identified by their themes. By listening to music, you learn to recognize the various themes of a composition. In this way you become aware of the structure, or sectional plan, of the composition.

UNITY

When all the constituent parts and sections of a composition combine to produce the effect of "oneness," *unity* is the underlying structural principle being used. A central theme which recurs throughout a composition produces unity, even though one or more subordinate themes may be introduced.

VARIETY

The principle of *variety* in music means modification (alteration) of essentially the same idea. When the theme of a composition reappears, but with certain changes, the principle of variety is at work. Variation of a thematic idea may be produced by several means, each based upon a musical element.

Melodic Variety. When the tones of a theme are altered, melodic variety is the result. This simple theme

may be altered melodically in this way

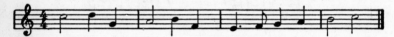

and tones may be added to the original melody without destroying its essential nature or recognizability, as below.

Another form of melodic variation is the addition of ornaments (such as trills, mordents, and figuration) to the basic tones.

Rhythmic Variety. By altering note values or changing the accents, the composer produces rhythmic variety.

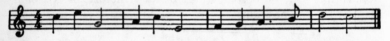

Also, the element of meter is employed in this illustration to create variety.

Harmonic Variety. A composer may choose to create harmonic variety by using different chords, as illustrated on the next page.

Tonal Variety. When the same theme appears in different keys or is changed from major to minor, tonal variety results. In the next example, our original theme in C major (page 78) now reappears in the key of G Major, then in C minor.

Change of Timbre. Assigning a given theme successively to different instruments of the orchestra produces variety of timbre (e.g., Ravel's *Boléro*).

Other Agents of Variety. The composer may obtain variety by changing the register of a theme (moving it from high to low, or vice versa) and by changing the accompaniment pattern. With all these resources at his disposal, he can produce unlimited variety in his thematic material. Obviously, any combination of the above methods can be used in successive appearances of the same theme. (Notice how Mozart varies the theme in the first movement of his *Sonata in A Major*, K. 331, which is illustrated in Chapter 13.)

CONTRAST

Whereas structural variety means modification of essentially the *same* theme, structural contrast means the juxtaposition of essentially *different* themes. Compositions which consist of several sections usually contain at least one contrasting section. Structural contrast is represented by letter formulas. For example, a composition in three sections, the middle section of which has a contrasting theme, would have the formula A B A. The principle of structural contrast is effected in several ways.

Thematic Contrast. One means of creating contrast is to introduce a new theme. Thus, a different theme is used to provide contrast with a preceding one. Contrasting themes will usually differ in several respects, such as melody, rhythm, and harmony.

Key Contrast. The use of a different key greatly enhances the effect of contrast. For example, in the structural plan A B A, the A sections might be in the key of C, while the B section might be in the key of G. The difference in key makes a greater contrast than would be the case if all sections were in the same key. Sectional changes from a major to a minor key, or from a minor to a major key, also provide contrast.

Tempo Contrast. The third method of achieving contrast is to introduce marked changes in tempo among the principal sections or movements of a larger composition. For example, the four movements of the Handel *Violin Sonata in D Major* have these tempo contrasts: slow, fast, slow, fast.

Other Methods of Providing Contrast. The effect of contrast can be further augmented by means of register (high against low), orchestral timbres (one color contrasted with another), sonorities (few instruments or parts contrasted with many), textures (homophonic textures contrasted with polyphonic textures), meters (three–four meter contrasted with four–four, etc.), and dynamics (loud sections contrasted with quiet sections).

LENGTH

Length in musical structure is a relative matter, but it may be a significant feature of a particular composition or of certain musical forms. Symphonies are usually longer than symphonic poems; operas are longer than cantatas; sonatas are longer than fugues. In general, the longer the composition is, the more complex the structure will be; and the shorter the composition, the simpler the structure.

Recommended Listening

The principles of theme, unity, variety, contrast, and length are to be found in virtually every composition but in varying degrees of prominence. The compositions listed below have been selected to help you develop your awareness of these general structural principles.

*Bach. *Cantata No. 140; Wachet auf, ruft uns die Stimme* (variety: opening chorus, second chorus for tenors, and final chorale all make use of the same hymn melody)

*————. *Passacaglia and Fugue in C Minor* (organ; theme and unity in both)

*————. *Suite No. 3 in D Major for Orchestra: Overture* (contrasting middle section)

————. *The Well-Tempered Clavier: Prelude No. 1 in C Major* (unity); *Fugue No. 1 in C Major* (theme, unity)

Beethoven. *Sonata No. 7 in D Major* (piano): III (*Menuetto;* contrasting middle section)

————. *Sonata No. 12 in A Flat Major* (piano): I (theme, unity, variety)

*————. *Symphony No. 5 in C Minor:* II (theme, variety)

*Brahms. *Symphony No. 3 in F Major:* III (contrasting middle section: A B A); IV (variety: modification of main theme)

————. *Variations on a Theme of Haydn,* Op. 56a (orchestra; theme and variety)

Chopin. *Étude in C Major,* Op. 10, No. 1 (piano; unity)

————. *Étude in E Minor,* Op. 25, No. 5 (piano; contrasting middle section)

————. *Étude in G Flat Major,* Op. 25, No. 9 ("Butterfly" Étude; unity, variety)

*————. *Sonata No. 2 in B Flat Minor,* Op. 35 (piano): III (contrasting middle section)

*Debussy. *Prélude à l'Après–midi d'un Faune (Prelude to the Afternoon of a Faun,* symphonic poem; theme, variety, contrast)

Handel. *Sonata No. 4 in D Major for Violin and Harpsichord,* Op. 1, No. 13 (contrast of movements, tempo)

*Haydn. *Quartet in E Flat Major,* Op. 33, No. 2 (strings): IV (theme, unity, contrast)

————. *Quartet in C Major,* Op. 76, No. 3 ("Emperor," for strings): II variety by accompaniment and register)

*Hindemith. *Sonata No. 3 for Piano:* IV (theme, unity)

Liszt. *Les Préludes* (theme)

*Mendelssohn. *Concerto in E Minor for Violin and Orchestra* (contrast of movements)

————. *A Midsummer Night's Dream* (orchestra; contrast of movements)

*Mozart. *Don Giovanni* (opera): *Overture* (contrast of tempo and key between *andante* introduction and *molto allegro*)

————. *Eine Kleine Nachtmusik (Serenade,* for small orchestra), K. 525 (themes, contrast of movements)

————. *Quintet in A Major for Clarinet and String Quartet,* K. 581: II (contrasting sections: A B A B)

*————. *Symphony No. 40 in G. Minor,* K. 550 (contrasting movements)

Paganini. *Caprice No. 24* (unaccompanied violin; theme, variety, unity)

*Ravel. *Boléro* (orchestra; theme, variety, unity)

————. *Concerto in G Major for Piano and Orchestra* (contrasting second movement)

Saint–Saëns. *Introduction and Rondo Capriccioso* (violin and orchestra; themes, contrast)

*Schubert. *Die Winterreise (The Winter Journey,* a song cycle): No. 11

("Spring Dream"; contrast of tempo and meter); No. 1 ("Good Night"; unity of accompaniment and theme, contrast of keys)

*Schumann. *Fantasiestücke* (*Fantasy Pieces*, piano): No. 2, "Aufschwung" ("Soaring"; contrast of keys and themes; unity of recurring main theme)

———. *Kinderscenen* (*Scenes of Childhood,* piano): No. 7, "Traumerei" ("Reverie"; theme, unity, variety, contrast)

*Strauss, R. *Till Eulenspiegel* (symphonic poem; theme, unity, variety, contrast)

*Tchaikovsky. *Nutcracker Suite* (orchestra; contrast of movements)

12. Simple Sectional Structures

The preceding chapter dealt with the general principles of musical structure. We shall now examine more specific principles which have to do with the sectional structure of music. Although scarcely any two compositions are identical in structure, there are certain structural principles which are followed in virtually all music.

PHRASE STRUCTURE

The smallest structural unit in music is the phrase. It is comparable to the sentence in prose composition in that it contains a complete musical idea. Like sentences, musical phrases vary greatly in length. The most common length of phrase is four measures. (*Home on the Range*, page 31, consists of four regular four–measure phrases: measures 1–4, 4–8, 8–12, and 12–16.)

Cadence. Just as sentences are punctuated by commas and periods, so phrases in music are punctuated by cadences. A *cadence* is a design or formula consisting of harmonic, rhythmic, and (usually) melodic elements which produce the effect of temporary or permanent completeness. Perhaps the most important determinant of a cadence is the harmonic progression. A cadence which ends on the tonic chord is a *complete cadence*. A cadence which ends on some other chord (usually dominant, sometimes subdominant), is an *incomplete* or *half cadence*. (See *Home on the Range*, page 31: complete cadences conclude the phrases in measures 8 and 16, and half cadences conclude the phrases in measures 4 and 12.) In the analogy of the sentence, the complete cadence is like the period; the half cadence is like a question mark or a semicolon. The cadence is usually marked by a rhythmic pause.

Antecedent and Consequent Phrases. A phrase which ends with a half cadence is called an *antecedent phrase.* It is followed by a phrase, called the *consequent phrase,* which ends with a complete cadence. (In *Home on the Range,* the first four measures are the antecedent phrase; the second four are the consequent phrase.)

Period Structure. When two or more phrases are joined in a continuous fashion so that together they constitute a sectional unit, the structure is called a *period.* (The first eight measures of *Home on the Range,* page 31, constitute a regular period of two four–measure phrases.)

Phraseology. The phrase structure of music is called *phraseology.* Music does not consist entirely of neatly arranged four–measure phrases grouped into regular period structures. Phrases not only vary greatly in length but also vary in degree of clarity. Consequently, it is not always easy to determine where one phrase ends and another begins. Varied phrase structure enhances the elasticity and the diversity of music.

PRINCIPAL SECTIONS

After phrase and period structures, the next larger (or longer) sections of musical structure should be considered. There is no single term to describe these larger sections. They are usually referred to by letters (A, B, C, etc.), as indicated above, or they may have functional names (which will be explained shortly). Two principles by which a single composition is divided into main sections are the *binary* and *ternary* plans.

Binary Structure. A piece of music which consists of two main sections is considered to be in binary form. There are several possibilities within this one concept.

First, the form may consist of two sections of essentially the same material, the second section being either an exact or a modified repetition of the first. This form is then represented by the formula A A or A A'. (The sign ' designates modification of the same theme.)

Second, the sections may consist of essentially different thematic material, in which case the structure is represented by the formula A B. Without changing the essentially binary form of the piece, either or both of these sections may be repeated with

or without modification: A A B (called *barform*), A A' B or
A B B or A A' B B'.

Ternary Structure. A composition in ternary form consists of
three main sections, the middle section of which is a contrasting
theme: A B A or A B A'. A familiar ternary structure on a larger
scale is the minuet movement of a sonata, a string quartet, or a
symphony. The minuet is represented by A; the middle section,
called a *trio,* is B; and the return to the minuet is again A.

Song Form. When the first section of a simple ternary form is
repeated (A A B A), the structure is usually referred to as *song
form* (because many folk songs have this structure) or as *rounded
binary.* (If we designate the phrases of *Home on the Range* as
main sections, we obtain the formula A A' B A', which is song
form or rounded binary.)

Further repetition of sections in a basically ternary structure
results in such schemes as A A B A B A and A A' B A" B A".

Functional Sections. In descriptions of musical structures, special terms are applied to certain sections which serve a special
purpose in the whole structure.

INTRODUCTION. A section appearing at the beginning of a composition and serving as a prologue or preface to the main part of
the piece is called an *introduction.* It does not necessarily introduce the thematic material of the main sections. (For examples
of short introductions, see Schubert's *Das Wandern, Der Erlkönig, Gretchen am Spinnrade,* and *Good Night,* and Mendelssohn's *Songs Without Words.*)

EXPOSITION. In larger forms the section which contains the
statement of the principal theme or themes is called the *exposition* (see Chapter 14).

RECAPITULATION. The repetition of the main section of a composition, usually after an intervening contrasting section, is called
the *recapitulation.* It is the second A in the formula A B A.
The recapitulation may be an exact repetition of the first main
section (as in the *da capo aria*) or it may be a modification
(A B A').

CODA. The term *coda* applies to a brief section at the end of
a composition. It functions as a conclusion or epilogue to the
whole composition.

TRANSITION, BRIDGE. The terms *transition* and *bridge* (or *bridge passage*) refer to sections of secondary importance. Their function is usually to effect a change of key (called *modulation*) from one main section of a composition to the next.

EPISODE. An *episode* is also a secondary section of a piece, apart from the main sections. The episode or *interlude,* as it is sometimes called, usually does not contain any of the main thematic materials; it is a digression from the main ideas of the composition.

Recommended Listening

The following list includes several songs which, because of their familiarity, will help you immediately to understand simple structural plans.

In listening to any of the following compositions, you will usually need to hear it several times to grasp its structure. Observe the main sections of the music and, so far as you can, the modification of the thematic ideas when they recur. Each piece listed under the various headings explained in this chapter has the main structural divisions indicated by the letter formula. You will notice that in some of the pieces the main divisions are only phrases, while in the longer compositions each section may consist of several phrases. For example, the Neapolitan boat song "Santa Lucia" has the following musical structure:

Now 'neath the silver moon Ocean is glowing } phrase a	}	section A
O'er the calm billow Soft winds are blowing; } phrase b		
Here balmy breezes blow Pure joys invite us, } phrase a	}	section A
And as we gently row, All things delight us. } phrase b		
Hark, how the sailor's cry Joyously echoes nigh: } phrase c	}	section B
Santa Lucia! Santa Lucia! phrase d		
Home of fair Poesy Realm of pure Harmony, } phrase c	}	section B
Santa Lucia! Santa Lucia! phrase d		

Hence, the structural formula of "Santa Lucia" is A A B B.

Regular phrases and periods:

Foster. *Swanee River*. First phrase, antecedent: "Way down upon the Swanee River, Far, far away" ending with half cadence on the dominant. Second phrase, consequent: "Dere's wha' my heart is turning ever, Dere's wha' de old folks stay," ending with complete cadence on the tonic. Both phrases together constitute a period.

Auld Lang Syne (Scottish folk song). First phrase, antecedent: "Should auld acquaintance be forgot, And never bro't to mind?" ending with cadence on the subdominant. Second phrase, consequent: "Should auld acquaintance be forgot. And days of auld lang syne?" ending with complete cadence on the tonic. Both phrases together constitute a period. The refrain has the same antecedent-consequent construction of phrases.

Haydn. *Oh Worship the King.* First phrase, antecedent: "Oh Worship the King all glorious above" ending with half cadence on the dominant. Second phrase consequent: "And gratefully sing His wonderful love" ending with complete cadence on the tonic. Both phrases together constitute a period.

Long phrases:

*Bach. *Suite No. 3 in D Major for Orchestra: Air*

————. *The Well-Tempered Clavier, Vol. I*: *Prelude No. 1 in C Major; Prelude No. 8 in E Flat Minor*

Handel. *Largo* (*Ombra mai fù,* from the opera *Xerxes*)

————. *Sonata No. 4 in D Major* for *Violin and Harpsichord* (or piano), Op. 1, No. 13: I

Wagner. *Die Meistersinger* (opera): "Prize Song" ("Morgenlicht leuchtend")

Simple binary structures:

Familiar songs and hymns:

    Abide with Me (A A')

    America (A B)

    The Linden Tree (*Der Lindenbaum;* No. 5 in Schubert's *Die Winterreise;* A A')

    London Bridge (A A')

    My Faith Looks Up to Thee (A B)

    Santa Lucia (A A B B; see page 83)

*Bach. *Cantata No. 140, Wachet auf, ruft uns die Stimme:* final chorale (barform, A A B for each verse)

————. *Christ lag in Todesbanden* (chorale prelude for organ; barform)

————. *St. Matthew Passion:* "O Haupt voll Blut und Wunden ("O sacred Head now wounded"; barform)

Beethoven. *Sonata No. 23 in F Minor* (piano, "Appassionata"): II, theme (A A B B)

Brahms. *Wiegenlied* (*Lullaby;* two periods of two phrases each: a a' b b' = total structure A B)

Chopin. *Préludes,* Op. 28 (piano): *No. 1 in C Major, No. 4 in E Minor, No. 5 in D Major, No. 7 in A Major* (all A A'); *No. 20 in C Minor* (A B B)

Couperin. *La Galante* (harpsichord; No. 40 in *Masterpieces of Music before 1750;* A A A' A'; i.e., the form A A' with each section repeated)

Lully. *Amadis de Gaule* (opera): "Bois Épais" (A B)

*Mozart. *Don Giovanni* (opera): *Serenade;* "Deh vieni alla finestra" (A A')

Neidhart von Reuenthal (thirteenth-century Minnesinger). *Willekommen Mayenschein* (A A B)

Purcell. *Dido and Aeneas* (opera): "When I am laid in earth" (barform)

Saint–Saëns. *Carnival of the Animals* (orchestra or two pianos): "Turtles" (phrases a a' b b'; structure A B)

Schubert. *An die Musik* (song): (A A)

————. *Du bist die Ruh* (A A' B B' each verse)

————. *Die Forelle* (each verse: A B)

————. *Die Schöne Müllerin:* No. 1, "Das Wandern" (phrases aa bc; main structure A B)

Schumann. *Dichterliebe:* "Ich grolle nicht" (A A')

Longer binary structures:

Bach. *Partita No. 5 in G Major* (piano or harpsichord): Allemande, Courante, Sarabande, Minuetto, Passepied, Gigue. (Each movement is an A A' form with each section repeated. However, in performance the sections are often not repeated.)

*Copland. *Music for the Theatre:* "Burlesque" (A B A B)

*Handel. *Messiah:* "But who may abide" (A A); "He shall feed His flock" (A A').

———. *Sonata No. 4 in D Major* (violin and harpsichord or piano), Op. 1, No. 13: I (A A')

Haydn. *The Creation:* "The heavens are telling" (A B B. The section beginning "The heavens are telling" is A; the section beginning "The wonder of His work" is B.)

Mozart. *Quintet in A Major* (clarinet and string quartet), K. 581: II (A B A B)

Pergolesi. *Stabat Mater:* "Cuius Animam" (A B); "Eja mater fons amoris" (A A' B)

Simple ternary structures:

*Bach. *Cantata No. 140; Wachet auf, ruft uns die Stimme:* "Wann kommst du, mein Heil," "Mein Freund ist mein" (both A B A)

———. *St. Matthew Passion.* The following numbers are *da capo arias* with the form A B A: "Buss und Reu," "Blute nur," "Gerne will ich mich bequemen," "Erbarme dich," "Können Thränen," "Mache dich mein Herze rein," and the final chorus, "Wir setzen uns mit Thränen nieder."

Chopin. *Prélude No. 15 in D Flat Major* (piano) (A B A')

Haydn. *The Creation:* "With verdure clad" (A B A')

Mendelssohn. *Elijah:* "Lift thine eyes" (A B A')

———. *Songs Without Words,* Op. 62, No. 28 in G Major (introduction, A B A coda)

Mozart. *The Marriage of Figaro:* "Voi che sapete" (A B A)

Pergolesi. *Stabat Mater:* "Vidit suum" (A B A)

Saint–Saëns. *Carnival of the Animals:* "The Elephant" (introduction, A B A, coda), "The Swan" (A B A)

Longer ternary structures:

Beethoven. *Quartet No. 2 in G Major* (strings): II (A B A')

———. *Sonata No. 7 in D Major* (piano): II (A B A')

———. *Sonata No. 18 in E Flat Major* (piano): III (A B A)

*———. *Symphony No. 5 in C Minor:* III (A B A)

*Brahms. *Symphony No. 3 in F Major:* III (A B A')

*Chopin. *Sonata No. 2 in B Flat Minor,* Op. 35: III (A B A)

*Haydn. *Quartet in E Flat Major* (strings), Op. 33, No. 2: II (A B A)

Mozart. *Concerto in A Major for Piano and Orchestra,* K. 488: II

*———. *Symphony No. 40 in G Minor:* III (A B A)

Song form (rounded binary):
Familiar songs:

    All through the Night (A A B A)
    America the Beautiful (A A' B A")
    Au Clair de la Lune (A A B A)
    Believe Me If All Those Endearing Young Charms (A A' B A')
    The Blue Bells of Scotland (A A B A)
    Drink to Me Only with Thine Eyes (A A B A)
    Home on the Range (A A' B A')
    Long, Long Ago (A A' B A')

Oh Susanna (verse: A A'; chorus: B A'; verse with chorus: A A' B A')
Oh Worship the King (A A' B A'')

Beethoven. *Sonata No. 12 in A Flat Major* (piano), Op. 26: I, theme (A A' B A')

Brahms. *Variations on a Theme of Haydn: theme* (A A' B A)

*Haydn. *Quartet in E Flat Major* (strings), Op. 33, No. 2: II, Minuet: A A B A B A. Trio: A A B A B A, or A A A' A A' A, since the thematic material is all quite similar. Returning minuet without repeats: A B A. The movement as a whole is A B A (minuet, trio, minuet)

Mendelssohn. *Songs Without Words:* Op. 19, *No. 4 in A Major;* Op. 30, *No. 9 in E Major;* Op. 62, *No. 27 in E Minor* (all have the plan: introduction, A A B A, coda. Some have a modified A in repetition); Op. 30, *No. 3 in E Major* (Introduction, A A' B A'', coda)

Mozart. *Sonata in A Major* (piano), K. 331: I, theme (A A' B A'')

————. *Variations on Ah vous dirai–je Maman,* K. 265, theme (A A B A)

Prokofiev. *Classical Symphony in D Major:* III (A A B A')

Schubert. *Die Winterreise (The Winter Journey,* song cycle): "Good Night" (A A B A')

13. Variation Forms

While the principle of variety discussed in Chapter 11 is opera-
tive to some extent in virtually all music, it is the principal structural feature of a number of types known as variation forms.

Theme and Variations. The commonest variation form is
known as *theme and variation* or *theme with variations.* The
plan of this form involves the following two steps: (1) There is
a statement of a theme, usually in a simple, straightforward manner. The theme, often a simple song form, may be original with
the composer, or he may borrow a theme which is already well-
known. (2) The theme is then restated several times, each time
with some scheme of modification or variation being applied.
Some of the variations, as these restatements are called, may in-
volve such extensive modification that the original idea is obscured. The means of variation (discussed in Chapter 11) are
numerous: melodic, harmonic, rhythmic, metric, tonal, textural,
and so forth. The illustration on page 91 from the first movement of Mozart's *Piano Sonata in A Major* (K. 331), shows how
extensive the melodic variation may be. In addition, the accompaniment style changes with each new variation.

Continuous Variations. The structure of the variation form
known as theme and variations is characterized by a definite
pause and separation between each variation. Another, somewhat older, type of variation is known as *continuous variations.*
Here, the theme (a harmonic progression of a short melody; see
the theme of the Bach *Passacaglia in C Minor,* page 26) is re-
iterated without pause between statements, and over the recurrent
theme there is a continuous flow of material. Continuous varia-

tions are designated by three terms: (1) *ground,* (2) *passacaglia,* and (3) *chaconne.*

GROUND. The variation form known as a *ground* is based upon a "ground bass," which is a short theme appearing in the bass. While the bass theme is stated over and over, often with little or no change, other materials of a constantly changing nature sound above it. In other words, the principle of variation is not active in the melodic theme itself, but rather in the materials which are added to it.

PASSACAGLIA. The terms *passacaglia* and *chaconne* are often confused. In fact, in the seventeenth and eighteenth centuries, these terms were used almost interchangeably. Both refer to continuous variations. If a distinction can be made, it is that the passacaglia is a type of "ground" in which contrapuntal material is superimposed on a recurrent bass theme. In some passacaglias, the theme occasionally moves from the bass to another register. Bach's famous *Passacaglia in C Minor* for organ is an example of this variation form.

CHACONNE. The term *chaconne* is sometimes applied to the variations-on-a-ground or the passacaglia, as explained above. In another type of chaconne, however, there is a recurrent chord progression above which varying melodies and contrapuntal material are superimposed. Bach's "Chaconne" from the *Partita No. 2 in D Minor* for unaccompanied violin is a famous example of this chaconne form.

Recommended Listening

In listening to any of the following compositions in variation form, you will do well to become thoroughly familiar with the theme by hearing it several times before listening to its subsequent variations. As you listen to each variation, try to determine just what the composer has done to modify the original theme.

Theme and variations:
Arenski. *Variations on a Theme by Tchaikovsky* (orchestra)
Ballantine. *Variations on Mary Had a Little Lamb* (piano)
Beethoven. *Sonata No. 12 in A Flat Major* (piano): I
———. *Sonata No. 23 in F Minor* (piano, "Appassionata"): II
———. *Symphony No. 3 in E Flat Major* ("Eroica"): IV
*———. *Symphony No. 5 in C Minor:* II (a free variation form on two themes)
Brahms. *Variations and Fugue on a Theme by Handel* (piano)
———. *Variations on a Theme of Haydn,* Op. 56a, 56b (orchestra or two pianos)
Britten. *Variations on a Theme by Frank Bridge* (string orchestra)

————. *The Young Person's Guide to the Orchestra*

Byrd. *The Bells* (harpsichord)

————. *The Carman's Whistle* (harpsichord)

Dohnányi. *Variations on a Nursery Theme* (piano and orchestra)

Elgar. *Enigma Variations* (orchestra)

Farnaby. *Loth to Depart* (harpsichord; No. 29 in *Masterpieces of Music before 1750*)

Franck. *Symphonic Variations* (piano and orchestra)

Ginastera. *Variaciones Concertantes* (orchestra)

Handel. *Suite No. 5 in E Major* (harpsichord): IV ("The Harmonious Blacksmith")

Haydn. *Quartet in C Major* ("Emperor," for strings): II

————. *Symphony No. 94 in G Major* ("Surprise"): II

Hindemith. *Symphonic Metamorphoses: Turandot*

D'Indy. *Istar Variations* (orchestra)

Liszt. *La Campanella* (piano)

————. *Variations on the Bach Prelude,* "Weinen, klagen"

Mendelssohn. *Variations Sérieuses in D Minor* (piano)

Mozart. *Concerto in C Minor for Piano and Orchestra*, K. 491: III

————. *Quintet in A Major for Clarinet and String Quartet*, K. 581: IV

————. *Sonata in A Major*, K. 331 (piano): I

————. *Variations on Ah vous dirai–je Maman*, K. 265 (piano)

Paganini. *Caprice No. 24* (unaccompanied violin)

Prokofiev. *Concerto No. 3 in C Major for Piano and Orchestra:* II

Rachmaninoff. *Variations on a Theme of Chopin* (piano)

————. *Variations on a Theme of Corelli* (piano)

*Ravel. *Boléro* (orchestral variations; each statement of the theme is presented by a different combination of instruments)

Reger. *Variations and Fugue on a Theme by Mozart* (orchestra)

Rósza. *Theme, Variations, and Finale* (orchestra)

Saint–Saëns. *Variations on a Theme by Beethoven* (2 pianos)

Schoenberg. *Variations on a Recitative* (organ)

Schubert. *Octet in F Major* (strings, horn, bassoon, and clarinet): IV

————. *Quartet No. 14 in D Minor* (strings, "Death and the Maiden"): II

————. *Quintet in A Major*, Op. 114 ("Trout"; piano, violin, viola, cello, and bass): IV

Strauss, R. *Don Quixote* (orchestra and cello solo; free orchestral variations)

Stravinsky. *Octet for Wind Instruments:* II

Sweelinck. *Variations on Mein junges Leben hat ein End* (organ)

————. *Variations on Unter den Linden grüne* (organ)

Tartini. *Variations on a Theme of Corelli* (cello and piano)

Thomson. *Variations on Sunday School Tunes* (organ)

Weber. *Variations on a Theme from Silvania* (clarinet and piano)

Widor. *Variations from Symphonie Gothique* (organ)

Passacaglia and ground:

Bach. *Mass in B Minor:* "Crucifixus"

*————. *Passacaglia in C Minor* (organ)

Bizet. *L'Arlésienne Suite No. 2* (orchestra): "Carillon"

Bloch. *Quartet No. 2* (strings): IV (Introduction, Passacaglia and Fugue)

Britten. *Passacaglia* from *Peter Grimes* (orchestra)

Copland. *Passacaglia* (piano)

Purcell. *Dido and Aeneas:* "When I am laid in earth" ("Dido's Lament")

Purcell. *A New Ground* (harpsichord; No. 38 in *Masterpieces of Music before 1750*)

Wolpe. *Passacaglia* (piano)

Chaconne:

Bach. *Goldberg Variations* (harpsichord)

———. *Partita No. 2 in D Minor for Unaccompanied Violin: Chaconne*

Brahms. *Symphony No. 4 in E Minor:* IV

Purcell. *Chaconne in G Minor* ("Great"; chamber orchestra)

14. The Larger Sectional Forms

Single pieces and movements of sonatas, suites, and other compound forms are usually constructed according to one of several plans, each of which is more complex than the structures described in Chapter 12. Although it is not essential that you grasp every detail of the more complex structures, you should certainly become familiar with the over–all plans.

EXPANDED TERNARY FORMS

If you listened to some of the longer ternary structures listed at the end of Chapter 12, you have already had the experience of hearing expanded ternary forms consisting of three main sections: A B A. In the expanded ternary form, often called *song form with trio,* each main section is itself a simple or (shorter) binary or ternary structure. An example of expanded ternary structure is the second movement (Scherzo and Trio) of Haydn's *Quartet in E Flat Major,* Op. 33. No. 2 (strings). There are four themes, which begin as shown in the following illustration.

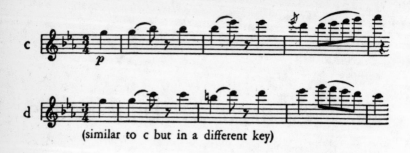

(similar to c but in a different key)

These four themes begin sections which have the following structure:

SCHERZO (A)   TRIO (B)   SCHERZO (A)

a :‖: b a :‖   c :‖: d c :‖   a b a

* The repeat signs (:‖: and :‖) mean that the scherzo will be played a a b a b a, and the trio c c d c d c.

The scherzo by itself is a song form (or rounded binary). The trio by itself is also a song form. The returning scherzo, played without repeats, is in simple ternary form. The three main sections, scherzo–trio–scherzo, constitute an expanded ternary form. Note that themes *a* and *b* are somewhat similar, that themes *c* and *d* are quite similar, and that the two pairs provide contrast.

RONDO FORMS

Several structural plans come under the heading *rondo forms*. The essential feature of all rondo structures is the recurrence of a main theme which alternates with one or more subordinate themes. Each theme may in itself be a short song form or a simple binary or ternary structure. Whereas the main theme (A) almost always appears unmodified in the tonic key, the other themes

(B, C, etc.) usually appear in contrasting keys. The themes of any rondo structure may be separated by episodes or transitions consisting of nonthematic (or of less thematic) material.

In a sense, the simple ternary plan, A B A, is a rondo (and is in fact sometimes called *first rondo*), but since there is only one recurrence of the main theme, it does not really belong to this category.

Simple Rondo. The simplest rondo structure (aside from the simple ternary form) is the one with only two thematic ideas (A and B) in alternation: A B A B A. Examples of this plan are the third and fourth movements of Haydn's *Quartet in E Flat Major,* Op. 33, No. 2 (strings).

Second Rondo. Perhaps the most common rondo form is the plan A B A C A, which contains two subordinate themes (B and C) in alternation with the main theme. This structure is called *second rondo.* An example which illustrates the rondo principle in general and the second rondo in particular is the second movement of Beethoven's *Sonata in G Major,* Op. 49, No. 2 (piano). The main theme (A) is a song form with the plan a a′ b a″ a‴.

A brief transition of eight measures modulates from the key of
G to the key of D with this material:

Transition

The second theme (B) then appears in the key of the dominant
(D major).

Another brief transition, suggesting the rhythm of the main
theme, takes us back to the key of G where the main theme (A)
is again stated in its entirety. The third theme (C) begins immediately after the conclusion of A. This theme is in the key of
C major.

At the end of C, a modulation returns once more to the key of G, where the main theme makes its final appearance. A short coda (see page 85) of 13 measures, using the main theme idea, concludes the movement. Hence, we have the following over–all plan of this rondo:

Theme:	A	tr.	B	tr.	A	C	A	coda
Key:	G		D		G	C	G	G

Third Rondo. The most elaborate and extended of the rondo forms is the plan A B A C A B A. Like the second rondo, illustrated before, it has two subordinate themes (B and C), but it also has further statements of A and B. The main theme (A) usually appears unmodified and in the tonic key. The second theme (B) first appears in the dominant key and appears the second time in the tonic key. The idea of this structure can be quickly grasped from Schumann's piano piece, "Fürchtenmachen" ("Frightening," No. 11 of *Kinderscenen*), which is a miniature third rondo of very short and sharply contrasted themes. The last movement of Beethoven's *Sonata in E Major,* Op. 14, No. 1 (piano), is a good example of a longer third rondo.

In the longer third rondo structure, when the middle section (C) is not essentially a different theme but rather a development of A and/or B, the form is referred to as *rondo–allegro* or *rondo–sonata*. The final movement of Beethoven's *Concerto No. 5 in E Flat Major for Piano and Orchestra* ("Emperor") is in rondo–allegro form.

SONATA–ALLEGRO FORM

The most flexible and certainly the most complex of all basic structural plans is the one called *sonata–allegro form* (or simply *sonata form*). It is also sometimes known as *first movement form* because it is most generally used as the first movement of sonatas; but it is quite often used as the form of slow movements and last movements as well. The sonata–allegro form is a large ternary structure consisting of three main sections:

A	B	A
Exposition	Development	Recapitulation

Each of these main divisions is separated into several thematic and functional sections.

Exposition. The exposition of sonata–allegro form contains the principal themes of the movement. Any number of themes may be introduced, but in the simple classical structure there are as a rule only two or three.

MAIN THEME. The main theme is usually vigorous and force-ful, containing rhythmic and melodic patterns known as *motives*. It is in the tonic key (the key of the movement). It may consist of one or several thematic ideas.

BRIDGE. Following the section containing the main theme or themes, there is a functional section called the *bridge* or *bridge passage,* which modulates to a contrasting key. If the movement is in a major key, the contrasting key will be the dominant. If the movement is in a minor key, the contrasting key will probably be the relative major key (a minor third higher than the tonic–the key with the same key signature as the major key).

SUBORDINATE THEME. The second principal section of the expo-sition is called the *subordinate theme* or *second theme*. Like the main-theme section, it may consist of more than one thematic idea. All this section is in the contrasting key (dominant or rela-tive major). The theme or themes of the subordinate section are usually more lyric and songlike than those in the main-theme section.

CLOSING THEME. The exposition usually concludes with a brief section called the *closing theme* or *codetta*. This section may have one or more themes of its own, or it may refer to themes already presented in the main-theme or subordinate-theme sections. It serves to bring the exposition to a close.

Development. One of the distinguishing features of the sonata–allegro form is the *development section,* the middle of the three main sections. This section employs any or all of the themes presented in the exposition. However, the themes are not usually present in their entirety but are broken up into motives; they are passed around among different registers and by various instruments (in orchestral compositions), put into different keys, and in general exploited or "developed." There are no standard lengths for the development section, no specified keys, and no conventional practices in regard to the material employed. Obviously, the principles of modification and variation come strongly into play in the development section.

Recapitulation. The recapitulation is essentially a restatement of the exposition, but with certain modifications. The chief difference between the exposition and the recapitulation is that the subordinate-theme and closing-theme sections in the latter are in the tonic key rather than in a contrasting key. The bridge passage is retained, but it does not establish a new key in the recapitulation.

Coda. The coda, a concluding section to the whole movement, is often employed. It may be a brief epilogue, or it may be a considerably extended section of the movement (as in the first movement of Beethoven's *Symphony No. 5 in C Minor*).

Introduction. The introduction, like the coda, is not essential to the sonata–allegro structure. When it is used to open a movement (e.g., Haydn's *Symphony No. 97 in C Major,* first movement), it is in a slow tempo. It may or may not include thematic material used in the exposition.

Total Structure. In order to obtain an over–all view of the basic plan of the sonata–allegro structure, let us examine the first movement of Mozart's *Symphony No. 40 in G Minor.* (The second and fourth movements of this symphony are also in the sonata–allegro form.)

Of the five thematic ideas, the first (*a*) is given by far the most extensive and prominent use. There is no introduction. The coda is a brief 12-measure extension of the closing-theme section. The development section uses the main-theme material exclusively and passes through several keys.

Structural Plan of Mozart's *Symphony No. 40 in G Minor*, I

Section	Material (letters indicate themes, page 103)	Key	Length (in measures)
Exposition			100
M.T.	a	G minor	20
bridge	a b c	G minor to B♭ major	23
S.T.	d	B♭ major	22
Cl. T.	e a	B♭ major	35
Development	a	F♯ minor, several other keys and back to G minor	64
Recapitulation			135
M.T.	a	G minor	19
bridge	a b c	G minor, E♭ major, G minor	43
S.T.	d	G minor	27
Cl. T. and coda	e a	G minor	46

Here are several suggestions for studying the form of this movement. First, become familiar with the thematic ideas on page 103.
Second, follow the movement from beginning to end, identifying
the themes as you hear them. Third, listen to the movement
again, consulting the chart (the structural plan) for guidance in
identifying the various sections. Finally, after repeated hearings,
concentrate upon the form as a whole without using the thematic
and structural guides.

It should be emphasized that sonata–allegro form, perhaps
more than any other structural plan, is a highly flexible concept,
not a rigid formula. Therefore, you should not be disturbed or
confused to find a movement of a sonata, quartet, or symphony
deviating in one or more respects from the general outline. Any
of the thematic sections may contain several themes or thematic
fragments; the composer may choose to vary the keys and materials considerably, not only in the development section, but also
in the exposition and recapitulation.

SONATINA FORM

The term *sonatina* (or *sonatine*) means a diminutive sonata; it is shorter and less involved than the regular sonata. The term is applied to a single–movement form when the development section is omitted or when it is replaced by a brief episode between the exposition and the recapitulation.

Recommended Listening

Especially in the study of larger structural forms, it is important to become familiar with the themes. With repeated hearings of the same composition, the structure will be come clear.

Song form and trio:
Beethoven. *Quartet No. 2 in G Major* (strings): III
———. *Sonata No. 12 in A Flat Major* (piano): II
*———. *Symphony No. 5 in C Minor:* III (*Scherzo*)
Chopin. *Étude in E Minor* (piano)
———. *Nocturne in F Sharp Major* (piano)
*———. *Sonata No. 2 in B Flat Minor,* Op. 35 (piano): II, III
Haydn. *Quartet in A Major,* Op. 20, No. 6 (strings): III
*———. *Quartet in E Flat Major,* Op. 33, No. 2 (strings): II
———. *Quartet in B Flat Major,* Op. 50, No. 1 (strings): II
———. *Symphony No. 94 in G Major* ("Surprise"): III
Mozart. *Eine Kleine Nachtmusik* (*Serenade,* for small orchestra), K. 525; III
———. *Quartet No. 14 in G Major* (strings), K. 387: II
*———. *Symphony No. 40 in G Minor,* K. 550: III
Tchaikovsky. *Quartet No. 1 in D Major* (strings): II

Rondo forms:
Bartók. *Rondos and Folk Dances* (piano)
Beethoven. *Concerto No. 3 in C Minor for Piano and Orchestra:* III
———. *Concerto No. 5 in E Flat Major for Piano and Orchestra* ("Emperor"): III (3rd rondo)
———. *Rondo in C Major* (piano) (A B A C A coda)
———. *Rondo in G Major* (piano) ("Rage over the Lost Penny")
———. *Sonata No. 3 in C Major* (piano): IV
———. *Sonata No. 8 in C Minor* (piano, "Pathétique"): II (A B A C A coda); III (3rd rondo)
———. *Sonata No. 9 in E Major* (piano): III (A B A C A B A)
———. *Sonata No. 15 in D Major* (piano): IV (A B A C A B A)
Debussy. *Minstrels* from *Préludes,* Book I, No. 12 (A B A C A)
Franck. *Sonata in A Major for Violin and Piano:* IV
———. *Symphony in D Minor:* II
Gershwin. *Prelude No. 3* (piano) (A B A C A)
Gluck. *Orfeo ed Euridice* (opera): "Che faro senza Euridice" (A B A C A)
Handel. *Concerto Grosso No. 9 in F Major:* II (A B A B A B A)
*Haydn. *Quartet in E Flat Major,* Op. 33, No. 2 (strings): III, IV (A B A B A)
———. *Sonata No. 7 in D Major for Piano:* III (A B A C tr. A)
———. *Symphony No. 97 in C Major* ("London" *Symphony No. 1*): IV
———. *Trio in G Major* (piano and strings): III (*Gypsy Rondo*)
Hindemith. *Quartet No. 3* (strings): IV

Kreisler. *Rondino on a Theme by Beethoven* (violin and piano; A B A C A D A. The themes are presented as follows: aa bb' a cc a dde a coda.)

Mendelssohn. *Rondo Capriccioso* (piano)

Mozart. *Concerto in A Major for Piano and Orchestra,* K. 488: III

——. *Eine Kleine Nachtmusik (Serenade, for small orchestra),* K. 525; II (A B A C A)

——. *Recitative and Rondo for Soprano,* K. 505 (soprano and orchestra)

——. *Rondo for Soprano,* K. 490 (soprano and orchestra)

——. *Rondo in B Flat Major,* K. 269 (violin and orchestra)

——. *Rondo in C Major,* K. 272 (violin and orchestra)

——. *Rondo in D Major,* K. 382 (piano and orchestra)

——. *Rondo in A Major,* K. 386 (piano and orchestra)

——. *Rondo in D Major,* K. 485 (piano)

——. *Rondo in A Minor,* K. 511 (piano)

Ravel. *Pavane pour une Infante Défunte (Pavane for a Dead Princess,* for piano and orchestra; A B A C A)

Saint–Saëns. *Introduction and Rondo Capriccioso* (violin and orchestra; A B A C A B A)

Schubert. *Quartet in A Minor* (strings): II (A B A C A)

——. *Rondo in A Major* (2 pianos)

——. *Rondo in A Major* (violin and strings)

*Schumann. *Fantasiestücke (Fantasy Pieces;* piano): No. 2, "Aufschwung" ("Soaring") (A B A' C A" B A); No. 4, "Grillen" ("Whims") (A B A C A B A)

——. *Kinderscenen (Scenes of Childhood;* piano): No. 11, "Fürchten-machen" ("Frightening"; A B A C A B A. Each section is very brief.)

*Strauss, R. *Till Eulenspiegel* (symphonic poem; A B A C A coda. *Note:* this is a very free rondo form in which the main theme is considerably modified in successive appearances.)

Stravinsky. *Le Sacre du Printemps (The Rite of Spring; a ballet):* finale (A B A C A)

Sonata-allegro form:

Beethoven. *Overture to Coriolanus*

——. *Overture to Egmont*

——. *Quartet No. 2 in G Major* (strings): I, IV

——. *Sonata No. 15 in D Major* (piano): I

——. *Sonata No. 20 in G Major* (piano): I

——. *Sonata No. 21 in C Major* (piano; "Waldstein"): I

——. *Symphony No. 1 in C Major:* I

*——. *Symphony No. 5 in C Minor:* I

Brahms. *Symphony No. 1 in C Minor:* I

*——. *Symphony No. 3 in F Major:* I

Dvořák. *Symphony No. 5 in E Minor* ("New World"): I

Haydn. *Quartet in F Major,* Op. 3, No. 5 (strings): I

*——. *Quartet in E Flat Major,* Op. 33, No. 2 (strings): I

——. *Symphony No. 94 in G Major* ("Surprise"): I

——. *Symphony No. 97 in C Major* ("London" *Symphony No. 1*): I

——. *Symphony No. 101 in D Major* ("Clock"): I

Mendelssohn. *A Midsummer Night's Dream: Overture*

*Mozart. *Don Giovanni: Overture*

——. *Eine Kleine Nachtmusik (Serenade;* for small orchestra), K. 525: I

——. *Quartet No. 14 in G Major* (strings), K. 387: I

——. *Quartet No. 15 in D Minor* (strings), K. 421: I

Mozart. *Quintet in A Major for Clarinet and String Quartet,* K. 581: I

*———. *Symphony No. 40 in G Minor,* K. 550; I (see analysis, pp. 101–103): II, IV

Schubert. *Symphony No. 8 in B Minor* ("Unfinished"): I

Sonatina form:

Bartók. *Sonatina in D Minor for Piano*

Beethoven. *Sonata No. 5 in C Minor* (piano): II

Brahms. *Quartet No. 1 in G Minor* (piano and strings): I

———. *Sonata No. 3 in D Minor* (violin and piano): II

Clementi. *Sonatinas,* Op. 36 (piano)

Milhaud. *Sonatina for Clarinet and Piano*

———. *Sonatine for Flute and Piano*

Mozart. *Sonata in B Flat Major* (piano), K. 189 f: II

15. The Principal Contrapuntal Forms

The forms described in the preceding chapters (12, 13, 14) are sectional structures. Forms of another kind, known as contrapuntal forms, will be considered in the present chapter. Instead of being based on sectional divisions, these forms are based on certain contrapuntal procedures. Contrapuntal or polyphonic textures (see Chapter 6) are occasionally used in sonata movements, song forms, variations, and so forth; but we are now interested primarily in the forms which are exclusively contrapuntal.

CANON

The *canon* is one of the most elementary contrapuntal forms. It is a very old type, dating back nearly 700 years. It consists of two or more parts (or voices) which carry the same melody but begin it at different times. The principle of the canon is illustrated by the following example:

Note that both parts present the same melody, but at different times (a device known as *imitation*), and that the second part, which begins the melody a measure later than the first, is also an octave lower. This can be compared to two people walking down the street at the same pace, with one of them lagging a few steps behind the other. In canons, the time lag between the parts may range from a few beats to several measures. Furthermore, the pitch difference between voices may range from unison (voices beginning on the same tone) to a difference of an octave or more. Once the time and pitch relationships have been introduced, however, they are kept constant throughout the canon.

Round. A special kind of vocal canon, familiar to all, is the *round*. It is a comparatively short and simple song. When each voice in turn reaches the end of the melody, it begins again. In the seventeenth and eighteenth centuries, these canons were called *catches;* they were especially popular in England. Well-known rounds are "Three Blind Mice," "Row, Row, Row Your Boat," "Frère Jacques," and "Merrily, Merrily." (See the accompanying illustration of a four-part round by Purcell.)

Inversion. A contrapuntal device known as *inversion* is sometimes used for canons. The second voice moves by the same intervals as the first but in the opposite direction. Such canons are known as *mirror canons*. In the following example the first voice begins by moving upwards in thirds, the second voice imitates the first by moving *downwards* in thirds, and so on.

Retrograde. When a melody is played backwards, the procedure is known as *retrograde motion*. Canons, such as the following, which make use of this procedure, are known as *cancrizans* or *crab canons*.

Augmentation. The device by which a melody is imitated by a second voice, moving in proportionately longer notes, is known as *augmentation*. In the following canon by augmentation, both voices begin together, but the lower voice moves in note values twice as long as the first, to create a sort of hare–and–tortoise situation:

Double Canon. Still another type of canon is the *double canon,* which consists of two *different* melodies moving simultaneously, each being imitated canonically by still another voice, with four parts in all. Bach's chorale prelude "In dulci jubilo" for organ is a good example of the double canon.

FUGUE

Perhaps the most important contrapuntal form is the *fugue.* It is based on the imitation of a short theme called a *subject.* In fugues the number of voices (or parts) may be three to five or more. Like the canon, the fugue may be written for either instrumental or vocal mediums, or, sometimes, for both combined (e.g., Bach's *Mass in B Minor,* "Kyrie").

The fugue subject contains rhythmic and melodic motives which make it easy to recognize. It is announced by one voice alone. A second voice then states the theme a fifth scale degree higher (or a fourth lower). This is called the *answer.* A third voice then comes in with the subject, a fourth with the answer, and so on until all the parts have made their entries. While the subject or the answer is being stated, the voice or voices which have already entered continue with other counterpoint. The counterpoint which appears consistently with the subject or answer (after the first statement of the subject by itself) is called the *countersubject.* The subject, answer, and countersubject of Bach's *Fugue in C Minor* (No. 2 in *The Well-Tempered Clavier,* Vol. 1) are shown in the next illustration.

After a brief episode of two measures, the third voice enters with the subject.

The subject is stated recurrently in one voice after another throughout the fugue. Passages during which the subject is not being stated are called *episodes*. While listening to a fugue, you will enjoy identifying the subject with each of its numerous appearances in the different parts of the texture.

CHORALE PRELUDE

The oldest technique in contrapuntal music is the procedure of writing counterpoint (i.e., adding a melody) to an existing tune which is called a *cantus firmus*. Some of the melodies thus "borrowed" were plainsong tunes; others were popular songs. The Reformation brought a vast number of hymn melodies called *chorales*. Chorales were sung by the congregation and were also employed as cantus firmi for choir ensembles and organ pieces called *chorale preludes* used in the Lutheran service. The cantus firmus is usually prominent in chorale preludes because of its longer note values, while the counterpoint woven around it moves in more lively rhythm. Here is the chorale tune *Christ lag in Todesbanden (Christ Lay in the Bonds of Death)* which

Bach used as a cantus firmus in the wonderful chorale prelude of the same title. In the chorale preludes "O Mensch, bewein' dein' Sünde gross" and "Das alte Jahr vergangen ist," the cantus firmus is highly ornamented instead of proceeding in long, sustained tones. There are sometimes contrapuntal introductions and interludes between the phrases of the chorale melody, as in "Wachet auf."

RELIGIOUS POLYPHONIC FORMS (VOCAL)

Two significant polyphonic forms are the *Mass* and the *motet*. Both are examples of liturgical music (i.e., composed to function as integral parts of the church service).

Mass. The polyphonic setting of the *Ordinary of the Mass* (see pages 176 f.) contains five main sections based on the liturgical text: (1) *Kyrie,* (2) *Gloria,* (3) *Credo,* (4) *Sanctus* (including the *Benedictus*), and (5) *Agnus Dei.* These Latin titles are the first words of the respective texts. The Renaissance Mass usually consisted only of these five parts (e.g., in Palestrina's *Missa Brevis*). Later on, these five parts were often subdivided into sections or movements (e.g., in Bach's *Mass in B Minor*).

Motet. The *motet* of the fifteenth and sixteenth centuries is a comparatively short polyphonic composition, usually for voices alone (*a cappella*). It usually employs contrapuntal imitation of several short thematic ideas. Its text, in Latin, is religious—often Biblical—but it is not from the Ordinary of the Mass. The motet may be a cantus firmus composition based on a plainsong or it may consist of "free" counterpoint originating entirely with the composer.

SECULAR POLYPHONIC FORMS

In the sixteenth century there developed a significant vocal literature of a secular nature, paralleling the superb literature of liturgical music.

Madrigal. Polyphonic music for four or five voices with secular texts in the vernacular language was developed in Italy and England. These compositions have no standard sectional structure. They have contrapuntal textures in which imitation is not as a rule extensively employed.

Chanson and Lied. The words *chanson* (French) and *Lied*

(German) simply mean song. The polyphonic chanson and the polyphonic Lied of the Renaissance are the French and German counterparts of the Italian and English madrigals. In all this secular music the poetry and music combine to create works of great charm.

Recommended Listening

From the following list of compositions, grouped according to the contrapuntal forms discussed in this chapter, you will be able to select representative compositions which will give you a more complete understanding of the various forms. You should listen to each composition several times before you go on to another in the same category.

Canons:
Bach. *The Art of Fugue (Die Kunst der Fuge)* (This is a set of fugues and canons based on one theme and revealing Bach's great contrapuntal genius.)
———. *Canonic Variations on Vom Himmel Hoch* (organ)
———. "Erscheinen ist der herrliche Tag" (Chorale prelude No. 15 in *Orgelbüchlein;* a double canon at the octave)
———. "In dulci jubilo" (Chorale prelude No. 35 in *Orgelbüchlein:* a double canon at the octave)
———. *Musical Offering (Das Musicalisches Opfer):* (a set of contrapuntal pieces including canons by retrograde, inversion, and augmentation)
Byrd. *Non nobis Domine (a cappella* choir; in *Pre-Baroque Sacred Music,* Fest. 70–202)
Diamond. *Rounds* (string orchestra)
Franck. *Sonata in A Major for Violin and Piano:* IV, opening theme
Hindemith. *Sonata for Two Flutes* (canonic)
Okeghem. *Missa Prolationum* (Each part of the Mass is a canon, each canon is at a successively wider interval of imitation. The "Sanctus," a double canon, appears in the record anthology *Masterpieces of Music before 1750,* No. 17.)

Fugues:
Bach. *The Art of Fugue*
———. *Brandenburg Concerto No. 5 in D Major* (concerto grosso): III
———. *Fugue in G Minor* ("The Little"; organ)
———. *Mass in B Minor:* "Kyrie," "Gratias Agimus," Dona Nobis Pacem"
*———. *Passacaglia and Fugue in C Minor* (organ)
———. *Toccata and Fugue in D Minor* (organ) (It is easy to hear where the fugue begins at the conclusion of the toccata.)
———. *The Well-Tempered Clavier,* Vols. I and II (This is a set of 48 preludes and fugues in all keys, major and minor.
Beethoven. *Great Fugue (Der Grosse Fuge;* string quartet)
Brahms. *Variations and Fugue on a Theme by Handel* (piano)
Franck. *Prelude, Fugue and Variations* (organ)
*Handel. *Messiah* (oratorio): "And He shall purify," "His yoke is easy," "And with His stripes we are healed," "He trusted in God" (These great choruses testify to Handel's mastery of the fugue form.)
Haydn. *The Creation* (oratorio): "For He has clothed the heavens and earth" (No. 10, following a chordal introduction)

Haydn. *Quartet in C Major,* Op. 20, No. 2 (strings): IV
———. *Quartet in F Minor,* Op. 20, No. 5 (strings): IV
———. *Quartet in A Major,* Op. 20, No. 6 (strings): IV
Hindemith. *Quartet in E Flat Major* (1943, strings): I
———. *Quartet No. 3* (strings): I
———. *Quartet No. 4* (strings): I, IV (passacaglia and fugue)
*———. *Sonata No. 3 for Piano: IV* (a double fugue)
Mozart. *Fantasy and Fugue in C Major,* K. 394 (piano)
———. *Mass in C Minor,* K. 427 ("The Great"): "Cum Sancto Spiritu"
Villa–Lobos. *Bachianas Brasileiras No. 1* (8 cellos): III (fugue for 8 cellos)

Chorale preludes:
Bach. *Ein Feste Burg ist Unser Gott* (organ)
———. *Komm süsser Tod* (organ)
———. *Orgelbüchlein* (*Little Organ Book*): (This is a set of 45 chorale
  preludes for the church year.)
    "Das alte Jahr vergangen ist" (No. 10)
    "Christ lag in Todesbanden (No. 5) (See chorale melody, page 111)
    "Ich ruf' zu dir, Herr Jesu Christ" (No. 30)
    "O Mensch, bewein' dein' Sünde gross" (No. 45)
———. *Wachet auf, ruft uns die Stimme* (organ, based on the same chorale
  as *Cantata No. 140* by the same title)
———. *Wenn wir in höchsten Nöten sein* (organ)

Masses and motets:
Bach. *Mass in B Minor*
Byrd. *Ergo Sum Panis Vivus* (motet for for a *cappella* choir)
Dufay. "Kyrie" from the Mass, *Se la Face ay Pale*
Josquin Des Prez. *Ave Maria* (motet for a *cappella* choir)
Lasso. *Tristis Est Anima Mea* (*Sad Is My Soul,* motet for a *cappella* choir)
Obrecht. *Parce, Domine* (motet for a *cappella* choir)
Okeghem. "Sanctus" from *Missa Prolationum* (a *cappella* choir)
Palestrina. *Improperia* (motet, a *cappella* choir)
*———. *Missa Brevis* (a *cappella* choir)
———. *Missa Papae Marcelli* (a *cappella* choir)
Victoria. *O Magnum Mysterium* (motet, a *cappella* choir)
———. *O Quam Gloriosum* (motet, a *cappella* choir)
  Note. Most of the Renaissance motets are not listed separately under the
composer's name in the record catalogues, but they are contained in a large
number of long-playing anthologies, some of which are suggested here.
    Anthologie Sonore (9 volumes containing over 40 12" discs)
    French Cathedral Service (Period 597)
    Masterpieces of Music before 1750: Nos. 15, 17, 18, 19, 23, 25
    Palestrina, Lassus, Byrd, etc. (Period 706)
    16th Century Venetian Motets (Vox 8790, 8030, 8610)

Secular polyphonic forms:
Bennet. *Thyrsis, Sleepest Thou* (madrigal)
Binchois. *Adieu m'amour et ma maistresse* (chanson)
Créquillon. *Pour ung plaisir* (chanson)
Marenzio. *S'io parto, i'moro* (madrigal)
  Note. Rennaissance polyphonic secular forms are to be found in a large
number of long-playing collections, some of which are suggested here.
    Anthology of Renaissance Music (Period 597)
    Courtly Music of the Renaissance (Acad. 308)

Elizabethan Madrigals (Eso 520)
English Madrigals (CHC–52)
French Masters of the Renaissance (AS 41)
French Renaissance Vocal Music (Decca 9629)
Pre–Baroque (Festival 70–202)
Treasury of Madrigals (Col. 3ML–4517)
Triumphs of Oriana (a collection of English madrigals recorded by several companies)

16. Free Forms

In the category of "free forms" are many generic terms which imply neither a sectional structure (as in sonata–allegro, song form, and ternary) nor a polyphonic texture (as in fugue, canon, and motet). Although any single composition in the free–form category may in itself have a definite, clear, conventional structural plan, the name of the form does not imply one. In some instances the term connotes a style.

Toccata. The *toccata* is usually written for a keyboard instrument (organ, harpsichord, piano). Having no standard structural scheme, it usually contains alternating passages or sections of scale work, figuration (pattern material), chordal material, and contrapuntal textures. The toccata may be a brilliant showpiece. Played in a free tempo, rhythm, and meter, it often conveys the impression of *improvisation;* i.e., an aimless, wandering effect as if the performer were "making it up" as he went along. Toccatas do not usually have central thematic organization.

Prelude. A form closely related to the toccata is the prelude. Originally it was a piece intended as an introduction (e.g., to a ceremony, service, or to music such as the suite). Later it became a detached piece not associated with anything else (e.g., the sets of piano preludes by Chopin, Rachmaninoff, Scriabin, and others). The prelude is usually a short composition. It may be polyphonic or homophonic, or it may consist of nonmelodic textures. (The chorale prelude discussed in the preceding chapter is a genre by itself.) The prelude has no set sectional plan, although, again, any single prelude may have a clear, conventional structure (e.g., Chopin's *Préludes No. 1, 4, 5, 7, 20*). Like the toccata, it is sometimes a brilliant display piece.

Fantasia and Capriccio. These terms, both of which indicate the fanciful, unrestricted nature of a composition, are even less uniform in meaning than toccata and prelude. In the Renaissance the terms fantasia and capriccio were often used as titles for pieces in strict contrapuntal textures, even fuguelike compositions. Later, the improvisational character of fantasias and caprices became more pronounced.

Character Pieces. In the nineteenth century a large number of descriptive terms came into general use, especially for single compositions for piano. These titles usually convey some underlying mood or style, but no structural principle. The most common terms in this category are: *album leaves, arabesque, bagatelle, ballade, caprice* (see above), *fantasy* (or *fantasia, fantasie, fancy;* see above), *impromptu, intermezzo, moment musical, nocturne* (literally a "night piece"), *novelette, rhapsody, romance* (or *romanza*), and *song without words.*

Lament. Another group of forms which may be regarded as character pieces comprises compositions of a sad or mournful character such as the *lament* (or *lamento, lamentation*), *elegy, plainte, threnody,* and *tombeau.*

Étude. A special type of free form, belonging primarily to the nineteenth century, is the *étude,* or *study,* which is designed to exploit some technical feature of performance. The étude, however, is not a mere finger exercise, but a composition of artistic worth suitable for concert performances.

Descriptive Titles. Instrumental pieces with descriptive titles are free forms which convey the idea or mood of the title. A few famous examples of music with descriptive titles are "The Bells" by William Byrd, "La Poule" ("The Hen") by Rameau, "Evening," "Soaring," and "Whims" by Schumann, "La Cathédrale Engloutie" ("The Sunken Cathedral") by Debussy, and "Jeux d'Eau" ("Fountains") by Ravel.

Symphonic Poem. Single–movement pieces for orchestra which carry descriptive titles are called *symphonic poems* or *tone poems.* Examples of this form are listed at the end of the present chapter. (See also the discussion of symphonic music in Chapter 18. Descriptive music in general will be discussed further in Chapter 25.)

Serialism. An important innovation in twentieth-century structures is the use of *serialism.* Serial music began with atonal tech-

niques based on the recurrence of a tone row (see page 36).
Then it added other elements: recurring patterns of tempo,
rhythm, dynamics, timbre, etc. Multiple serialism, in which the
various elements are staggered rather than synchronized, results
in complexity of structure. Serialism is also an important property
of electronic music (see page 63).

Aleatory Music. *Aleatory music* (also *chance music*) is one of
the most radical trends of this century. It is a concept based on
random selection of musical materials by the composer, the per-
former(s), or both. There are neither laws nor limits imposed on
the procedures. In general the composer selects, often by chance,
certain basic elements or ideas which may be notated in conventional score, or, more often, in some contrived set of symbols.
The performers then "improvise" on those ideas. Each performance is unique. Each creation is preserved only through on-the-
scene recording. Aleatory music is often allied with electronic
and computer music. It has even transcended musical boundaries
when combined with random poetry reading, improvised audience participation, and other irrelevancies. Needless to say, such
indeterminacy precludes any adherence to musical form.

Recommended Listening

While listening to any of the following music, you may wish to identify
the composition with the particular category of free forms with which it is
associated, but it is more important to observe the structural plan and the
kinds of materials used (thematic, scale work, figuration, chords, counterpoint, and so forth). In the case of a descriptive title, it is always interesting
to observe how the composer conveys the mood or idea of the title.

Toccatas:
Bach. *Toccata and Fugue in D Minor* (organ)
———. *Toccata in F Major* (organ)
———. *Toccatas* (harpsichord): *in C Minor, D Major, D Minor, E Minor*
Chávez. *Toccata for Percussion*
Cowell. *Toccata for Flute, Soprano, Cello, and Piano*
Pachelbel. *Toccatas* (organ)
Prokofiev. *Toccata in D Minor* (piano)
Schumann. *Toccata in C Major*, Op. 7 (piano)
Sweelinck. *Toccata in A Minor* (organ)

Preludes:
Bach. *The Well–Tempered Clavier* (2 volumes: 48 preludes and fugues in all
    keys, major and minor)
Chopin. *Préludes*, Op. 28
Debussy. *Préludes* (piano, 2 books; pieces with descriptive titles)
Franck. *Prelude, Fugue and Variations* (organ)
Gershwin. *Preludes* (3, for piano)

Kabalevsky. *Preludes* (24, piano)
Messiaen. *Préludes* (2, piano)
Rachmaninoff. *Preludes,* Opp. 3, 10, 23 (piano)
————. *Prelude in C Sharp Minor,* Op. 3, No. 2
Ravel. *Le Tombeau de Couperin:* "Prélude"
Shostakovitch. 24 *Preludes,* Op. 34 (piano)

Fantasia and capriccio:
Bach. *Chromatic Fantasy and Fugue* (harpsichord)
————. *Fantasia and Fugue in G Minor* ("The Great," for organ)
Brahms. *Capriccios:* Opp. 76, 116 (piano)
Britten. *Phantasy Quartet for Oboe and Strings*
Chopin. *Fantasy-Impromptu in C Sharp Minor,* Op. 66
Griffes. *Fantasy Pieces,* Op. 6 (3, piano)
Harris. *Fantasy for Piano and Orchestra*
Ibert. *Capriccio* (orchestra)
Locke. *Consort of Four Parts* (fantasies for small string ensembles; contrapuntal pieces)
Mendelssohn. *Capriccio Brillant* (piano)
Mozart. *Fantasy in C Minor,* K. 475 (piano)
Paganini. *Caprice No. 24* (virtuoso variations for unaccompanied violin. See Rachmaninoff *Rhapsody.*)
Purcell. *Fantasias in 3, 4, and 5 Parts* (string fantasies, contrapuntal)
Stravinsky. *Capriccio for Piano and Orchestra*
Telemann. *Fantasias* (12, for harpsichord)
Vaughan Williams. *Fantasia on a Theme of Thomas Tallis* (string orchestra)
Wieniawski. *Caprices in A Minor, E Flat Major* (violin)

Character pieces:
Beethoven. *Bagatelles,* Opp. 33, 119, 126 (piano)
Brahms. *Ballade in G Minor,* Op. 118 (piano)
————. *Ballades,* Op. 10 (4, piano)
————. *Intermezzi,* Opp. 76, 116, 117, 118, 119 (piano)
————. *Rhapsodies,* Opp. 79, 119 (piano)
————. *Romanze in F Major,* Op. 118, No. 5 (piano)
Chausson. *Poème for Violin and Orchestra*
Chopin. *Ballade No. 3 in A Flat Major,* Op. 47 (piano)
————. *Impromptus,* Opp. 29, 36, 51 (piano)
————. *Nocturnes* (piano), *E Flat Major,* Op. 9, No. 2; *F Sharp Major,* Op. 15, No. 2
*Copland. *Music for the Theatre* (orchestra): I (*Prologue*), III (*Interlude*)
Debussy. *Rhapsodie for Saxophone and Orchestra*
————. *Rhapsodie No. 1 for Clarinet and Piano*
Dvořák. *Nocturne in B Major for Strings*
Fauré. *Impromptu for Harp Solo*
————. *Nocturne in A Flat Major* (piano)
Franck. *Pièce Héroïque* (organ)
Gershwin. *Rhapsody in Blue* (piano and orchestra)
Griffes. *Poem for Flute and Orchestra*
Křenek. *Bagatelles* (4, piano)
————. *Pieces for Piano*
Liszt. *Hungarian Rhapsody No. 2 in C Sharp Minor* (piano or orchestra)
Mendelssohn. *Songs Without Words,* Op. 102 (piano)
Milhaud. *Pastorale for Oboe, Clarinet, and Bassoon*
Persichetti. *Pastoral for Winds*

Poulenc. *Nocturne in D Major* (piano)

Rachmaninoff. *Rhapsody on a Theme of Paganini* (piano and orchestra. See Paganini *Caprice No. 24.*)

————. *Romance in E Flat Major* (piano)

Satie. *Gymnopédies* (piano or orchestra)

Schoenberg. *Drei Klavierstücke* (*Three Piano Pieces*), Op. 11

————. *Klavierstücke* (*Piano Pieces*), Op. 24

Schubert. *Moments Musicaux* (*Musical Moments;* piano)

————. *Nocturne in E Flat Major,* Op. 40 (piano, violin, and cello)

Schumann. *Arabesques* (piano)

————. *Blumenstücke* (*Flower Pieces;* piano)

————. *Bunte Blätter* (*Bright Leaves;* piano)

————. *Carnaval,* Op. 9 (piano pieces with titles)

————. *Davidsbündlertanze,* Op. 6 (18 piano pieces)

*————. *Fantasiestücke* (*Fantasy Pieces;* piano), Opp. 12, 73, 111

————. *Humoresque,* Op. 20 (piano)

————. *Intermezzi,* Op. 4 (piano)

————. *Kinderscenen* (*Scenes of Childhood;* a set of piano pieces with descriptive titles)

————. *Novelette No. 4 in D Major* (piano)

————. *Papillons* (*Butterflies;* a set of short piano pieces with descriptive titles)

————. *Romances,* Opp. 28, 93 (piano)

Tcherpnine, *Arabesques* (4, for piano)

————. *Bagatelles,* Op. 5 (10 pieces for piano)

————. *Nocturne in G Sharp Major* (piano)

Turina. *Poema Fantastico* (piano)

Laments:

Hindemith. *Trauermusik* (*Funeral Music,* for viola and orchestra)

Ravel. *Le Tombeau de Couperin* (piano)

Stravinsky. *Élégie* (unaccompanied violin)

Études:

Chopin. *Études in: C Major,* Op. 10, No. 1; *E Minor,* Op. 25, No. 5; *G Flat Major,* Op. 25, No. 9 (all for piano)

Debussy. *Études* (2 books, piano)

Liszt. *Étude de Concert No. 3 in D Flat Major* ("Un Sospiro," for piano)

Martinu. *Études* (3, for piano)

Schumann. *Symphonic Études* (each étude is a variation, for piano)

Descriptive titles:

Bartók. *Mikrokosmos* (6 books of graded piano pieces with descriptive titles)

Bloch. *Schelomo* (cello and orchestra)

Byrd. *The Bells* (variations, harpsichord)

————. *The Carman's Whistle* (variations, harpsichord)

Couperin. *La Galante* (harpsichord)

————. *Les Folies françoises* (a set of mood pieces for harpsichord)

Debussy. *La Cathédrale Engloutie* (*The Sunken Cathedral,* piano)

————. *Children's Corner Suite* (piano): *Golliwog's Cake-walk*

————. *L'Isle Joyeuse* (piano)

————. *Préludes* (piano pieces with descriptive titles)

————. *Suite Bergamasque* (suite of piano pieces with descriptive titles, including "Clair de Lune")

Farnaby. *Loth to Depart* (harpsichord)

Granados. *Goyescas* (piano pieces from the opera *Goyescas*)

Handel. *Suite No. 5 in E Major* (harpsichord: IV ("The Harmonious Blacksmith," a set of variations)

Liszt. *La Campanella* (piano)

MacDowell. *Woodland Sketches* (descriptive piano pieces, including the famous "To a Wild Rose")

Mendelssohn. "Spinning Song" (from *Songs Without Words*, Op. 67, No. 4, piano)

Milhaud. *The Household Muse* (short piano pieces with descriptive titles)

Ravel. *Gaspard de la Nuit* (piano)

————. *Jeux d'Eau* (*Fountains*, for piano)

————. *Pavane pour une Infante Défunte* (*Pavane for a Dead Princess*, piano or orchestra)

Saint–Saëns. *Carnival of the Animals* (descriptive pieces for orchestra)

Satie. *Three Pieces in the Form of a Pear* (piano)

Schumann. (See items listed under *Character pieces*)

*Tchaikovsky. *Nutcracker Suite* (movements with descriptive titles, for orchestra)

Villa-Lobos. *The Baby's Family* (piano pieces)

Symphonic poems:

Debussy. *Prélude à l'Après-midi d'un Faune* (*Prelude to the Afternoon of a Faun*)

Dukas. *The Sorcerer's Apprentice*

Griffes. *The White Peacock* (orchestra)

Honegger. *Pacific 231*

Liszt. *Les Préludes* (based on Lamartine's *Méditations Poétiques*)

Mossolov. *Iron Foundry*

Rachmaninoff. *Isle of the Dead*

Saint–Saëns. *Danse Macabre* (orchestra)

Sibelius. *Finlandia*

————. *The Swan of Tuonela*

Smetana. *The Moldau* (from the symphonic cycle, *My Fatherland*)

Strauss, R. *Don Quixote* (orchestra and cello solo)

————. *Ein Heldenleben* (*A Hero's Life*)

*————. *Till Eulenspiegel*

Wagner. *A Siegfried Idyll*

Serialism:

Berg. *Violin Concerto*

Webern. *Concerto for Nine Instruments*

Aleatory music:

Bernstein. *Four Improvisations by the* [New York Philharmonic] *Orchestra*

Cage. *Concert for Piano and Orchestra*

————. *Variations III*

Stockhausen. *Klavierstücke XI*

Xenakis. *Strategie*

17. Compound Structures

So far in this unit on musical form (Chapters 11–16) we have been dealing mainly with the basic structural plans of single compositions or movements. We shall now consider compound structures consisting of more than one movement. A *movement* is a composition which may be heard as a complete and independent work by itself, but which forms a part of such larger compositions as sonatas, suites, symphonies, and so forth. Movements are referred to according to tempo (fast movement, slow movement, allegro, andante, etc.) and by their consecutive position (first movement, second movement, last movement or finale).

SONATA

The term "sonata form" is commonly used to mean the single-movement sonata–allegro structure described in Chapter 14. In the present chapter we are dealing with the form of the sonata as a whole, and the general plan of its movements.

The *sonata* is a compound structural concept employed in a number of mediums: solo sonata (for violin, cello, flute, clarinet, etc., usually with piano accompaniment), piano sonata, string quartet and other chamber music ensembles, symphony and concerto.

The term sonata was once used for diverse instrumental pieces. It signified a composition to be played on one or more instruments, as opposed to a composition to be sung. Later the term came to have a more specific meaning. There are two main sonata types: (1) the *baroque sonata,* which was popular in the late seventeenth and the first half of the eighteenth centuries and (2) the *classical sonata,* which constitutes a general structural plan to be found in instrumental music from the mid-eighteenth century to the present. The over–all plan of the sonata, like the one–movement structures discussed in Chapter 14, is subject to many deviations from the "rule."

Baroque Sonata. The most common structure of the sonata in the late Baroque period (as seen in the works of Bach, Handel, Corelli, Vivaldi, and others) is a four–movement plan alternating between slow and fast movements: S F S F. The structure and style of the individual movements were not standardized, nor were the later structural types (sonata–allegro, minuet and trio, rondo, and so on) used. The *baroque sonata* is more often polyphonic than homophonic.

Classical Sonata. In the late eighteenth century, the *classical sonata* assumed a somewhat more standard structural plan. It became a form generally consisting of three or four movements.

First Movement. The first movement is in fast tempo. It is in the tonic key (i.e., the key of the whole sonata). It is usually in sonata–allegro form. Interesting exceptions are the first movement of Beethoven's "Moonlight" *Sonata in C Sharp Minor* (piano), Op. 27, No. 2; of his *Sonata in A Flat Major* (piano), Op. 26; and of Mozart's *Sonata in A Major* (piano), K. 331.

Second Movement. The second movement is usually in slow tempo, in a contrasting key (most commonly the subdominant key). A number of different structural plans are used for the slow movement: sonata–allegro, theme and variations, sonatina, binary, ternary, and, occasionally, one of the rondo forms.

Third Movement. If a sonata has four movements, the minuet–and–trio (or scherzo–and–trio) form is used. It is in the tonic key; its tempo ranges from moderate to fast. In some sonatas of the eighteenth century, the minuet movement is omitted.

In a relatively few instances the minuet or scherzo (if included at all) appears as the second movement, exchanging places with the slow movement.

Fourth Movement (Finale). The fourth movement is in fast tempo. It is in the tonic key. Its structure is sonata–allegro or one of the rondo forms (A B A C A or A B A C A B A).

In the nineteenth century, sonatas and symphonies occasionally employed more than four movements (e.g., Beethoven's *Symphony No. 6 in F Major* ("Pastorale"), Berlioz' *Symphonie Fantastique*). In the twentieth century, composers have experimented with sonata structures of one, two, and three movements. Also, after the eighteenth century, the structure, style, and keys of movements became more varied. It is well to keep in mind that every sonata has its own individuality.

CONCERTO

The *concerto,* like the sonata and symphony (page 62), is a multiple–movement form. In the baroque solo concerto and concerto grosso, there is no standard number or type of movements. The classical concertos of the eighteenth and nineteenth centuries parallel the classical sonata plan, but the minuet movement is omitted. Near the end of the first movement, and sometimes in other movements as well, appears the *cadenza.* This is a section for the solo instrument alone, consisting of brilliant, virtuoso material which displays the technique of the performer.

SUITE

Another classification of compound forms is the *suite.* Three broad divisions of this class are: (1) the *baroque suite* (*dance suite*), (2) the *descriptive suite* (usually for orchestra or piano solo), and (3) the *ballet suite.* (See also Baroque Dances, page 155.)

Baroque Suite. The *baroque suite* (also called *partita*) consists of a series of dances, derived from social or court dances of the time. The four principal dances of the baroque suite are (1) the *allemande,* (2) the *courante,* (3) the *sarabande,* and (4) the *gigue.* Additional dances often included in the suite are the *minuet, bourrée, gavotte, passepied, polonaise, rigaudon, anglaise, loure,* and *hornpipe.* Baroque suites frequently begin with a prelude.

In music of the Baroque period, the term *sonata* was often used for a suite of dance movements (*sonata da camera* or *chamber sonata*). Baroque suites were written for harpsichord solo, chamber ensembles, and orchestra. The *dance suite* virtually disappeared after 1750.

Descriptive Suite. The *descriptive suite,* especially that for orchestra, came into favor during the nineteenth century. It consists of several movements with descriptive titles; there is no standard structural form for the movements.

Ballet Suite. Orchestral suites arranged from opera and ballet came into wide vogue late in the nineteenth century, and they continue to be an important category of orchestral music in the twentieth century. (See further discussion of *ballet suites* in Chapter 20.)

OPERA, ORATORIO, CANTATA, MASS

The preceding compound forms are all instrumental. Mediums which are essentially vocal and consist of numerous sections, pieces, or movements include the opera, oratorio, cantata, and settings of the Mass. (These will be taken up in Chapters 19 and 24.)

Recommended Listening

In listening to the following compositions, you should determine the number of movements, general tempo, mood, and as far as possible the structure of each movement. Listening to at least one composition in each category of compound forms will enable you to appreciate the differences among them.

Baroque sonata:
Bach. *Sonata No. 3 in E Major* (violin and harpsichord or piano)
———. *Trio Sonata in C Minor* (flute, violin, continuo; in *The Musical Offering*)
Corelli. *Sonata in G Minor*, Op. 5, No. 5 (violin and harpsichord)
Handel. *Sonata in F Major for Flute and Continuo*, Op. 1, No. 11
———. *Sonata No. 4 in D Major for Violin and Harpsichord* (or piano), Op. 1, No. 13
———. *Trio Sonata in B Flat Major for Flute, Oboe, and Continuo*
Telemann. *Trio Sonata in E Minor for Flute, Oboe, and Continuo*
Vivaldi. *Sonata in A Major* (violin and piano)

Sonata (after 1750; classical, romantic, modern):
*Bartók. *Quartet No. 5* (strings; 5 movements)
Beethoven. *Quartet No. 2 in G Major* (strings)
———. *Sonata No. 2 in A Major* (piano)
———. *Symphony No. 1 in C Major*
*———. *Symphony No. 5 in C Minor*
*Brahms. *Symphony No. 3 in F Major*
*Chopin. *Sonata No. 2 in B Flat Minor*, Op. 35 (piano)
*Haydn. *Quartet in E Flat Major*, Op. 33, No. 2 (strings)
———. *Symphony No. 94 in G Major* ("Surprise")
Hindemith. *Quartet No. 3* (strings)
———. *Sonata for Trumpet and Piano*
*———. *Sonata No. 3 for Piano*
Mozart. *Quartet No. 14 in G Major* (strings), K. 387
———. *Quintet in A Major for Clarinet and String Quartet*, K. 581
*———. *Symphony No. 40 in G Minor*, K. 550
Schubert. *Quintet in A Major* (strings)
———. *Symphony No. 8 in B Minor*

Concerto:
Beethoven. *Concerto No. 5 in E Flat Major for Piano and Orchestra* ("Emperor")

Liszt. *Concerto No. 1 in E Flat Major for Piano and Orchestra*
*Mendelssohn. *Concerto in E Minor for Violin and Orchestra*
Mozart. *Concerto in E Flat Major for Piano and Orchestra,* K. 271 (See also the list of concertos and concerti grossi at the end of Chapter X.)

Baroque suite:
Bach. *English Suite No. 2 in A Minor* (harpsichord)
————. *Partita No. 2 in D Minor for Unaccompanied Violin*
————. *Partita No. 5 in G Major* (harpsichord or piano)
*————. *Suite No. 3 in D Major for Orchestra*
Corelli. *Sonata in E Minor,* Op. 5, No. 2 (violin and piano)
Couperin. *Suite No. 24* (harpsichord)
Handel. *Suite No. 5 in E Major* (harpsichord)

Descriptive suite:
Bizet. *L'Arlésienne Suite No. 2* (orchestra)
*Copland. *Music for the Theatre* (orchestra)
Debussy. *Children's Corner Suite* (piano)
————. *Ibéria* (orchestra)
————. *La Mer* (suite for orchestra)
————. *Suite Bergamasque* (piano)
Grieg. *Peer Gynt Suite No. 1* (orchestra)
Holst. *The Planets* (orchestra)
————. *St. Paul Suite* (string orchestra)
Ippolitov–Ivanov. *Caucasian Sketches* (orchestra)
MacDowell. *Woodland Sketches* (piano)
Mendelssohn. *A Midsummer Night's Dream* (orchestra)
Milhaud. *Suite Française* (orchestra)
————. *Suite Provençale* (orchestra)
Mussorgski. *Pictures at an Exhibition* (piano or orchestra; transcribed from piano by Maurice Ravel)
Prokofiev. *Lieutenant Kije Suite* (orchestra)
————. *Scythian Suite* (orchestra)
Ravel. *Ma Mère l'Oye* (*Mother Goose Suite;* 2 pianos or orchestra)
————. *Le Tombeau de Couperin* (piano)
Respighi. *The Fountains of Rome* (orchestra)
————. *The Pines of Rome* (piano)
Rimsky–Korsakov. *Scheherazade* (orchestra)
Saint-Saëns. *Carnival of the Animals* (orchestra)
Taylor. *Through the Looking Glass* (orchestra)
Thomson. *Suite from The Plow that Broke the Plains* (documentary film; orchestra)

Ballet suite:
Bernstein. *Fancy Free* (orchestra)
Copland. *Appalachian Spring* (orchestra)
————. *Billy the Kid* (orchestra)
Falla. *El Amor Brujo* (*Love the Sorcerer*)
————. *El Sombrero de Tres Picos* (*The Three-Cornered Hat*)
Hindemith. *Nobilissima Visione* (orchestral suite from the ballet *St. Francis*)
Menotti. *Sebastian Ballet Suite* (orchestra)
Piston. *Suite from The Incredible Flutist*
Prokofiev. *Cinderella Ballet Suite* (orchestra)
Ravel. *Daphnis et Chloé Suite No. 2* (orchestra)
Roussel. *Bacchus et Ariane, Ballet Suite No. 2* (orchestra)

Shostakovitch. *Polka and Dance* from the ballet *The Golden Age*
Stravinsky. *Le Baiser de la Fée* (*The Fairy's Kiss*)
————. *Card Game*
————. *Firebird Suite* (orchestra)
————. *Petrouchka* (orchestra)
————. *Scènes de Ballet* (orchestra)
*Tchaikovsky. *Nutcracker Suite* (orchestra)
————. *The Sleeping Beauty* (suite)
————. *Swan Lake Ballet* (suite)
Thomson. *Filling Station*

PART FIVE

Categories of Music Literature

Parts Two, Three, and Four have dealt with the materials, properties, mediums, and forms of music. In Part Five we shall consider categories of music literature which do not come specifically under those headings. It will be important to keep in mind, however, that all of these new categories to be discussed are related to and overlap with the others. Also, you should constantly strive to integrate new information with that already acquired and with your musical experience in general.

18. Symphonic Music

You have already had some experience with symphonic music through your own listening as well as through the study of Chapter 10 and various chapters on musical form. In this chapter we shall be concerned with the forms of symphonic music.

The term *symphony* is used in two senses: (1) to mean a particular organization of players (e.g., the Boston Symphony, the B. B. C. Symphony) and (2) to mean a particular composition for symphony orchestra (e.g., Beethoven's *Symphony No. 5 in C Minor,* or Haydn's "Surprise" *Symphony No. 94 in G Major*).

SYMPHONY ORCHESTRA

Before we take up the forms of symphonic music, let us first review the chief characteristics of the *symphony orchestra.*

Size. The modern symphony orchestra is a large ensemble made up of approximately 125 players. The entire ensemble is likely to be used in the performance of symphonic music of the nineteenth and twentieth centuries; but for baroque orchestral music (Bach, Handel, Corelli, Vivaldi) and eighteenth–century classical music (Haydn, Mozart, Beethoven), as well as for some twentieth–century music, a much smaller orchestra is required.

Instruments. As previously mentioned, the symphony orchestra includes four classes of instruments: woodwinds, brasses, percussion, and strings.*

* The drawings on pages 138–142 have been reproduced from the scriptographic booklet *The ABC's of Symphonies* by special permission of the copyright owner, Channing L. Bete Co., Inc., Greenfield, Mass.

WOODWINDS. The woodwind instruments generally found in a full symphonic score include a piccolo, two flutes, two oboes, two clarinets, a bass clarinet, a bassoon, a contrabassoon, and (sometimes) an English horn.

BRASSES. The brasses used include two or three trumpets, two to four (usually three) trombones, four or more French horns, and one or two tubas.

PERCUSSION. The percussion group (see page 61) varies considerably with individual compositions. A fairly standard arrangement comprises two or three timpani, snare and bass drums, a triangle, cymbals, a harp (a plucked string instrument usually classed as percussion in the orchestral score), and occasionally, in twentieth–century music, a piano.

STRINGS. The string choir in a symphony orchestra consists of five parts: first violins, second violins, violas, cellos, and basses. Compositions occasionally call for subdivisions of these groups to make a string orchestra of six to eight or more parts.

Score. The standard plan in scoring (i.e., writing the musical score) for symphony orchestra is to place the woodwinds at the top, the brasses next, then the percussion, and, at the bottom of each page, the strings. Here is a specimen page of five measures from an orchestral score (Tchaikovsky's *Symphony No. 5 in E minor,* fourth movement), which calls for the following instruments indicated in the score by abbreviations:

Woodwinds	*Percussion*
3 flutes	3 timpani
2 oboes	
2 clarinets	
2 bassoons	*Strings*
	first violins
	second violins
Brass	violas
4 horns	cellos (violoncello)
2 trumpets	string basses (contrabasses)
3 trombones	
1 tuba	

Note that the woodwind instruments are playing in unison (indicated in the score by the designation "a 2") and that in the third measure the second violins and violas are divided (indicated in the score by the abbreviation "div.").

Seating Arrangement. Although conductors of symphony orchestras do not all employ the same seating arrangement for the players, the most conventional plan is the one shown in the following diagram.

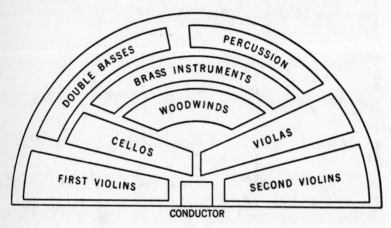

SYMPHONIC FORMS

The Symphony. The symphony is a compound form which may consist of from one (e.g., Sibelius' *Symphony No. 7*) to five (e.g., Beethoven's "Pastorale" *Symphony No. 6 in F Major*) or more movements; conventionally, however, there are four movements. The structure of the individual movements is highly variable, but the same conventional plan is used for symphonies, quartets, and sonatas (see pages 122 ff.). Eminent composers from Haydn and Mozart to the present have written symphonies which belong to the world's greatest music.

The Program Symphony. Occasionally, nineteenth-century composers wrote symphonies which were intentionally designed to describe nonmusical ideas. Compositions with descriptive associations of this kind are called *program music*. Famous examples of program symphonies are Beethoven's *Symphony No. 6 in F*

Major ("Pastorale") are Berlioz' *Fantastic Symphony (Symphonie Fantastique).*

Concerto. Since the beginning of the eighteenth century, the term *concerto* has meant a composition for one or more solo performers and orchestra. Usually, the concerto has three movements, and makes use of a sonata structure (see page 124).

Symphonic Poem. In the second half of the nineteenth century, Franz Liszt conceived the idea of writing one–movement compositions for orchestra based on extramusical associations, i.e., program music. Such works are called *symphonic poems* or *tone poems*. They are free forms, for they have no standard structure or style. (Examples are Liszt's *Les Préludes* and Debussy's *Prélude à l'Après-midi d'un Faune.*)

Symphonic Suite. Somewhat akin to the symphonic poem is the *symphonic suite,* which in the nineteenth century consisted of descriptive movements instead of the dance movements which had characterized the orchestral suite in the Baroque period (see page 124). The symphonic suite, as its name implies, is a work in several movements, but it has no standard structure or style of movements. (Famous examples are Respighi's *The Pines of Rome,* Debussy's *La Mer,* and Rimsky–Korsakov's *Scheherazade.*)

Ballet Music. This category includes music originally intended to accompany ballet, but subsequently rearranged for concert performance, usually in the form of a suite. Also, some single–movement works (e.g., Ravel's *Boléro* and *La Valse*) are heard more frequently as concert pieces than as accompaniment to the dances for which they were written.

Incidental and Entr'acte Music. Since the seventeenth century, composers have been intrigued with the idea of providing *incidental music* to dramas, sometimes to be performed during the course of the play, either as interpolated or background music (incidental music), or else as music to be played between the scenes or acts of a play (*entr'acte music*). Some of these works have become famous as concert pieces (e.g., Mendelssohn's incidental music to *A Midsummer Night's Dream*). Music in this category is usually in the form of a suite in several movements.

Providing background music for motion pictures is now a major field of endeavor in the world of music. In a few instances this music has been rearranged for concert purposes (e.g., Prokofiev's

Lieutenant Kije Suite, Thomson's *Suite from The Plow that Broke the Plains,* and Copland's *Our Town*).

Overture. In the early history of opera it came to be common practice to introduce an opera with an instrumental prelude of some sort. Two forms of overture were employed in the seventeenth century: the French *overture* ("ouverture") and the Italian *sinfonia.*

FRENCH OVERTURE. The *French overture* consists of three main sections: a slow, majestic section in dotted rhythms; a fast, fugal middle section; and a concluding slow section similar to the first. (The overture to Lully's *Armide* is a good example of this form.)

ITALIAN SINFONIA. The *Italian sinfonia* has the opposite plan of tempos in three sections: fast, slow, fast. The slow section is usually very short. This form of overture, the forerunner of the classical symphony, is seldom heard today. French and Italian overture types were used also as opening movements to oratorios, cantatas, suites, and other instrumental forms.

CONCERT OVERTURE. The practice of writing a single–movement composition as an introduction to an opera or oratorio did not disappear in the eighteenth century. Some of the operatic overtures, usually in sonata–allegro form (see Chapter 14), came to be performed separately as concert pieces. Then, in the nineteenth century, composers wrote orchestral pieces called overtures which were not introductions or preludes to any larger work. Such works are referred to as *concert overtures.* Concert overtures usually have descriptive titles (e.g., Mendelssohn's *Hebrides Overture*), and some are even programmatic (e.g., Schumann's *Manfred Overture*).

These types of overture, especially operatic and concert overtures, are commonly included in programs of symphonic music.

Symphonic Variations. A number of works for symphony orchestra are in theme–and–variation form (see Chapter 13), in addition to the symphonies which use that form for a single movement. A number of famous orchestral works are variations (e.g., Brahms's *Variations on a Theme by Haydn,* Elgar's *Enigma Variations*).

Orchestral Music with Narrator. In the twentieth century a new type of symphonic music has made its appearance. The new idea is to have a narrator who speaks lines during the course of the music. The subject is usually a dramatic one. Such orchestral compositions are usually in one movement, though they may be divided into sizable sections. (Prokofiev's *Peter and the Wolf* is a favorite in this category.)

Orchestral Music with Chorus and Solo Voices. This type of symphonic music is somewhat akin to oratorio and cantata, but it properly belongs in the category of symphonic music. A famous example of a symphony utilizing chorus and solo voices is Beethoven's *Symphony No. 9 in D Minor* ("The Choral Symphony"), the last movement of which employs a mixed chorus and solo voices in a setting of Schiller's "Ode to Joy."

A few modern composers have written symphonic works which utilize a chorus without text for the purpose of obtaining added color effects. In his celebrated orchestral suite *The Planets,* Holst employed this medium in the movement called "Neptune the Mystic"; likewise, the "Sirènes" of Debussy's *Nocturnes* is an example of wordless choral effects.

Miscellaneous Orchestral Music. The principal categories of symphonic music have been mentioned. There are, however, compositions appearing on symphonic programs which do not properly belong to any of these categories, or which are hybrid pieces having characteristics of two or more categories. For example, Franck's *Symphonic Variations* (listed at the end of this chapter under the heading of "symphonic variations") features a solo instrument (the piano) and is therefore related to the concerto medium. Again, *Don Quixote,* by Richard Strauss, is listed as a symphonic poem, but it is also a free variation form, and it employs a cello soloist.

FREE FORMS. As indicated in Chapter 16, there are a number of free forms, the terms for which do not imply specific structures or styles. These are encountered frequently in orchestral music. In the list of miscellaneous orchestral music at the end of this chapter are compositions with such titles as "caprice," "rhapsody," and "fantasia."

DANCES. Single dance pieces and marches not derived from opera or ballet are not uncommon in symphonic music. Such pieces as Tchaikovsky's *Marche Slave,* Liszt's *Mephisto Waltz,* Dvořák's *Slavonic Dances,* and Ravel's *Pavane for a Dead Princess* belong to this miscellaneous category of orchestral music.

PICCOLO
FLUTE
OBOE
CLARINET
BASS CLARINET
BASSOON

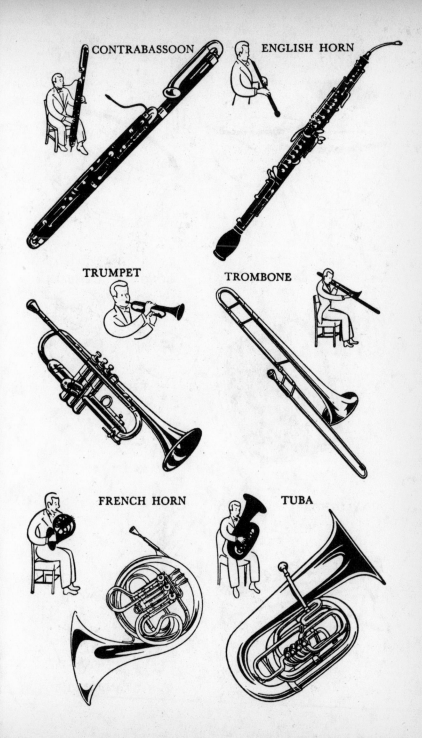

CONTRABASSOON

ENGLISH HORN

TRUMPET

TROMBONE

FRENCH HORN

TUBA

TIMPANI

SNARE DRUM

BASS DRUM

GONG

CYMBALS

TRIANGLE

XYLOPHONE

CASTANETS

TAMBOURINE

HARP

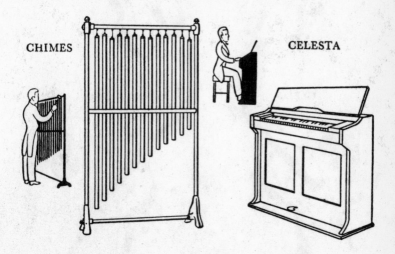

CHIMES

CELESTA

PIANO

VIOLIN

VIOLA

CELLO

DOUBLE BASS

Program symphonies:

Beethoven. *Symphony No. 6 in F Major* ("Pastorale")
Berlioz. *Symphonie Fantastique (Fantastic Symphony)*
Bloch. *Israel Symphony*
Chávez. *Sinfonia India*
Hindemith. *Mathis der Maler*
Liszt. *A Faust Symphony* (orchestra, tenor solo, and male chorus)
Shostakovitch. *Symphony No. 7* ("Leningrad")
Concerto (See list on page 72 f.)

Symphonic Poems:

Borodin. *On the Steppes of Central Asia*
*Debussy. *Prélude à l'Après-midi d'un Faune (Prelude to the Afternoon of a Faun)*
Delius. *Brigg Fair*
Dukas. *The Sorcerer's Apprentice*
Gershwin. *An American in Paris*
Gillis. *The Alamo*
Griffes. *The Pleasure-dome of Kubla Khan*
———. *The White Peacock* (orchestra)
Honegger. *Pacific 231*
Liszt. *Les Préludes* (based on Lamartine's *Méditations Poétiques*)
Loeffler. *Memories of My Childhood*
Mossolov. *Iron Foundry*
Mussorgski. *Night on Bald Mountain*
Rachmaninoff. *Isle of the Dead*
Saint-Saëns. *Danse Macabre*
Scriabin. *Poem of Ecstasy*
———. *Prometheus; The Poem of Fire*
Sibelius. *Finlandia* (orchestra)
———. *The Swan of Tuonela*
Smetana. *The Moldau* (from the symphonic cycle, *My Fatherland*)
Strauss, R. *Don Quixote* (orchestra and cello solo)
———. *Ein Heldenleben (A Hero's Life)*
*———. *Till Eulenspiegel*
Stravinsky. *Fireworks*
Varèse. *Ionization* (for percussion orchestra)

Symphonic suites:

*Bach. *Suite No. 3 in D Major for Orchestra* (baroque dance suite)
Bizet. *L'Arlésienne Suite No. 2*
*Copland. *Music for the Theatre*
Debussy. *Ibéria*
———. *La Mer*
———. *Nocturnes* (3 pieces for orchestra)
Falla. *Nights in the Gardens of Spain* (piano and orchestra)
Grieg. *Peer Gynt Suite No. 1* (incidental music to Ibsen's play)
Grofé. *Grand Canyon Suite*
Handel. *Water Music* (baroque orchestral suite including nondescriptive dance movements)
Holst. *The Planets*
———. *St. Paul Suite*
Ippolitov–Ivanov. *Caucasian Sketches*
Kodály. *Háry János Suite*

The Johann Strauss waltzes (*Blue Danube Waltz, Tales from t Vienna Woods,* etc.) are more likely to appear on "pop" concei than on more serious symphonic programs.

TRANSCRIPTIONS. When a composition written for one mediu is arranged for a different medium, the latter work is known a *transcription.* Bach's organ music transcribed for orchestra an example of this kind of music. (See, for example, the orchestr recordings of Bach's *Toccata and Fugue in D Minor* and h *Passacaglia and Fugue in C Minor.*)

Recommended Listening

The following compositions, listed according to the various categories di cussed above, are major symphonic works you are likely to encounter in symphony concert or broadcast.

Symphonies:
Beethoven. Nine symphonies, among the greatest in the literature. The follov ing ones are most often performed:
———. *Symphony No. 1 in C Major*
———. *Symphony No. 3 in E Flat Major* ("Eroica")
*———. *Symphony No. 5 in C Minor*
———. *Symphony No. 7 in A Major*
Brahms. Four symphonies:
———. *No. 1 in C Minor*
———. *No. 2 in D Major*
*———. *No. 3 in F Major*
———. *No. 4 in E Minor*
Dvořák. *Symphony No. 5 in E Minor* ("New World")
Franck. *Symphony in D Minor*
Hanson. *Symphony No. 2* ("Romantic")
Harris. *Symphony No. 3* (in one movement)
Haydn. *Symphony No. 94 in G Major* ("Surprise")
———. *Symphony No. 97 in C Major* ("London Symphony No. 1")
———. *Symphony No. 101 in D Major* ("Clock")
Hindemith. *Symphony in E Flat*
Mendelssohn. *Symphony No. 4 in A Major* ("Italian")
Milhaud. *Symphony No. 2*
*Mozart. *Symphony No. 40 in G Minor,* K. 550
———. *Symphony No. 41 in C Major,* K. 551 ("Jupiter")
Prokofiev. *Classical Symphony in D Major*
Schubert. *Symphony No. 7 in C Major*
———. *Symphony No. 8 in B Minor* ("Unfinished")
Schumann. *Symphony No. 3 in E Flat Major* ("Rhenish")
Shostakovitch. *Symphony No. 5*
Sibelius. *Symphony No. 1 in E Minor*
———. *Symphony No. 5 in E Flat Major*
Stravinsky. *Symphony in Three Movements*
Tchaikovsky. *Symphony No. 5 in E Minor*
———. *Symphony No. 6 in B Minor,* Op. 74 ("Pathétique")
Vaughan Williams. *Symphony No. 2* ("London")

Mendelssohn. *A Midsummer Night's Dream* (incidental music to Shakespeare's play)
Milhaud. *Suite Française*
———. *Suite Provençale*
Mussorgski. *Pictures at an Exhibition*
Prokofiev. *Lieutenant Kije Suite* (music from a Russian moving picture)
———. *Scythian Suite*
———. *Summer Day Suite* (children's suite for little symphony)
Ravel. *Ma Mère l'Oye* (*Mother Goose Suite;* originally for two pianos; later arranged for orchestra by Ravel)
———. *Le Tombeau de Couperin* (originally for orchestra; later arranged for piano by Ravel)
———. *Rhapsodie Espagnole*
Respighi. *The Fountains of Rome*
———. *The Pines of Rome*
Rimsky–Korsakov. *Scheherazade*
Saint–Saëns. *Carnival of the Animals*
Stravinsky. *Ode*
Taylor. *Through the Looking Glass*
Thomson, V. *Suite from The Plow that Broke the Plains*
Weill. *Lady in the Dark* (from the moving picture of the same name)

Ballet music:
Bernstein. *Fancy Free*
Borodin. *Polovetsian Dances* (from the opera *Prince Igor*)
Copland. *Appalachian Spring*
———. *Billy the Kid*
Delibes. *Sylvia*
Falla. *El Amor Brujo* (*Love the Sorcerer*)
———. *El Sombrero de Tres Picos* (*The Three-cornered Hat*)
Hindemith. *Nobilissima Visione* (orchestral suite from the ballet *St. Francis*)
Khachaturian. *Saber Dance* (from the ballet *Gayaneh*)
Menotti. *Sebastian Ballet Suite*
Milhaud. *Le Boeuf sur le Toit* (comic ballet)
Piston. *Suite from the Incredible Flutist*
Ponchiella. *Dance of the Hours* from *La Gioconda*
Prokofiev. *Cinderella Ballet Suite*
———. *Romeo and Juliette Suite No. 2*
*Ravel. *Boléro*
———. *Daphnis et Chloé Suite No. 2*
———. *La Valse*
Roussel. *Bacchus et Ariane Ballet Suite No. 2*
Schubert. *Rosamunde* (incidental music, ballet; overture)
Schuman. *Judith* (choreographic poem for orchestra)
———. *Undertow* (choreographic episodes for orchestra)
Shostakovitch. *Polka and Dance,* from the ballet *The Golden Age*
Stravinsky. *Le Baiser de la Fée* (*The Fairy's Kiss*)
———. *Card Game*
———. *Firebird Suite*
———. *Petrouchka*
———. *Scènes de Ballet*
*Tchaikovsky. *Nutcracker Suite*
———. *The Sleeping Beauty* (suite)

Tchaikovsky. *Swan Lake* (suite)

Thomson, V. *Filling Station*

Overtures:

*Bach. *Suite No. 3 in D Major for Orchestra: Overture*

Beethoven. *Overture to Coriolanus*

———. *Overture to Egmont*

———. *Overture to Leonore, No. 3*

———. *Overture to Prometheus*

Berlioz. *Overture to Benvenuto Cellini*

———. *Overture: The Roman Carnival* (prelude to the second act of *Benvenuto Cellini*)

*Bizet. *Prelude to Carmen*

Brahms. *Academic Festival Overture* (concert overture)

———. *Tragic Overture* (concert overture)

Bruckner. *Overture in G Minor* (concert overture)

Donizetti. *Overture to La Fille du Régiment* (*Daughter of the Regiment*)

Glinka. *Overture* to the opera *Russlan and Ludmilla*

Gluck. *Overture* to the opera *Alceste*

*Handel. *Overture to Messiah* (French overture)

Humperdinck. *Prelude to Hansel and Gretel.*

Lully. *Overture to Armide* (French overture; No. 36 in *Masterpieces of Music before 1750*)

Mendelssohn. *Overture: The Hebrides* (*Fingal's Cave;* concert overture)

———. *Overture to Ruy Blas* (a play by Victor Hugo)

Menotti. *Overture to The Old Maid and the Thief*

*Mozart. *Overture to Don Giovanni*

———. *Overture to The Magic Flute*

———. *Overture to The Marriage of Figaro*

Nicolai. *Overture to The Merry Wives of Windsor*

Rimsky–Korsakov. *Russian Easter Overture* (concert overture)

Rossini. *Overture to The Barber of Seville*

———. *Overture to La Gazza Ladra* (*The Thieving Magpie*)

———. *Overture to The Italian Woman in Algiers*

———. *Overture to William Tell*

Schubert. *Overture to Rosamunde*

Schumann. *Overture to Manfred* (programmatic concert overture based on Byron's poem)

Smetana. *Overture to The Bartered Bride*

Strauss, J. *Overture* to the operetta *Die Fledermaus* (*The Bat*)

Tchaikovsky. *Overture, 1812* (concert overture)

———. *Romeo and Juliet* (overture fantasy)

Vaughan Williams. *Overture* to the comedy, *The Wasps,* of Aristophanes

Verdi. *Prelude to Aida*

Wagner. *Overture to The Flying Dutchman*

———. *Overture to Tannhäuser*

———. *Preludes to Act I and Act III of Lohengrin*

———. *Prelude to Die Meistersinger*

———. *Prelude to Tristan and Isolde*

Weber. *Overture to Euryanthe*

———. *Overture to Der Freischütz*

———. *Overture to Oberon*

Symphonic Variations:

Arenski. *Variations on a Theme by Tchaikovsky*

Brahms. *Variations on a Theme of Haydn*
Britten. *The Young Person's Guide to the Orchestra*
Dohnányi. *Variations on a Nursery Theme* ("Ah vous dirai-je Maman," piano
and orchestra)
Elgar. *Enigma Variations*
Franck. *Symphonic Variations* (piano and orchestra)
D'Indy. *Istar Variations*

Orchestral Music with Narrator:
McDonald. *Builders of America*
Prokofiev. *Peter and the Wolf*
Schoenberg. *A Survivor from Warsaw*
Thompson, R. *Testament of Freedom*
Walton. *Façade*

Symphonic Works with Chorus:
Beethoven. *Symphony No. 9 in D Minor* ("Choral"): *Finale*
Brahms. *Alto Rhapsody* (contralto, male chorus, and orchestra)
Debussy. *Nocturnes: Sirènes* (female chorus without text)
Holst. *The Planets:* "Neptune, the Mystic" (female chorus without text)
Liszt. *A Faust Symphony* (male chorus, tenor solo, and orchestra)
Mahler. *Symphony No. 2 in C Minor* (alto solos, mixed chorus)
Stravinsky. *Symphony of Psalms* (mixed chorus and orchestra)

Miscellaneous Orchestral Music:
*Bach. *Passacaglia and Fugue in C Minor* (transcribed for orchestra)
————. *Toccata and Fugue in D Minor* (transcribed for orchestra)
Bloch. *Schelomo: Hebrew Rhapsody for Cello and Orchestra*
Britten. *The Young Person's Guide to the Orchestra*
Chabrier. *España: Rhapsody for Orchestra*
Copland. *El Salón México*
————. *A Lincoln Portrait*
Debussy. *Fantaisie for Piano and Orchestra*
Diamond. *Rounds* (string orchestra)
Dvořák. *Slavonic Dances* (8 pieces for orchestra)
Enesco. *Rumanian Rhapsody in A Major*
Gershwin. *Rhapsody in Blue* (piano and orchestra)
Gould. *Interplay for Piano and Orchestra*
Hindemith. *Symphonic Metamorphoses on a Theme of Weber*
Lalo. *Symphonie Espagnole* (violin and orchestra)
Liszt. *Mephisto Waltz* (originally for orchestra; transcribed for piano; both
versions recorded)
Rachmaninoff. *Rhapsody on a Theme of Paganini* (piano and orchestra)
Ravel. *Pavane pour une Infante Défunte* (*Pavane for a Dead Princess*;
orchestra)
————. *Tzigane, Rhapsody for Violin and Orchestra*
Rimsky–Korsakoff. *Capriccio Espagnole*
Stravinsky. *Capriccio for Piano and Orchestra*
————. *Circus Polka:* "Ballet for an Elephant"
Toch. *Circus Overture*
Vaughan Williams. *Fantasia on a Theme by Thomas Tallis* (string orchestra)
Wagner. *A Siegfried Idyll* (tone poem)
Weill. *Lady in the Dark* (from the moving picture)
Weinberger. *Polka and Fugue* from the opera *Schwanda*

19. Opera

Music has been associated with drama since the times of ancient Greece. Since the beginning of the seventeenth century a number of musico–dramatic forms have come into existence. Dramatic music of all kinds constitutes a significant portion of music literature, and opera is the most important of these.

Opera is a drama set to music. It embraces such arts as poetry, scenery, costumes, acting, and dancing, in addition to vocal and instrumental music. Rarely are the respective fields in perfect balance; usually either the drama or the music predominates. In its 350–year history, opera has changed many times in form and style. We will deal here only with general and structural aspects of the music.

APPRECIATION OF OPERA

To some extent it is possible to enjoy opera merely by listening to it, as in hearing opera broadcasts or recordings. To grasp the full experience of opera, however, it must be seen as well as heard. To appreciate opera it is necessary at least to visualize the action, scenery, and costuming, and to know the dramatic plot of the story as well as to be familiar with the music and the forms.

COMPONENTS OF OPERA

Synopses of opera plots, lists of characters, and references to important musical selections from the opera may be found in opera guides (see page 220). In this chapter we shall merely outline the principal musical ingredients and the main types of opera.

Libretto. The text of an opera is called the *libretto*. The libretto is sometimes adapted from a novel or drama (e.g., Debussy's *Pelléas et Mélisande* from Maeterlinck's play); most often it is specially written for a particular composer (by da Ponte for Mozart, by Boito for Verdi, etc.) ; and sometimes, though less often, it is created by the composer himself (Wagner, Pizzetti, Menotti).

The performance of an opera in a foreign language may constitute a barrier to appreciation. Here it is especially important that the listener know the story. As an aid to understanding the dialogue, most recordings of complete operas are issued with the libretto and its translation printed side by side.

Overture. The instrumental composition which serves as an introduction to the opera is called an *overture,* or, sometimes, a *prelude*. The main types of overture were outlined in Chapter 18. Mention should also be made of the *potpourri* or *medley* overtures used in light opera, which consist of chains of themes from the opera. In general, composers are more concerned in the overture with presenting the prevailing mood of the opera than with introducing its themes.

Recitative. The *recitative* is sung dialogue. Here the composer's interest is primarily in declamation, i.e., in making the words intelligible rather than in constructing a beautiful song. In recitative the words are more important than the music, but the latter enhances the emotion of the former.

Aria. In contrast to the recitative, the aria is a song which poetically and musically reflects dramatic feeling rather than contributing to the dialogue or the dramatic action. Arias constitute an important literature for vocal solo, and familiarity with famous arias is one basis for developing an appreciation of opera.

Duo, Trio, and Other Small Ensembles. When two singers are engaged in performing an aria, it is called a *duo* (or *duet*); an aria for three is a *trio,* for four a *quartet,* for five a *quintet,* and for six a *sextet*. The "Quartet" from *Rigoletto* and the "Sextet" from *Lucia* are examples of famous operatic ensembles.

Chorus. Operas which include scenes involving crowds of people make use of large choral ensembles. Examples of famous operatic choruses are "The Anvil Chorus" from *Il Trovatore,* "The Pilgrim's Chorus" from *Tannhäuser,* "The Triumphal

Chorus" from *Aida,* and "Tutto nel mondo è burla" from *Falstaff.*

Orchestra. The role of the orchestra does not end with the overture. It is heard by itself in innumerable instrumental interludes of various lengths. In some operas it provides merely the accompaniment to arias, recitatives, choruses, and dancing. In others it plays a more significant role by bringing continuity and excitement to the action, portraying characters, and creating the emotional atmosphere of a scene. The orchestra occupies an especially prominent position in Wagner's operas.

Ballet. Dances of a formal and stylized nature are not infrequently introduced into opera as interludes not essential to the plot. Ballet is particularly important in French opera. Ballet music has already been mentioned in connection with compound structures (page 124 f.) and symphonic forms (page 135), and more will be said about the subject in Chapter 20 on dance music.

Acts and Scenes. Opera, like drama, is customarily divided into main sections, or *acts.* These are usually subdivided into shorter sections, or *scenes.*

Leitmotif. In some operas, especially those by Wagner, a device known as *leitmotif* (leading motive) is employed. It is a theme used recurrently throughout the opera to represent a character, an object, or a situation. Examples of leitmotifs are the "Ring motive" in Wagner's *Ring* cycle and the "love motive" in *Tristan and Isolde.*

TYPES OF OPERA

The term opera without a modifying adjective usually implies a heroic or tragic drama. This was formerly called *opera seria* (serious opera) or *grand opera.*

Comic Opera. There are several types of comic opera: (1) *opéra–comique* (French), (2) *opera buffa* (Italian), (3) *ballad opera* (eighteenth–century English comic opera), and (4) *Singspiel* (German). Operas of this class usually make use of parody (or farce) and spoken dialogue, and the music is less profound than that of serious opera.

Operetta. An operetta is an opera which is light, popular, romantic, and often humorous. Like most types of comic opera, operettas use spoken dialogue instead of recitative.

Folk Opera. Recently there has been an awakened interest in light opera based upon local legend, color, and folklore. Such operas are referred to as *folk operas*. (Examples are Weill's *Down in the Valley,* Foss's *The Jumping Frog of Calaveras County,* and Gershwin's *Porgy and Bess.*)

Continuous Opera. Since about the middle of the nineteenth century, there has been a trend toward eliminating the components as separate sections (arias, recitatives, choruses, etc.) and thus making the drama one continuous flow of music. Wagner was the first fully to realize this concept in his *music–dramas.* Continuous opera is now the predominant form.

Radio and Television Opera. In recent years radio and television have provided a new medium for dramatic musical productions. Menotti's *The Old Maid and the Thief* (radio) and *Amahl and the Night Visitors* (television) are examples of dramatic music written specifically for these modern outlets.

Recommended Listening

You may already have become familiar with some of the great operatic arias listed at the end of Chapter 9. You will undoubtedly want to make further preparation for listening to an entire opera by reading a synopsis of the story from an opera guide. While listening to one of the operas listed below, observe the interplay of the various components of opera and notice how the composer has used music to serve his dramatic purpose.

Serious opera:
Bellini. *Norma*
———. *La Sonnambula*
Berg. *Wozzeck*
*Bizet. *Carmen*
Borodin. *Prince Igor*
Charpentier. *Louise*
Debussy. *Pelléas et Mélisande*
Delibes. *Lakmé*
Donizetti. *Lucia di Lammermoor*
Flotow. *Martha*
Glinka. *A Life for the Czar*
———. *Russlan and Ludmilla*
Gluck. *Alceste*
———. *Orfeo ed Euridice*
Gounod. *Faust*
Halévy. *La Juive*
Humperdinck. *Hansel and Gretel* (fairy-tale opera)
Leoncavallo. *I Pagliacci*
Mascagni. *Cavalleria Rusticana*
Massenet. *Manon*
———. *Thaïs*
Menotti. *Amahl and the Night Visitors* (opera for television)
———. *The Consul*
———. *The Medium*

Menotti. *The Saint of Bleeker Street*
Meyerbeer. *L'Africaine*
——. *Le Prophète*
Monteverdi. *Il Combattimento di Tancredi e Clorinda*
——. *L'Incoronazione di Poppea*
——. *Orfeo*
*Mozart. *Don Giovanni*
——. *The Magic Flute*
Mussorgski. *Boris Godounov*
Nicolai. *The Merry Wives of Windsor*
Offenbach. *Tales of Hoffmann*
Ponchielli. *La Gioconda*
*Puccini. *La Bohème*
——. *Madama Butterfly*
——. *Manon Lescaut*
——. *La Tosca*
Purcell. *Dido and Aeneas*
Rimsky–Korsakoff. *May Night*
——. *Sadko*
Rossini. *William Tell*
Saint–Saëns. *Samson and Dalila*
Strauss, R. *Der Rosenkavalier*
——. *Salomé*
Stravinsky. *The Rake's Progress*
Tchaikovsky. *Eugen Onegin*
Thomas. *Mignon*
Thomson. *Four Saints in Three Acts* (opera on text by Gertrude Stein)
Verdi. *Aida*
——. *Falstaff*
——. *Otello*
——. *Rigoletto*
——. *La Traviata*
——. *Il Trovatore*
Wagner. *Götterdämmerung* (*The Twilight of the Gods*)
——. *Die Meistersinger*
——. *Parsifal*
——. *Siegfried*
——. *Tannhäuser*
*——. *Tristan and Isolde*
——. *Die Walküre*
Weber. *Euryanthe*
——. *Der Freischütz*

Comic opera, operetta, folk opera:
Auber. *Fra Diavolo* (comic opera)
Blitzstein. *No for an Answer* (comic opera)
Cimarosa. *Il Matrimonio Segreto* (*The Secret Marriage;* opera buffa)
Foss. *The Jumping Frog of Calaveras County* (folk opera)
Friml. *Rose Marie* (operetta)
——. *The Vagabond King* (operetta)
Gershwin. *Porgy and Bess* (folk opera)
Gilbert and Sullivan. *The Gondoliers* (operetta)
——. *H.M.S. Pinafore* (operetta)
——. *Iolanthe* (operetta)

———. *Mikado* (operetta)

———. *Trial by Jury* (operetta)

Herbert. *Naughty Marietta* (operetta)

———. *The Red Mill* (operetta)

———. *Sweethearts* (operetta)

Menotti. *Amelia Goes to the Ball* (*Amelia al Ballo;* modern comic opera)

———. *The Old Maid and the Thief* (modern comic opera)

———. *The Telephone* (modern comic opera)

Mozart. *Cosi fan' tutte* (opera buffa)

———. *The Impresario* (*Der Schouspieldirektor;* Singspiel)

———. *The Marriage of Figaro* (opera buffa)

Pergolesi. *The Music Master* (opera buffa)

———. *La Serva Padrona* (opera buffa)

Ravel. *L'Heure Espagnole* (one-act comic opera)

Romberg. *The Student Prince* (operetta)

Rossini. *The Barber of Seville* (opera buffa)

Smetana. *The Bartered Bride* (opera buffa)

Strauss. J. *The Gypsy Baron* (operetta)

Stravinsky. *Mavra* (opera buffa)

———. *Renard* (burlesque chamber opera)

Weill. *Down in the Valley* (folk opera)

———. *Three-Penny Opera* (adapted from Gay and Pepusch's *The Beggar's Opera,* a ballad opera)

Wolf–Ferrari. *The Secret of Suzanne* (a one–act comic intermezzo)

20. Dance Music

At least since the beginning of recorded history, dancing has been a significant activity in the life of man. The dance has always been used for seasonal ceremonies (harvest, spring, etc.), for war, and for all sorts of religious and social rites. Wherever and whenever dances have been performed, some kind of musical accompaniment has been utilized, if only the beat of a primitive drum. Thus, of all types and categories of music, dance music has the longest and most nearly universal tradition. Dance forms constitute a significant portion of all music literature.

FUNCTIONAL DANCE MUSIC

When music serves as an accompaniment to dancing, it is functional. The orchestras and bands that play for social dances are performing functional dance music. Most of the recorded popular music of dance bands is functional dance music.

STYLIZED DANCE MUSIC

When dance music is composed or arranged for listening enjoyment rather than as a background for actual dancing, it is called *stylized* dance music. Stylized dance music usually retains the general rhythmic and metric character of the original dance, and often its structure as well. But the composer may introduce counterpoint, ornamentation, or other factors to such an extent that it is no longer feasible to dance to the music. The baroque suite is an example of stylized dance music. A twentieth–century example is Ravel's *La Valse*.

INFLUENCE OF DANCE STYLES

Not only is dance music stylized for concert purposes, but dance styles have infiltrated other musical forms. The influence of dance is clearly to be heard in such compositions as Stravinsky's *Dumbarton Oaks Concerto,* in the first and last movements of Ravel's *Concerto in G Major for Piano and Orchestra,* and in Gershwin's *Rhapsody in Blue* and his three *Preludes* for piano. The inclusion of the stylized minuet in the classical sonata form (see page 123) is further evidence of the strong impact of dance forms on concert music.

Dance music is basically instrumental, but dance forms are to be found in vocal music too; e.g., in Brahms's *Liebeslieder Waltzes* for vocal ensemble, the arias "L'amour est un oiseau rebelle" (a habanera) and "Près des remparts" (a seguidilla), both in Bizet's *Carmen,* and the tarantella song *La Danza* by Rossini.

PRINCIPAL DANCE FORMS

The number of dance forms is extremely large. The following list includes only the dances most frequently encountered in music literature, summarized according to the historical periods in which they were most common, and to the nationality, tempo, and meter of the individual dance forms.

Medieval Dances
ESTAMPIE (French, usually $\frac{3}{4}$, fast)
DANSE ROYALE (French court dance)

Renaissance Dances (These were often in pairs, the first in slow tempo, the second in fast.)
PAVANE (Spanish, slow, $\frac{4}{4}$); GALLIARD (French, fast, $\frac{3}{4}$)
BASSE–DANSE (French, slow, $\frac{3}{4}$); TOURDION (French, fast, $\frac{4}{4}$)
TANZ–NACHTANZ (German dance pairs)

Baroque Dances (Dances of the Baroque period, 1600–1750, were stylized in the baroque suite. See Chapter 17.)
ALLEMANDE (German, moderate tempo, duple meter)
COURANTE (French); CORRENTE (Italian) (fast, triple meter)
SARABANDE (Spanish, slow, triple meter)
GIGUE, GIGA, JIG (English or Irish, fast tempo, compound triple meter, $\frac{6}{8}$ or $\frac{9}{8}$)

In addition to the foregoing dances, "optional" dances are variously included in the baroque suite.

BOURRÉE (French, fast, duple)

GAVOTTE (French, moderate tempo, $\frac{4}{4}$, begins on third count of the measure)

LOURE (French, moderate, $\frac{6}{4}$)

MINUET, MENUET, MENUETTO (French, moderate, $\frac{3}{4}$)

HORNPIPE (English sailor dance, moderate, $\frac{3}{2}$ or $\frac{4}{4}$)

PASSEPIED (French, fast $\frac{3}{8}$ or $\frac{6}{8}$)

RIGAUDON (French, moderate, $\frac{4}{4}$)

POLONAISE (Polish, moderate, triple meter)

Late Eighteenth–Century Dances. Composers in the second half of the eighteenth century produced no new types of dances. The minuet (see above) became very prominent as a court dance and also was incorporated into the sonata. A country dance of English or Scottish origin, called the *écossaise,* became popular in England and France during the late eighteenth century.

Nineteenth–Century Dances. A number of new dance types appeared in the nineteenth century and were well represented in the piano music of the time.

QUADRILLE (French square dance, alternating $\frac{2}{4}$ and $\frac{6}{8}$ meters)

CONTREDANSE, CONTRATANZ, COUNTRY DANCE (English origin)

GALOP (Fast, duple)

POLKA (Bohemian, fast, duple)

MAZURKA (Polish, moderate tempo, triple meter)

TARANTELLA (Italian, fast, $\frac{6}{8}$)

WALTZ (Austrian origin, moderate or fast, $\frac{3}{4}$)

LÄNDLER (A slow waltz)

POLONAISE (Polish, moderate tempo, triple meter; continued from the eighteenth century.)

Twentieth–Century Dances. Popular native dance music continues to hold favor with composers, who use their rhythms in stylized dance compositions. Many of these dances are of Spanish and Latin American origin. They include *bolero* (Cuban), *habanera* (Spanish-Cuban), *tango* (Argentine), *fandango* (Spanish), *rumba* (Afro-Cuban), *jota* (Spanish), *conga* (Afro-Latin-American), and *samba* (Brazilian).

A number of twentieth-century dances originated in the United States. Among them are the foxtrot, Charleston, shimmy, black bottom, and jitterbug. Chapter 21 deals with dance and dance-oriented music in the United States.

BALLET

Ballet music has been mentioned in our discussion of symphonic music and as an adjunct to opera. The modern full ballet is a dramatic whole which conveys a complete dramatic action through the pantomime of the dancers. This dramatic form developed in the late nineteenth century; in the twentieth century, ballet music has become a major form of expression. It is generally highly stylized.

Components. The ballet includes staging, scenery, costumes, dancing, and music, but no dialogue and no singing.

Choreography. The counterpart of the libretto in opera is *choreography* in ballet. This is the detailed plan of the dancing and pantomime in accordance with the plot of the drama. The composer collaborates with the choreographer to achieve the most effective music for the action of the dancers.

Recommended Listening

The enjoyment of dance music stems directly from pleasurable associations with the dance itself, from "feeling" bodily movements stimulated by the rhythms. Most of the music listed below belongs to the category of stylized dance music. Some of the compositions are more stylized than others, but all are highly rhythmic in character. Whatever dance music you select, you will enjoy observing its relationship to the dance itself and noting the recurrence of rhythmic patterns.

Medieval and Renaissance Dances

Estampie (medieval dance; No. 12 in *Masterpieces of Music before 1750*)
Jenkins. *Pavan for Four Viols*
Lute dances of the sixteenth century (dance pair; No. 22 in *Masterpieces of Music before 1750*)

Baroque Dances

Bach. *English Suites* (6; harpsichord or piano)
———. *English Suite No. 2 in A Minor* (*Allemande, Courante, Sarabande, Bourrée, Gigue*)
———. *French Suites* (6; harpsichord or piano)
———. *Partita No. 2 in D Minor for Unaccompanied Violin* (*Allemande, Courante, Sarabande, Gigue*)
———. *Partita No. 5 in G Major* (piano or harpsichord; *Allemande, Courante, Sarabande, Menuetto, Passepied, Gigue*)
*———. *Suite No. 3 in D Major for Orchestra* (*Gavotte, Bourrée, Gigue*)
Couperin. *Suite No. 24* (harpsichord)

Froberger. *Suite in E Minor* (harpsichord: *Allemande, Courante, Sarabande, Gigue;* No. 35 in *Masterpieces of Music before 1750*)

Handel. *Suite No. 5 in E Major* (harpsichord; *Allemande, Courante*)

———. *Water Music* (orchestra; *Bourrée, Hornpipe*)

Eighteenth–Century Minuets

Haydn. *String Quartet in C Major* ("Emperor"), Op. 76, No. 3: III

———. *Symphony No. 94 in G Major* ("Surprise"): III

*Mozart. *Don Giovanni* (opera): *Minuet* (Act I)

———. *Eine Kleine Nachtmusik* (*Serenade,* orchestra), K. 525: III

*———. *Symphony No. 40 in G Minor,* K. 550: III

Nineteenth–Century Dances

Waltz:

Brahms. *Liebeslieder Waltzes* (for vocal ensemble)

———. *Waltzes,* Op. 39 (piano)

Casella. *Five Pieces for String Quartet: Valse Ridicule* (a twentieth–century parody of the waltz)

Chopin. *Waltz in C Sharp Minor,* Op. 64, No. 2 (piano)

———. *Waltz in D Flat Major* ("Minute"; piano), Op. 64, No. 1

Liszt. *Mephisto Waltz* (piano or orchestra)

*Puccini. *La Bohème* (opera): "Quando m'en vo' " (Musetta's waltz)

Ravel. *La Valse* (orchestra)

Schubert. *Ländler* (piano)

Sibelius. *Valse Triste* (orchestra)

Strauss, J. *Blue Danube Waltz* (orchestra)

———. *Tales from the Vienna Woods* (orchestra)

Tchaikovsky. *Eugen Onegin: Waltz* (Act II)

*———. *Nutcracker Suite* (orchestra): "Waltz of the Flowers"

Contra dances: Beethoven. *Contra Dances* (orchestra)

Mazurka: Chopin. *Mazurka in A Flat Major,* Op. 59, No. 2 (piano)

Polka: Weinberger. *Polka and Fugue* from the opera *Schwanda* (orchestra)

Polonaise: Chopin. *Polonaise No. 6 in A Flat Major,* Op. 53 (piano)

Tarantella: Rossini. *La Danza* (voice and piano)

Twentieth–Century Dances

Spanish:

Albéniz. *Spanish Dances* (8, for orchestra))

Chabrier. *España: Rhapsody for Orchestra* (includes the jota and malagueña)

Glinka. *Jota Aragonesa* (orchestra)

Granados. *Spanish Dances* (orchestra)

*Ravel. *Boléro* (orchestra)

———. *Rhapsodie Espagnole* (orchestra): II (Malagueña); III (Habanera)

American dance styles:

Casella. *Five Pieces for String Quartet:* "Fox-trot"

*Copland. *Music for the Theatre* (orchestra): II (*Dance*)

Creston. *Symphony No. 2:* II (*Interlude and Dance*)

Debussy. *Children's Corner Suite* (piano): *Golliwog's Cake-walk*

Gershwin. *Preludes* (3, for piano)

Goeb. *Three American Dances* (orchestra)

Gould. *Interplay for Piano and Orchestra*

———. *Tap Dance Concerto* (orchestra)

Riegger. *New Dance* (orchestra; originally for 2 pianos)

Stravinsky. *Danses Concertantes* (orchestra)
————. *Ebony Concerto* (dance band)
————. *Piano Rag Music*
————. *Ragtime* (piano)

Some National Dances

Albéniz. *Tango in D Major* (for piano)
Bartók. *Bulgarian Dances* (6, for piano)
Borodin. *Polovetsian Dances* from the opera *Prince Igor*
Brahms. *Hungarian Dances* (orchestra)
Cowell. *Fiddler's Jig* (Irish, orchestra)
Dvořák. *Slavonic Dances* (8, for orchestra)
Grieg. *Norwegian Dances* (orchestra)
Mozart. *German Dances* (orchestra)
Milhaud. *Saudades do Brazil* (for piano; music suggested by Brazilian dance rhythms)
Kodály. *Galanta Dances* (Hungarian gypsy, for orchestra)

Ballet Music

(See "Ballet Suite," pp. 124–125, and "Ballet Music," pp. 145–146.)

Miscellaneous Dance Music

Antheil. *Valentine Waltzes* (piano)
Bennett. *Suite of Old American Dances* (band): "Cake Walk," "Schottische," "Western One-Step," "Wallflower Waltz," "Rag"
Creston. *Choric Dances*
Falla. "Ritual Fire Dance" from *El Amor Brujo* (orchestra or piano)
Grieg. *Peer Gynt Suite No. 1: In the Hall of the Mountain King; Anitra's Dance*
Holst. *St. Paul Suite* (string orchestra): I (*Jig*)
Khachaturian. *Saber Dance* from the ballet *Gayaneh*
Ponchielli. *La Gioconda* (opera): "Dance of the Hours"
Prokofiev. *Classical Symphony in D Major:* III (*Gavotte*)
Ravel. *Pavane pour une Infante Défunte* (*Pavane for a Dead Princess;* piano or orchestra)
————. *Le Tombeau de Couperin:* "Forlane," "Rigaudon," "Minuet"
Saint-Saëns. *Danse Macabre* (orchestra)
Schumann. *Davidsbündlertanze* (18 pieces for piano)
Shostakovitch. *Polka and Dance,* from the ballet *The Golden Age* (orchestra)
Stein. *Hassidic Dances* (3, for orchestra)
Stravinsky. *Circus Polka:* "Ballet for an Elephant"
*Tchaikovsky. *Nutcracker Suite* (orchestra): "Arabian Dance," "Chinese Dance," "Dance of the Reed Flutes," "Dance of the Sugar-Plum Fairy," "Russian Dance," "Waltz of the Flowers"
Weber. *Invitation to the Dance* (orchestra)

21. Jazz

Distinctly a twentieth-century phenomenon and essentially a popular American art, *jazz* is a significant category in its own right as well as having considerable influence on serious composed music.

Jazz has no standard definition. Some authorities limit the term to improvised instrumental dance music (specifically "hot jazz" or "pure jazz"); to others it means almost any form of popular music. In the following summary, it will be used in a broad sense, but excluding most popular song types, country-Western music, neofolk songs, hit tunes, and "protest" songs (most of which nevertheless often form the basis of jazz improvisations or arrangements). Jazz is notably an ephemeral art, continually changing in style and technique, and with one of its categories overlapping another.

Ragtime. Probably originating in the minstrel shows of the late nineteenth century, *ragtime* lasted from about the turn of the century to the end of World War I. It was essentially dance music for piano solo, but the style was also used in early dance bands. Prominent traits were persistent syncopation over left-hand accompaniment of alternating octaves and chords, and "strains" (period forms) of eight, sixteen, and thirty-two bars.

Blues. A style known as *blues* originated in Afro-American work songs and spirituals and became popular in the early 1900s. It was a type of solo song, which soon permeated jazz bands. Blues songs deal with melancholy subjects. The style is characterized by twelve-bar periods of three four-measure phrases, lowered third and seventh scale degrees, and "bending" (slurring) melodic tones upward or downward from the normal pitch.

Dixieland. Concurrent with ragtime and blues was *Dixieland* jazz, a dance-band style that began in New Orleans. Dixieland bands usually consisted of cornet, trombone, clarinet, banjo, and drums. The musicians, most of whom could not read musical scores, improvised on well-known tunes with ingenious counterpoint. Impromptu groups of musicians assembled in what were called *jam sessions,* to play jazz, sometimes in private, sometimes before informal audiences.

Swing. A trend toward larger bands began in the late 1920s and continued through the 1930s. The style called *swing* relied on written arrangements of popular tunes rather than on improvisation. Although the arranger became all important, considerable latitude was provided for solo passages. A new brilliance of sound characterizes this style. Big bands provided concert entertainment as well as ballroom dance music.

Associated with big name bands, a vocal style called *crooning* had a popular vogue (Rudy Vallee, Bing Crosby). It was characterized by soft and sentimental singing with sliding and moaning effects.

Boogie-Woogie. Concurrent with swing was a piano solo style, known as *boogie-woogie,* which consisted of an ostinato figure (a recurring melodic and rhythmic pattern) in the left hand over which melodic and harmonic material was improvised.

Bop. A style known as *bop, bebop,* or *rebop* was the main current in the 1940s. It was characterized by a return to smaller ensembles (called "combos," including amplified guitar), faster tempo, improvised melody over fixed harmonic progressions, more dissonant harmony, and complex rhythms.

Jazz since 1950. After World War II, jazz underwent numerous and rapidly changing fads, variously labelled *progressive jazz, cool jazz, funky hard bop regression, third-stream music, soul jazz, rock and roll,* and *punk rock.* In general these styles are more diversified, somewhat less dance oriented, have greater variety of medium within relatively small combos, and are more diverse in terms of melody, rhythm, and harmony. They also incorporate electronic mediums and procedures.

Rock is essentially a vocal medium (soloist or small group) with accompaniment of one or more guitars and bass. It is characterized by a very strong beat, incessant repetition of melodic and rhythmic patterns, and often, with amplification in live performance, an extremely high decibel level ("acid rock"). Rock music is associated with discothèques (night clubs or other public places for dancing to recorded music), rock festivals, concerts, and an enormous volume of recorded music—all are an impressive part of the current scene.

Recommended Listening

The following list is a mere sampling of various types of jazz. Current record catalogs provide a wide selection.

Ragtime:
Joplin. *Gladiolus Rag*
———. *Maple Leaf Rag*
Bowman. *Twelfth Street Rag*
Confrey. *Kitten on the Keys*
Morton. *Tiger Rag*

Blues:
Bessie Smith (singer). *Put it Right There*
———. *Any Woman's Blues*
Handy. *St. Louis Blues*

Dixieland:
When the Saints Go Marching In (traditional)
The Darktown Strutter's Ball (traditional)

Swing:
Porter. *Begin the Beguine* (Artie Shaw recording)
Ellington. *Take the A Train* (Duke Ellington band)
Jam Session (Benny Goodman band).

Bop:
A Night in Tunisia (Gillespie and Parker recording)

Progressive:
Great Expectations. Miles Davis and ensemble
Brubeck. *A Dialogue for Jazz Combo and Orchestra*

Rock:
See record catalogs for recordings by any of the following rock groups: The Beatles, Rolling Stones, Led Zeppelin, Temptations, Supremes, Jefferson Airplane, Blood Sweat and Tears, ABBA, Cream, Weather Report.

Jazz-influenced compositions:
Note. Most of the following compositions show influences of "The Golden Age of Jazz" in the 1920s.
Casella. *Five Pieces for String Quartet:* "Fox-trot"
*Copland. *Music for the Theatre: II* ("Dance")
———. *Piano Concerto*
Creston. *Symphony No. 2: II* ("Interlude and Dance")
Debussy. *Children's Corner Suite* (piano): "Golliwog's Cake-Walk"
Gershwin. *Concerto for Piano and Orchestra*
———. *Preludes* (piano)
———. *Rhapsody in Blue* (piano and orchestra)

Goeb. *Three American Dances* (orchestra)
Gould. *Interplay for Piano and Orchestra*
———. *Chorale and Fugue in Jazz*
———. *Tap Dance Concerto*
Milhaud. *La Création du Monde* (*The Creation of the World*)
Riegger. *New Dance* (orchestra; originally for 2 pianos)
Stravinsky. *Danses Concertantes* (orchestra)
———. *Ebony Concerto* (composed for Woody Herman dance band)
———. *Piano Rag Music*
———. *Ragtime* (piano)

22. Art Song

A well-rounded appreciation of music requires consideration of the art song—an important area of music literature. The art song can provide a boundless source of enjoyment, exploration, and discovery in musical experience.

Unlike folk song, art song is the creation of a composer. As opposed to the aria, which is an integral part of a large compound structure, the art song is a single composition. Differing from both the folk song and the popular song, the art song is a sophisticated type of music, a personal artistic creation. It is a relatively short composition of a decidedly intimate nature.

COMPONENTS

Art song, which depends upon the union of poetry and music, has the following components: (1) text, (2) vocal melody, and (3) accompaniment.

Text. An appreciation of art song requires an awareness of the beauty of the poetry itself. This may become difficult for the listener when the text is in a foreign language. For this reason, program notes and record jackets usually provide translations which enable the listener to follow the thought of the song.

Vocal Melody. The melody is the most important musical component of an art song. As noted in Chapter 4, the melodic properties characteristic of a song are: rhythm, dimensions, register, direction, and progression. All these factors are combined in a given song to create musical expression of the text.

Accompaniment. The art song is usually composed with a piano accompaniment. Solo songs of an earlier period were written with accompaniments for harpsichord, lute, and other instruments. Occasionally, composers have employed orchestral accompaniments for more elaborate songs (e.g., Mahler's *Kindertotenlieder*).

The accompaniment functions as a support to the vocal melody, and it provides a brief introduction and interludes.

Composers give considerable attention to the accompaniment which, like the melody, aids the effective musical expression of the text. The elements of harmony, rhythm, tempo, meter, texture, and key combine to create the desired effect. An example of the effective use of accompaniment is Schubert's *Gretchen am Spinnrade* (*Gretchen at the Spinning Wheel*). The piano clearly imitates the whirling of the wheel, which pauses momentarily on the word "kiss" while Gretchen reflects, then haltingly begins again as the song resumes. Again, in Schubert's "The Post," from the song cycle *Die Winterreise,* the accompaniment suggests the galloping of the horses while the vocal melody occasionally imitates the sound of the post horn call.

FORM

The musical form of an art song is partly determined by its poetic structure, although composers exhibit some freedom in their setting of the text. Poetry is usually written in units of several lines, known as stanzas or strophes. These strophes constitute the structural units of a song, subdivided into phrases or periods (see Chapter 12). The total length of a song is determined by the length and number of strophes. There are two main structural categories in art song: (1) strophic and (2) through-composed.

Strophic Form. In strophic settings, each stanza of the poem is set to the same music. For example, Schubert's *Das Wandern* (*The Wanderer*) has five stanzas, each musically identical and each with the musical structure *a a b c*. (The letters stand for phrases.)

Through–Composed Form. The term *through–composed* comes from the German word *Durchkomponiert*. Through–composed songs have different music for each stanza of the poem in order to follow the changing ideas or moods of the text. Schubert's *The Erlking* is an example of through–composed song; another is "Frozen Tears" from *Die Winterreise*.

Although most art songs belong to one or the other of these

categories, occasionally, if there is some recurrence of melody, an art song may be a mixture of both types. Schubert's "Linden Tree" (from *Die Winterreise*), for example, has the following structure:

Strophe	Melodic material
1	a
2	b
3	a′ (in minor key)
4	b
5	c
6	a
6*	b

The five strophes of Schubert's "Serenade" have the musical structure *a b a b c,* a mixture of strophic and through–composed plans.

SONG CYCLE

A group of art songs which are settings of several poems on a central subject are known as *song cycles.* Song cycles have a rather indefinite narrative, and the individual songs can be heard and enjoyed apart from the whole group. The most famous song cycles are listed at the end of this chapter.

Recommended Listening

Before listening to any selections of songs that are sung in a foreign language, try to obtain a translation of the text. In all songs, notice how the composer has utilized musical resources to enhance the beauty and meaning of the poetry.

Songs:

Bach. *Bist du bei mir (If thou art with me;* song in *Anna Magdalena Bach's Notebook)*

Binchois. *Adieu m'amour et ma maistresse (Farewell my love;* a fifteenth-century French song, No. 16 in *Masterpieces of Music before 1750)*

Brahms. *An die Nachtigal (To the Nightingale)*

———. *Dein Blaues Auge (Thy Blue Eyes)*

———. *Feldeinsamkeit (Meadow Loneliness)*

———. *Von ewiger Liebe (Of Eternal Love)*

———. *Ein Wanderer (A Wanderer)*

———. *Wiegenlied (Lullaby)*

* The last strophe of the poem is repeated in the song, but with different material.

Carpenter. "When I bring you colour'd toys," and "The sleep that flits on baby's eyes," from the song cycle *Gitanjali*

Duparc. *Chanson Triste (Melancholy Song)*

Dvořák. *Songs My Mother Taught Me*

Fauré. *Après un rêve (After a Dream)*

———. *Au cimetière (At the Cemetery)*

Gretchaninov. *The Mournful Steppe*

Grieg. *Ich liebe dich (I Love Thee)*

———. *Solvejg's Song* (from *Peer Gynt*)

Landino. *Chi più le vuol sapere (Who wishes to know them more;* ballata, No. 14 in *Masterpieces of Music before 1750)*

Mendelssohn. *Auf Flügeln des Gesanges (On Wings of Song)*

———. *Du bist wie eine Blume (Thou Art Like a Flower)*

Mozart. *Das Veilchen (The Violet)*

Mussorgski. *The Song of the Flea*

Neidhart von Reuenthal. *Willekommen Mayenschein (Welcome Art Thou, May's Bright Sun;* a thirteenth-century song, No. 5 in *Masterpieces of Music before 1750)*

Purcell. *I Attempt from Love's Sickness to Fly*

Rachmaninoff. *Oh Do Not Sing Again*

Rossini. *La Danza (Tarantella Napolitana)*

Schubert. *An die Musik (To Music)*

———. *An die Nachtigal (To the Nightingale)*

———. *Ave Maria*

———. *Du bist die Ruh (Thou Art Repose)*

———. *Der Erlkönig (The Erlking)*

———. *Die Forelle (The Trout).* The melody of this song was used in Schubert's *Quintet in A Major,* Op. 114, referred to as the *Trout Quintet.*

———. *Gretchen am Spinnrade (Gretchen at the Spinning Wheel)*

———. *Heidenröslein (Hedge Rose)*

———. *Liebesbotschaft (Love's Message)*

———. *Das Wandern (The Wanderer;* No. 1 in *Die Schöne Müllerin)*

———. *Ständchen (Serenade;* from the song cycle *Schwanengesang,* No. 4)

———. *Die Winterreise (The Winter Journey,* a song cycle): No. 1 ("Good Night"), No. 5 ("The Linden Tree"), No. 13 ("The Post")

Schumann. *Die beiden Grenadiere (The Two Grenadiers)*

———. *Frühlingsnacht (Spring Night)*

———. *Ich grolle nicht (I shall not complain,* No. 7 in the song cycle *Dichterliebe)*

———. *Mondnacht (Moonlight,* No. 5 in the song cycle *Liederkreise)*

———. *Widmung (Dedication)*

Tchaikovsky. *None but the Lonely Heart*

Trouvère Song (thirteenth century): ("Or la Truix"; No. 4 in *Masterpieces of Music before 1750)*

Wolf. *Anakreons Grab (Anacreon's Grave)*

———. *Verborgenheit (Secrecy)*

Song cycles:

Beethoven. *An die ferne Geliebte (To the Distant Beloved)*

Carpenter. *Gitanjali*

Debussy. *Chansons de Bilitis (Songs of Bilitis)*

Fauré. *La Bonne Chanson (The Good Song)*

Hindemith. *Das Marienleben (Life of the Virgin Mary)*

Mahler. *Kindertotenlieder* (*Songs of Children's Death;* a cycle of five songs with orchestra)

Mussorgski. *Songs and Dances of Death*

————. *Sunless*

Schoenberg. *Pierrot Lunaire;* song cycle with chamber ensemble, performed in "Sprechstimme" (half–spoken, half–sung)

Schubert. *Die Schöne Müllerin* (*The Miller's Daughter*)

*————. *Die Winterreise* (*The Winter's Journey,* a song cycle)

Schumann. *Dichterliebe* (*Poet's Love*)

————. *Frauenliebe und Leben* (*Women's Love and Life*)

————. *Liederkreise* (Eichendorff)

Vaughan Williams. *On Wenlock Edge* (song cycle for tenor voice, piano, and string quartet)

23. Folk and Ethnic Music, Nationalism

This chapter deals with three separate but related categories of music: *folk music, ethnic music,* and *nationalism* in music. The first two categories include songs, dances, or both combined.

FOLK MUSIC

Folk music is the traditional and spontaneously developed music of a people, race, region, or nation. As opposed to art song, which is sophisticated and is created by musically trained composers, folk music is unstudied and of humble origin. Since folk music is preserved by tradition, the original composer is often unknown. Folk tunes undergo continual change; consequently, there are often many different versions of the same song, both in words and melody.

Folk songs are characteristically simple in terms of melody, rhythm, harmony, and sectional structure (binary, ternary, song form).

Folk songs and folk dances constitute a wealth of melodic material that, aside from its intrinsic beauty, has provided thematic ideas for many compositions.

ETHNIC MUSIC

The categories of folk and ethnic music have much in common; they overlap in several respects. Both are indigenous to a people, race, region, or nation; both are generally unsophisticated music as opposed to composed art song or "art music." The distinction lies mainly in the fact that ethnic music is associated with non-

Western cultures, whereas the folk music tradition is primarily Western. Also, ethnic music includes that produced by ancient or by primitive peoples.

Ethnic music is predominantly characterized by a wide diversity of scale systems (pentatonic, microtonic, etc.), which may sound strange to Western ears. It may also differ markedly in respect to concepts of rhythm, timbre (from non-Western instruments), and structure.

Exceptions to the general distinctions between folk and ethnic music should be noted. For example, a Chinese folk song is ethnic music to Western ears. The folk music of some so-called ethnic minorities in the United States (Puerto Rican, Chicano, Afro-American) is not necessarily ethnic music; but American Indian music is ethnic music. The *ragas* and *talas* of India are ethnic music despite their highly complex and sophisticated structure.

Worldwide dissemination of folk and ethnic music has brought about considerable musical acculturation, especially notable being the influence of popular Occidental music on non-Western music. Modern techniques of recording and study, called *ethnomusicology*, have created widespread interest in the music of all lands and peoples, ancient and modern.

NATIONALISM

Nationalism in music began in the second half of the nineteenth century as a forceful European movement. Many composers strove to create music that would reflect the spirit of their own countries. They emphasized the distinctive characteristics of their native folk songs and dances, either directly quoting as thematic material or simulating them. Folklore and national legends were also employed in operas and symphonic poems.

Nationalism is especially evident in the music of Russia, Bohemia, Norway, Spain, Brazil, and Mexico.

The twentieth century has seen the fading of strong nationalism and its replacement by an eclecticism in which composers borrow styles and materials from countries other than their own. For example, European and American composers utilize ethnic music from Asia, the Middle East, and Africa. Thus folk and ethnic music are not only significant in themselves but also play important roles in sophisticated composition.

Recommended Listening

The most comprehensive representation of ethnic and folk music is by Folkways Records, whose catalogs list music according to major geographical areas (continents), subdivided into countries. To show how comprehensive is the recorded music in these series, under "Africa" more than 400 discs, representing 160 African countries and tribes, are listed. Although ethnic and folk music are not listed separately, it is clear that music listed under "Asia" would be almost entirely ethnic, while music under "Europe" would be mostly Western folk music.

Folk Songs

We shall list here some of the more familiar folk songs.

American:
Casey Jones (folk song-ballad)
Deep River (Negro spiritual)
Down in the Valley (See folk opera by Kurt Weill.)
The Erie Canal
Frankie and Johnny (folk song balad)
Home on the Range (cowboy folk song)
Turkey in the Straw (folk song and dance tune)
Stephen Foster songs. (Though composed, such songs as *Old Black Joe, Oh Susanna,* and *Swanee River* belong to this category.)
Wayfaring Stranger
Yankee Doodle

English:
Barbara Allen
Drink to Me Only with Thine Eyes
The Foggy, Foggy Dew
John Peel
London Bridge

French:
Ah vous dirai-je Maman. (See the variations on this tune by Mozart and Dohnányi listed at the end of Chapter 13.)
Malbrough s'en va-t-en guerre
Sur le pont d'Avignon
Au clair de la lune
Alouette (French-Canadian folk song)

German:
Ach du lieber Augustin
Der Tannenbaum

Irish:
Believe Me if All Those Endearing Young Charms
Irish Washerwoman (folk song, jig)
Londonderry Air

Italian:
Santa Lucia

Russian:
Song of the Volga Boatmen

Scotch:
Blue Bells of Scotland

Comin' through the Rye
Lord Randal

Spanish:
Juanita

Welsh:
All through the Night

National Music

See also Twentieth-Century Dances (page 158) and Some National Dances (page 159).

American:
Bennett. *Suite of Old American Dances* (band)
Copland. *Billy the Kid* (ballet music)
*———. *Music for the Theatre* (orchestra)
Foss. *The Jumping Frog of Calaveras County* (folk opera)
Gershwin. *An American in Paris* (orchestra)
———. *Porgy and Bess* (blues folk opera)
———. *Rhapsody in Blue* (piano and orchestra)
Goeb. *Three American Dances* (orchestra)
Gould. *Tap Dance Concerto* (orchestra)
Grofé. *Grand Canyon Suite* (orchestra)
Gruenberg. *Concerto for Violin and Orchestra*
Thomson. *Suite from The Plow that Broke the Plains* (orchestra; documentary film music)
Weill. *Down in the Valley* (folk opera based on folk tune by the same name; see above)

Bohemian:
Dvořák. *Slavonic Dances* (8 pieces for orchestra)
Smetana. *The Bartered Bride* (comic opera)
———. *The Moldau* (from the symphonic cycle, *My Fatherland*)

Brazilian:
Villa–Lobos. *Bachianas Brasileiras No. 5* (8 cellos and soprano)

Bulgarian:
Bartók. *Bulgarian Dances* (6 pieces for piano)

English:
Delius. *Brigg Fair* (orchestra)
Gilbert and Sullivan. *H.M.S. Pinafore* (operetta)
Vaughan Williams. *Symphony No. 2* ("London")

Finnish:
Sibelius. *Finlandia* (tone poem)
———. *The Swan of Tuonela* (orchestra)

French:
*Debussy. *Prélude à l'Après-midi d'un Faune* (*Prelude to the Afternoon of a Faun;* French Impressionism in music)
Milhaud. *Suite Française* (orchestra)
——— .*Suite Provençale* (orchestra)

German: The spirit of German nationalism is perhaps best exemplified in the operas of Wagner, especially the operas of the *Ring* cycle and *Die Meistersinger.*

Hungarian:
Bartók. *Rondos and Folk Dances* (piano)

Brahms. *Hungarian Dances* (orchestra; really "borrowed nationalism")
Kodály. *Háry János Suite* (orchestra)
Liszt. *Hungarian Rhapsody No. 2 in C Sharp Minor* (orchestra or piano)
Jewish:
Bloch. *Baal Shem* (violin and piano)
———. *From Jewish Life* (cello and piano)
———. *Israel Symphony* (orchestra and vocal parts)
———. *Schelomo* (cello and orchestra)
Bruch. *Kol Nidrei* (cello and orchestra)
Mexican:
Chávez. *Sinfonia India*
Revueltas. *Cuauhnahuac* (orchestra)
———. *Sensemaya* (orchestra)
Norwegian:
Grieg. *Norwegian Dances* (orchestra)
———. *Peer Gynt Suite No. 1* (orchestra)
Polish:
Chopin. *Mazurka in A Flat Major,* Op. 59, No. 2 (piano)
———. *Polonaise No. 6 in A Flat Major,* Op. 53 (piano)
Rumanian:
Enesco. *Rumanian Rhapsody in A Major* (orchestra)
Russian:
Borodin. *On the Steppes of Central Asia* (symphonic poem)
———. *Prince Igor* (opera)
Glinka. *Russlan and Ludmilla* (opera)
Ippolitov–Ivanov. *Caucasian Sketches* (symphonic suite)
Mussorgski. *Boris Godounov* (opera)
———. *Night on Bald Mountain* (symphonic poem)
Rimsky–Korsakov. *Russian Easter Overture*
———. *Sadko* (opera)
Stravinsky. *Fireworks* (orchestra)
*———. *Petrouchka* (ballet suite for orchestra)
Tchaikovsky. *Overture, 1812*
———. *Nutcracker Suite* (orchestra)
———. *Symphony No. 6 in B Minor*
Spanish:
Albéniz. *Spanish Dances* (8 pieces for orchestra)
———. *Tango in D Major* (piano)
Falla. *El Amor Brujo* (*Love the Sorcerer;* a ballet)
———. *Nights in the Gardens of Spain* (symphonic suite for piano and orchestra)
———. *El Sombrero de Tres Picos* (*The Three-Cornered Hat;* ballet)
Granados. *Spanish Dances* (orchestra)

Borrowed Nationalism

*Bizet (French. *Carmen* (opera; Spanish)
Chabrier (French). *España: Rhapsody for Orchestra* (Spanish)
Copland (American). *El Salón México* (orchestra; Mexican)
Debussy (French). *Ibéria* (orchestra; Spanish)
Dvořák (Bohemian). *Quartet in F Major* (string): "American"
———. *Symphony No. 5 in E Minor* ("New World," American)
Glinka (Russian). *Jota Aragonesa* (orchestra; Spanish)

Lalo (French). *Symphonie Espagnole* (Spanish)

Mendelssohn (German). *Hebrides Overture* (*Fingal's Cave;* Scotch)

Milhaud (French). *Le Boeuf sur le Toit* (Brazilian)

————. *Saudades do Brazil* (Brazilian)

*Puccini (Italian). *La Bohème* (opera; French)

————. *Madama Butterfly* (opera; Japanese)

*Ravel (French). *Boléro* (Spanish)

————. *L'Heure Espagnole* (comic opera; Spanish)

————. *Tzigane; Rhapsody for Violin and Orchestra* (Gypsy)

Rimsky-Korsakov (Russian). *Capriccio Espagnole* (orchestra; Spanish)

————. *Scheherazade* (orchestral suite; Oriental exoticism)

24. Religious Music

Music has served humanity's religious needs and thoughts from earliest times. Some of the world's greatest music, like some of its greatest painting and architecture, has a religious purpose and can be enjoyed for its artistic significance as well as for its religious import.

There are two main categories of religious music: (1) *liturgical music,* which is composed for a specific function in the church ceremony, and (2) *nonliturgical music,* which is composed more for concert purposes than for performance in church, even though it is of a serious religious nature.

LITURGICAL MUSIC

The purpose of liturgical music is to create or enhance attitudes of worship. This form of music should be included in the study of music appreciation because (like painting and architecture) it is frequently experienced as an art, entirely apart from the religious function for which it was originally intended. For the fullest understanding and enjoyment of liturgical music, however, it is best to bear in mind its basic functional purpose.

Plainsong. Perhaps the greatest body of liturgical melody is *plainsong* (also called *plainchant* and *Gregorian chant*). The characteristics of plainsong which, taken together, set it apart from other melodic styles are that it is: (1) monophonic, (2) nonmetric, (3) rhythmically free, (4) modal, and (5) until recently sung in Latin in the Roman Catholic Church.

Chorale. Another great body of religious melody is the Protestant *chorale,* which had its origin during the Lutheran Reformation in the sixteenth century. Some of the finest hymns in use today belong to this category of religious melody. Chorale melody differs from Catholic plainsong in that it is: (1) more often harmonized and accompanied, (2) more regular in meter and rhythm, (3) more major and minor than modal, and (4) sung in the vernacular language instead of in Latin.

The chorale, like plainsong, forms the cantus firmus basis of much fine polyphonic music, both instrumental and vocal (see pages 111 f).

Mass. The Catholic liturgical Mass consists of two main divisions: (1) the Ordinary of the Mass, the Latin text of which remains the same in all services, and (2) the Proper of the Mass, which varies from Sunday to Sunday.

ORDINARY. The *Ordinary* of the Mass consists of five sections: *Kyrie, Gloria, Credo, Sanctus,* and *Agnus Dei.* These parts are usually sung in monophonic plainsong or in polyphonic settings (see page 112).

PROPER. The parts of the *Proper* of the Mass which are sung are the *Introit, Graduale, Alleluia, Offertorium,* and *Communio.* These parts are sung in plainsong or else in polyphonic settings called *motets* (see below).

REQUIEM MASS. A special kind of Mass is the *Requiem* (also called the *Missa pro defunctis,* or *Mass for the Dead*). It is similar in construction to the Ordinary of the Mass except that the Gloria and the Credo are omitted and a section called *Dies Irae* (based on a plainsong sequence of the thirteenth century) is added.

Motet. The motet (see Chapter 15) is a liturgical form extensively employed in the Renaissance (fifteenth and sixteenth centuries). Some of the greatest liturgical literature of all time belongs to this category. The term appears from the Middle Ages to the eighteenth century (e.g., Bach's motet *Singet dem Herrn* and Mozart's *Ave Verum Corpus*), but most motet literature belongs to the Renaissance. The Renaissance motet not only represents a perfection of contrapuntal technique in the *a cappella* (unaccompanied) style, but also constitutes the perfect vehicle for religious contemplation: impersonal in style, yet deeply expressive of spiritual ideas.

Church Cantata. The liturgical cantata is to Protestant music what the Mass and motet are to Catholic music. It is a later form, arising from the innovations of dramatic music in the early seventeenth century. It flourished in the Baroque period.

The church cantata is composed for voices and instruments. It may include recitative, arias, duets, and choral pieces, and it often makes use of chorale melody. In this sense the cantata is a composite form comparable to opera and oratorio, but it is shorter than either of these, and is more reflective than narrative.

Anthem. The principal liturgical form in the Anglican Church and in other Protestant denominations is the *anthem,* a form which employs a chorus with English text and usually with organ accompaniment. If parts for solo singers are included, the form is referred to as *verse anthem.*

Instrumental Church Music. Although religious music is composed principally for vocal mediums, there are a few important instrumental liturgical forms. The most important of these is the chorale prelude for organ, which uses a chorale melody as a cantus firmus (see Chapter 15). The chorale prelude reached its highest development in the work of Bach during the eighteenth century.

Another instrumental form, presumably used in church, was the baroque *sonata da chiesa* (church sonata). This form, consisting of several movements, often of dancelike character, though not so labelled, was distinguished from the *sonata da camera* (chamber sonata), which was actually a dance suite (see "baroque suite," Chapter 17).

NONLITURGICAL FORMS

The introductory remarks for this chapter pointed out the artistic significance of all religious music, liturgical and nonliturgical alike. The borderline between these two categories is sometimes vague. In fact, compositions in the liturgical forms, especially the Mass and Requiem, are sometimes essentially nonliturgical, because inappropriate operatic styles (Mozart's "Coronation" *Mass in C Major,* Verdi's *Requiem*) or great length (Beethoven's *Missa Solemnis,* Bach's *Mass in B Minor*) make them impractical for normal use in the church service. However, such masterpieces are neither less great as works of art nor necessarily less religious because of these nonliturgical aspects.

Oratorio. Since the early seventeenth century, composers have written dramatic religious works of a nonliturgical intent. The principal form of this kind of music is the *oratorio,* a religious dramatic work which employs operatic forms but is performed without staging, costuming, or scenery.

COMPONENTS. An oratorio includes recitative, arias and solo ensembles (duets, trios, quartets, etc.), chorus, and orchestra. The story, usually Biblical, is told by a *narrator* in recitative style. The chorus is more extensively employed in oratorio than in opera. The oratorio is longer and more dramatic than the church cantata.

PASSION ORATORIOS. Oratorios based on the Easter story as related by the Biblical Evangelists (Matthew, Mark, Luke, John) are called *passion oratorios*. Bach's *St. Matthew Passion* is a magnificent example of such music.

Miscellaneous Music of a Religious Nature. Although the principal form of nonliturgical music is the oratorio, it does not represent all the great music in this category.

OPERA. There are a few operas which have a strong religious emphasis but which are perhaps more secular than sacred in their purpose. Examples are Massenet's *Thaïs* and Wagner's *Parsifal*.

SYMPHONIC WORKS. A considerable number of works for orchestra, with or without chorus, manifest religious ideas. Such are Beethoven's *Symphony No. 9 in D Minor* with choral finale, Britten's *Sinfonia da Requiem* (for orchestra), and Respighi's *Concerto Gregoriano*.

RELIGIOUS SONGS. Not all the solo songs discussed in Chapter 22 are settings of poems about love and other secular topics. Some of them deal with religious subjects. Schubert's familiar *Ave Maria* and Hindemith's *Marienleben* (a song cycle) are notable examples of solo song literature dealing with religious subjects.

Recommended Listening

In order to obtain a rounded knowledge of religious musical forms, you should select compositions from each of the categories of liturgical and nonliturgical music listed below. It is interesting to hear religious music from different historical periods; for example, a Mass by Machaut (fourteenth century), one by Palestrina (sixteenth century), Bach (eighteenth century), Bruckner (nineteenth century), and Stravinsky (twentieth century).

Liturgical Music

Gregorian chant:

(Some 15 albums of Gregorian chant are listed in the record catalogues. The chants listed here are to be found in *Masterpieces of Music before 1750*.)

Alleluia: Vidimus Stellam No. 2

Antiphon: Laus Deo Patri No. 1

Psalm: Laudate Pueri No. 1

Sequence: Victimae Paschali No. 3

Mass (including festival, nonliturgical, and Requiem masses):

Bach. *Mass in B Minor*

Beethoven. *Missa Solemnis in D Major*

Benevoli. *Festival Mass* (for 53 voices)

Berlioz. *Requiem*

Bruckner. *Mass No. 3 in F Minor* ("Great")

Dufay. "Kyrie" from the Mass, *Se la Face ay Pale* (fifteenth century, a cappella; No. 15 in *Masterpieces of Music before 1750*)

Fauré. *Requiem*

Kodály. *Missa Brevis in Tempore Belli* (voices and organ)

Machaut. *Notre Dame Mass* (fourteenth-century Mass)

Mozart. *Mass in C Major*, K. 317 ("Coronation")

————. *Mass in C Minor*, K. 427 ("The Great")

————. *Requiem*, K. 626

Okeghem. *Missa Prolationum* (fifteenth-century Mass; a cappella)

*Palestrina. *Missa Brevis* (sixteenth-century Mass, a cappella)

————. *Missa Papae Marcelli* (sixteenth century Mass, a cappella

Stravinsky. *Mass* (for boys' choir and brass instruments)

Vaughan Williams. *Mass in G Minor*

Verdi. *Requiem*

Motets:

Bach. *Singet dem Herrn* (baroque motet, a cappella)

Byrd. *Ergo Sum Panis Vivus* (sixteenth century; No. 25 in *Masterpieces of Music before 1750*)

————. *Non nobis Domine* (a cappella)

Gabrieli. *Motets* (late sixteenth century)

Josquin Des Prez. *Ave Maria* (fifteenth century, a cappella; No. 19 in *Masterpieces of Music before 1750*)

Lasso. *Tristis Est Anima Mea* (sixteenth century, a cappella; No. 23 in *Masterpieces of Music before 1750*)

Mozart. *Ave Verum Corpus* (eighteenth century)

Obrecht. *Parce, Domine* (fifteenth century, a cappella; No. 18 in *Masterpieces of Music before 1750*)

Palestrina. *Improperia* (sixteenth century, a cappella)

————. (See motets by Palestrina and other Renaissance composers in album by Sistine Choir.)

Victoria. *O Magnum Mysterium* (sixteenth century, a cappella)

————. *O Quam Gloriosum* (sixteenth century, a cappella)

Church cantatas:

Bach. *Cantata No. 4, Christ lag in Todesbanden*

————. *Cantata No. 80, Ein Feste Burg ist unser Gott*

*————. *Cantata No. 140; Wachet auf, ruft uns die Stimme*

Gabrieli. *Symphoniae Sacrae* (chorus)

Schütz. *Kleine Geistliche Konzerte* (religious pieces)

Miscellaneous church music (mostly liturgical):

Bach. *Magnificat in D Major* (chorus, orchestra)

Britten. *Te Deum in C Major* (chorus and organ)

Bruckner. *Te Deum* (choir and orchestra)

Handel. *Te Deum for the Peace of Utrecht*

Pergolesi. *Stabat Mater*

Rossini. *Stabat Mater*

Chorale preludes:

Bach. *Orgelbüchlein* (a collection of chorale preludes for the church year):
    'Das alte Jahr vergangen ist" (No. 10)
    "Christ lag in Todesbanden" (No. 5)
    "Erscheinen ist der herrliche Tag" (No. 15)
    "Ich ruf' zu dir, Herr Jesu Christ" (No. 30)
    "In dulci jubilo" (No. 35)
    "O Mensch, bewein' dein' Sünde gross" (No. 45)

————. *Canonic Variations on Vom Himmel hoch* (organ)

————. *Ein Feste Burg ist unser Gott* (See also Bach's cantata No. 80, and the finale of Mendelssohn's *Symphony No. 5*, "Reformation," which use the same chorale tune.)

————. *Jesu Joy of Man's Desiring* (chorale chorus from *Cantata No. 147;* also arranged for organ and for piano)

————. *Komm süsser Tod* (organ)

*————. *Wachet auf, ruft uns die Stimme* (chorale prelude, organ; see also *Cantata No. 140*)

————. *Wenn wir in höchsten Nöten sein* (organ)

Reger. *Chorale Preludes,* Op. 67

Nonliturgical Forms

Oratorio:

Berlioz. *L'Enfance du Christ* (*The Childhood of Christ*)
Carissimi. *Jepthe* (seventeenth century)
Elgar. *The Dream of Gerontius* (nineteenth century)
Franck. *Les Béatitudes* (nineteenth century)
Handel. *Judas Maccabaeus* (eighteenth century)
*————. *Messiah* (eighteenth century)
Haydn. *The Creation* (eighteenth century)
Honegger. *King David* (twentieth century)
Mendelssohn. *Elijah* (nineteenth century)
————. *St. Paul*
Walton. *Belshazzar's Feast* (twentieth century)

Passion music:

Bach. *St. John Passion*
————. *St. Matthew Passion*
Schütz. *St. John Passion* (seventeenth century)
————. *St. Matthew Passion*
Stainer. *The Crucifixion* (Easter cantata)
————. *Seven Words from the Cross* (Easter cantata)

Miscellaneous religious works:

Beethoven. *Symphony No. 9 in D Minor* ("Choral"): *Finale*
Bloch. *Israel Symphony* (orchestra and vocal parts)
Brahms. *A German Requiem* (*Ein deutsches Requiem;* an oratorio-like work not based on the liturgical text)
Britten. *Sinfonia da Requiem* (orchestra)
Bruckner. *Psalms 112 and 150* (choir and orchestra)
Corelli. *Concerto Grosso No. 8 in G Minor,* Op. 6 ("Christmas")
Dello Joio. *Psalm of David* (chorus and orchestra)
Dupré. *The Stations of the Cross* (organ)
Franck. *Chorale No. 3 in A Minor* (for organ)
Hindemith. *Das Marienleben* (*Life of the Virgin Mary,* a song cycle)
Ives. *Sixty-Seventh Psalm* (8-part chorus)

Massenet. *Thaïs* (a secular opera on a religious subject)

Mendelssohn. *Symphony No. 5 in D Major*, Op. 107 ("Reformation"; last movement employs the Bach chorale *Ein Feste Burg*)

Respighi. *Concerto Gregoriano* (violin and orchestra)

Schubert. *Ave Maria* (solo song)

Stravinsky. *Symphony of Psalms* (chorus and orchestra)

Wagner. *Parsifal* (opera of a deeply religious nature)

Familiar hymns:

Barnby. *Now the Day Is Over*

Haydn. *Oh Worship the King*

Luther. (*Ein Feste Burg ist unser Gott*) *A Mighty Fortress Is Our God*

Mason. *My Faith Looks Up to Thee*

———. *Nearer My God to Thee*

Monk. *Abide with Me*

25. Absolute and Program Music

The terms *absolute* and *program* are concerned with two broad categories of instrumental music; the use of these terms depends on whether or not the music is intended to convey nonmusical ideas.

ABSOLUTE MUSIC

Instrumental music which stands entirely on its own merits and which has no intrinsic association with extramusical ideas is called *absolute music.* Absolute music bears such titles as *Symphony No. 40 in G Minor, Sonata in D Major, Toccata and Fugue in D Minor*—titles which are not descriptive of anything but the music itself.

PROGRAM MUSIC

The opposite of absolute music is *program music:* instrumental music which by the composer's intention is designed to convey some extramusical idea. Descriptive titles, such as *Carnival, The Afternoon of a Faun,* and *The Pines of Rome,* imply program music.

Music literature which has extramusical associations but which generally falls outside consideration of the program category includes all vocal music (opera, oratorio, songs, etc.), dance music (music associated with the dance), national music (music associated with nations or regions), and religious music (both liturgical and nonliturgical music associated with religious ideas).

Mood or Atmosphere. Most music in the program category attempts little more than to convey the general mood or "atmosphere" of the indicated idea. For example, the main purpose of Debussy's *The Afternoon of a Faun,* based on a poem by Mallarmé, is to convey the warm, dreamy, and rather vague nature of the poem.

Narrative Program Music. The programmatic basis of a composition may be carried to a higher degree of realism when the music is intended to tell a story or depict a series of related events. Examples of this sort of narrative program music are Strauss's symphonic poems *Till Eulenspiegel* and *Don Quixote,* and Berlioz's *Fantastic Symphony* in which each of the five movements depicts a different episode in the life of an artist.

Realism. Program music sometimes attempts direct realism by reproducing or imitating sounds of nature, such as bird calls (e.g., Beethoven's "Pastorale" *Symphony No. 6*), trumpet fanfares and hunting horns, storms, battle scenes, wind, etc. Such effects usually add nothing to the artistic merits of the music.

Program Music and Appreciation. The approach to music appreciation through program music was once thought to be the soundest one. The prevailing opinion today minimizes the importance of program music as such and holds that extramusical association is unessential or even detrimental to true appreciation, that it serves merely as a crutch to listening, and that overemphasis on the programmatic aspect of music detracts from perceptive listening. The listener who requires extramusical associations of ideas (even of his own invention) in order to enjoy music, will never be able to appreciate fully the beauty and the meaning of music itself. There are innumerable masterpieces of program music which can be appreciated for their own sake even though the composer has "attached a program."

Style. The style of program music differs in no essential or consistent way from that of absolute music. Unless one knows the title or programmatic intent of the composer, it is impossible to distinguish a piece of program music from absolute music. A piece of absolute music can be very romantic and emotional without being even remotely related to a specific program.

ERAS AND MEDIUMS

Program music occurs most extensively in nineteenth-century music for symphony orchestra (in the symphonic poem and symphonic suite) and piano (short descriptive pieces).

Absolute music predominated through the eighteenth century. It encompassed all instrumental forms and mediums: chamber music, keyboard music, and orchestral music. In the twentieth century, although program music continues to play an important role, absolute music predominates.

Recommended Listening

The literature in both categories, but especially in absolute music, is, of course, extensive, The following list of compositions has been selected from music listed in preceding chapters. Select a composition from each category, preferably in the same medium, and compare them musically in as many ways as you can.

Absolute Music

Bach. *Brandenburg Concerto No. 5 in D Major* (concerto grosso)
——. *Christ lag in Todesbanden* (chorale prelude for organ)
Note: This and other chorale preludes are listed here, even though they belong to the category of religious music and have titles of an extramusical nature. These pieces in concert performance have little programmatic connotation; instead, they are enjoyed as examples of absolute music.
——. *Chromatic Fantasy and Fugue* (harpsichord)
——. *Fantasia and Fugue in G Minor* ("The Great"; for organ)
——. *Musical Offering* (*Das Musicalische Opfer*)
——. *Partita No. 5 in G Major* (piano or harpsichord)
*——. *Passacaglia and Fugue in C Minor* (organ)
*——. *Suite No. 3 in D Major for Orchestra*
——. *Toccata and Fugue in D Minor* (organ)
——. *The Well–Tempered Clavier* (48 preludes and fugues representing all keys, major and minor; piano or harpsichord)
Barber. *Adagio for Strings*
Bartók. *Concerto No. 3 for Piano and Orchestra*
*——. *Quartet No. 5* (strings)
Beethoven. *Quartet No. 12 in E Flat Major* (strings)
——. *Sonata No. 23 in F Minor* (piano; "Appassionata")
Note: The title "Appassionata" was not affixed by Beethoven, nor was his intention programmatic. This is true of other parenthetical titles listed here.
*——. *Symphony No. 5 in C Minor* (This symphony is sometimes called "The Fate Symphony" because of a remark supposedly made by Beethoven that the opening motive represented "fate knocking at the door." This story is probably untrue; it certainly offers no basis for giving the symphony a programmatic connotation.)
Brahms. *Capriccios:* Opp. 76 and 116 (piano)
——. *Intermezzi* (piano)
——. *Quartet No. 2 in A Minor* (strings)
——. *Symphony No. 1 in C Minor*
*——. *Symphony No. 3 in F Major*

————. *Trio in E Flat Major* (piano, violin, horn)

Chopin. *Ballade No. 3 in A Flat Major,* Op. 47 (piano)

————. *Nocturne in E Flat Major,* Op. 9, No. 2 (piano)

————. *Préludes,* Op. 28 (piano)

————. *Waltz in D Flat Major* ("Minute"; piano), Op. 64

Copland. *Passacaglia* (piano)

Creston. *Symphony No. 2*

Franck. *Prelude, Fugue and Variations,* Op. 18 (organ)

————. *Symphonic Variations* (piano and orchestra)

Gershwin. *Preludes* (3, for piano)

Handel. *Concerto Grosso No. 5 in D Major,* Op. 6

————. *Sonata No. 4 in D Major for Violin and Harpsichord* (or piano), Op. 1, No. 13

Harris. *Symphony No. 3* (in one movement)

*Haydn. *Quartet in E Flat Major,* Op. 33, No. 2 (strings)

————. *Symphony No. 94 in G Major* ("Surprise")

Hindemith. *Sonata for Two Flutes* (canonic)

*————. *Sonata No. 3 for Piano*

————. *Symphony in E Flat*

Kreisler. *Rondino on a Theme by Beethoven* (violin and piano)

Martin. *Concerto for Harpsichord and Small Orchestra*

Martinu. *Sonata for Flute and Piano*

*Mendelssohn. *Concerto in E Minor for Violin and Orchestra*

Milhaud. *Sonatina* (clarinet and piano)

Mozart. *Concerto in E Flat Major for Piano and Orchestra,* K. 271

————. *Eine Kleine Nachtmusik,* K. 525

————. *Quartet in G Major* (strings), K. 387

————. *Quintet in A Major* (clarinet and string quartet), K. 581

————. *Sonata in A Major* (piano), K. 331

*————. *Symphony No. 40 in G Minor,* K. 550

Poulenc. *Trio for Piano, Oboe, and Bassoon*

Prokofiev. *Classical Symphony in D Major*

————. *Concerto No. 2 in G Minor for Violin and Orchestra*

————. *Toccata in D Minor* (piano)

Purcell. *Fantasias in 3, 4, and 5 Parts* (strings)

Rachmaninoff. *Concerto No. 2 in C Minor for Piano and Orchestra*

Ravel. *Concerto in G Major for Piano and Orchestra*

Riegger. *Quartet No. 2* (strings)

Saint–Saëns. *Introduction and Rondo Capriccioso*

Scarlatti, D. *Sonata in D Major* (harpsichord)

Schoenberg. *Drei Klavierstücke* (*Three Piano Pieces*), Op. 11

————. *Quartet No. 4* (strings), Op. 37

Schubert. *Symphony No. 8 in B Minor* ("Unfinished")

Schumann. *Concerto in A Minor for Piano and Orchestra*

Shostakovitch. *Preludes* (24, for piano)

————. *Symphony No. 5*

Sibelius. *Symphony No. 1 in E Minor*

Stravinsky. *Symphony in Three Movements*

Tchaikovsky. *Concerto in D Major for Violin and Orchestra*

————. *Symphony No. 5 in E Minor*

Program Music

Beethoven. *Symphony No. 6 in F Major* ("Pastorale")

Note: Unlike *Symphony No. 5,* The "Fate Symphony" (see above), each movement of the "Pastorale Symphony" bears Beethoven's inscription of a program: "Feelings on arriving in the country," "Beside the brook," etc.

Berg. *Concerto for Violin and Orchestra* ("To the Memory of an Angel")

Berlioz. *Symphonie Fantastique* (*Fantastic Symphony*)

Bizet. *L'Arlésienne Suite No. 2* (orchestra)

Borodin. *On the Steppes of Central Asia* (orchestra)

Byrd. *The Bells* (harpsichord)

———. *The Carman's Whistle* (harpsichord)

Copland. *Appalachian Spring* (ballet suite for orchestra)

Couperin. *La Galante* (harpsichord; No. 40 in *Masterpieces of Music before 1750*)

Debussy. *La Cathédrale Engloutie* (*The Sunken Cathedral;* piano)

———. *La Mer* (symphonic suite)

———. *Nocturnes* (3 pieces for orchestra)

*———. *Prélude à l'Après-midi d'un Faune* (*Prelude to the Afternoon of a Faun;* symphonic poem)

Delius. *Brigg Fair* (symphonic poem)

Dukas. *The Sorcerer's Apprentice* (symphonic poem)

Elgar. *Enigma Variations* (orchestra)

Griffes. *The Pleasure-dome of Kubla Khan*

———. *The White Peacock* (piano or orchestra)

Grofé. *Grand Canyon Suite* (orchestral suite)

Hindemith. *Mathis der Maler* (orchestra, three movements)

Holst. *The Planets* (orchestral suite)

Honegger. *Pacific 231* (symphonic poem)

D'Indy. *Istar Variations* (orchestra)

Ippolitov–Ivanov. *Caucasian Sketches* (symphonic suite)

Liszt. *La Campanella* (piano)

———. *Les Préludes* (symphonic poem based on Lamartine's *Méditations Poétiques*)

MacDowell. *Woodland Sketches* (descriptive pieces, including *To a Wild Rose*)

Mendelssohn. *Hebrides Overture* (concert overture)

———. *Songs Without Words*, Op. 67, No. 4 ("Spinning Song," piano)

Milhaud. *The Household Muse* (collection of descriptive pieces for piano)

Mossolov. *Iron Foundry* (orchestra)

Mussorgski. *Night on Bald Mountain* (orchestra)

———. *Pictures at an Exhibition* (piano or orchestra)

Prokofiev. *Lieutenant Kije Suite* (orchestra)

Rachmaninoff. *Isle of the Dead* (symphonic poem pased on a painting by Boecklin)

Ravel. *Gaspard de la Nuit* (suite for piano)

———. *Jeux d'Eau* (*Fountains,* for piano)

———. *Ma Mère l'Oye* (*Mother Goose Suite;* orchestra or 2 pianos)

Respighi. *The Fountains of Rome* (orchestral suite)

———. *The Pines of Rome* (orchestral suite)

Rimsky–Korsakov. *Scheherazade* (orchestral suite)

Saint-Saëns. *Carnival of the Animals* (orchestral suite)

———. *Danse Macabre* (orchestra)

Schumann. *Carnaval* (descriptive pieces for piano)

*———. *Fantasiestücke* (*Fantasy Pieces,* piano)

———. *Papillons* (*Butterflies;* descriptive piano pieces)

Scriabin. *Poem of Ecstasy* (orchestra)

Sibelius. *Finlandia* (tone poem for orchestra)

——. *The Swan of Tuonela* (symphonic poem)

——. *Valse Triste* (orchestra)

Smetana. *The Moldau* (from the symphonic cycle, *My Fatherland*)

Strauss, R. *Don Quixote* (symphonic poem in the form of free variations, each variation being an episode in the story of Cervantes' knight represented by cello theme)

——. *Ein Heldenleben* (*A Hero's Life;* symphonic poem)

*——. *Till Eulenspiegel* (symphonic poem; episodes in the life of a legendary medieval character)

Stravinsky. *Fireworks* (symphonic poem)

Taylor. *Through the Looking Glass* (orchestral suite based on Lewis Carroll's humorous classic of the same title)

*Tchaikovsky. *Nutcracker Suite* (orchestral suite from ballet)

Note: Ballet music arranged for concert performance is of a descriptive, programmatic nature, but, like opera and vocal music, it has generally been excluded from this list because it is a functional category, an integral part of a creation that includes activities in addition to music.

——. *Overture, 1812*

——. *Romeo and Juliet* (overture fantasy)

26. Humor in Music

Not all music is of a serious or profound nature. Humor plays a significant role in music literature, as it does in fiction and drama. The various kinds of humor that exist in music are sources of considerable pleasure and amusement.

Humor in music does not constitute such a clearly defined and separate category as do symphonic music, opera, art song, and others. Humor is to be found in virtually all musical forms, mediums, and categories.

Humor as Relief. In highly dramatic works, comic relief is provided for release from intense emotion. The comic scenes in Shakespeare's plays function precisely in this way. Early in the history of opera, comic *intermezzi* were inserted between the serious acts. This was the origin of comic opera.

Scherzo. In large instrumental works such as sonatas and symphonies, a contrasting movement in lighter vein is similar to the intermezzo in that it is a device for relieving tension. The generic name for such movements is *scherzo,* an Italian word meaning a joke or play. The musical scherzo embraces all shades of humor from the merely clever, gay, witty, or jocund (e.g., the *Scherzo* from Mendelssohn's *A Midsummer Night's Dream*) to the thoroughly farcical, grotesque, or even hilarious (e.g., the movement entitled "Scherzophrenia" in Don Gillis' *Symphony No. 5½*).

Parody. Parody is an important aspect of musical humor. In vocal music, comedy can be evoked by setting texts of a serious or heroic nature to light, frivolous music, or by setting a humorous text in a deliberately ponderous manner.

Caricature. By exaggerating the idiosyncrasies or mannerisms of the style of a certain composer or era, effective musical humor can be produced. Satire and caricature are commonly employed in the twentieth century. An interesting study of style caricatures is Edward Ballantine's *Variations on Mary Had a Little Lamb* (two sets of variations for piano), in which he cleverly imitates the familiar styles of such composers as Bach, Franck, Richard Strauss, Gershwin, and others.

Incongruity. Another humorous device, somewhat related to parody, is the introduction of marked incongruities into music. This is often brought about by sudden changes in rhythm, tempo, dynamics, harmony, and other musical elements. Beethoven's scherzos are notable in this respect. Haydn, too, was fond of humorous surprises. The sudden fortissimo chord in the second movement of Haydn's *Symphony No. 94* ("Surprise"), after a very quiet beginning, is a deliberately humorous trick. Another instance of humor in Haydn's music occurs at the end of the last movement of his *String Quartet No. 38* (Op. 33, No. 2, in E Flat), where several long pauses are introduced which deceive the listener several times into thinking the conclusion has been reached, so that when the final phrase has actually been played, the audience is not sure that it is the end. A similar instance of humor is Johann Strauss's *Perpetuum Mobile: A Musical Joke* ("Perpetual Motion"), the fast, continuous flow of which is suddenly broken off in mid–air.

Wrong Notes. The intentional introduction of "wrong notes" into the melody or harmony may result in a comic incongruity. Examples of this kind of humor are Shostakovitch's "Polka" from *The Golden Age,* Goossens' "Hurdy-Gurdy Man" from the suite *Kaleidoscope,* and Mozart's *Musical Joke.*

Borrowed Melody. A humorous effect can be produced by borrowing a well–known melody and placing it in an incongruous setting. Debussy does this in his "Golliwog's Cake-walk" from *The Children's Corner Suite,* a droll dance piece which introduces the "love motive" from Wagner's *Tristan and Isolde.* The last movement of Berlioz' *Fantastic Symphony,* entitled "Dream of a Witches' Sabbath," introduces the famous plainsong "Dies Irae" of the Requiem Mass in order to produce an element of diabolical humor. Still another instance is Stravinsky's amusing quotation of a theme from Schubert's *Marche Militaire* in his *Circus Polka* ("Ballet for an Elephant").

Humor in Vocal Music. Humorous texts call for appropriate musical treatment. There are many examples of humor in songs, operas and operettas, and choral music. Mussorgski's *Song of the Flea,* Pergolesi's *The Music Master,* and Purcell's *'Tis Women Makes Us Love* (see page 108) are just a few examples.

Other Instances of Musical Humor. Mozart's *Musical Joke,* mentioned above, is a famous example of musical humor. This divertimento pokes fun at the unskilled composer who sprinkles his score with banalities, and also at the unskilled performer who plays wrong notes. The piece ends with a humorously impressive dissonance.

Henry Purcell wrote a five-part fantasy for strings in which one part plays the same note throughout the whole piece. Peter Cornelius wrote a song called *The Monotone* in which the vocal line is on just one tone while the melody in the accompaniment provides a humorous contrast by moving around in a wide range.

A sort of grotesque humor is exhibited in the trio section of the Scherzo of Beethoven's *Symphony No. 5,* where rapid scales and figures are given to the unwieldly string basses (doubled by cellos). The rustic peasant dance in Beethoven's *Symphony No. 6* ("Pastorale"), third movement, portrays an amateur orchestra in which the bassoon player repeatedly "comes in late."

Erik Satie was an exponent of musical satire. His piano pieces carry such humorous titles as *Three Pieces in the Form of a Pear, Cold Pieces, Unpleasant Glances, Automatic Descriptions,* and *Next-to-last Thoughts.*

Recommended Listening

Many of the humorous compositions listed below have already been mentioned. Remember that humor in music is not necessarily comic or funny, but may be witty, merry, whimsical, or mildly amusing. In any case, you should try to ascertain what the degree of humor is and how it is brought about musically.

Bach. *Cantata No. 211 (Coffee Cantata;* humorous secular cantata composed by a usually very serious composer)
Ballantine. *Variations on Mary Had a Little Lamb* (piano)
*Bartók. *Quartet No. 5* (strings): II *(Scherzo)*
*Beethoven. *Symphony No. 5 in C Minor:* III *(Scherzo)*
————. *Symphony No. 6 in F Major* ("Pastorale"): III
Berlioz. *Symphonie Fantastique (Fantastic Symphony):* V "Dream of a Witch's Sabbath"
Casella. *Five Pieces for String Quartet:* III ("Valse Ridicule"); V ("Foxtrot")
Claflin. *Lament for April 15* (settings for sections of the federal income tax instructions)
Debussy. *Children's Corner Suite* (piano): *Golliwog's Cake-walk*

Dukas. *The Sorcerer's Apprentice* (symphonic poem; the grotesque and furious dance of the broom is entertaining humor)

Gershwin. *An American in Paris* (orchestra; contains jaunty café tunes and simulates French taxi horns)

Gilbert and Sullivan. *H.M.S. Pinafore* (operetta)

———. *Mikado* (an operetta with many humorous elements)

*Haydn. *Quartet in E Flat Major* (strings), Op. 33, No. 2: IV

———. *Symphony No. 94 in G Major* ("Surprise"): II

*Hindemith. *Sonata No. 3 for Piano:* II

Mendelssohn. *A Midsummer Night's Dream* (orchestra): *Scherzo* (a light, gay movement)

Menotti. *The Telephone* (a gay, witty comic intermezzo)

Milhaud. *Le Boeuf sur le Toit* (comic ballet)

*Mozart. *Don Giovanni* (opera): (Leporello, Don Giovanni's servant, is a comic character. See, for example, the opening monologue of Leporello, and "Madamina," his famous "Catalogue Song.")

———. *The Impresario* (*Der Schauspieldirektor,* a Singspiel in two acts)

———. *Musical Joke* (*Musikalischer Spass*), K. 522 (sextet for string quartet and two horns)

Mussorgski. *The Song of the Flea* (comic song)

Pergolesi. *The Music Master* (short comic opera)

Prokofiev. *Peter and the Wolf* (a children's fairy tale for narrator and orchestra. The themes of Peter, Grandfather, the bird, the cat, the duck, and the wolf, provide amusing uses of the *leitmotif* in the story's mildly comic situations.)

Rameau. *La Poule* (*The Hen,* for harpsichord. An amusing piece in which the sounds of chickens are portrayed.)

Saint–Saëns. *Carnival of the Animals* (orchestra or two pianos)

Satie. *Descriptions Automatiques* (piano)

———. *Next-to-last Thoughts* (piano)

———. *Three Pieces in the Form of a Pear* (piano)

———. *Unpleasant Glances* (piano)

*Schumann. *Fantasiestücke* (*Fantasy Pieces;* piano)

Strauss, J. *Perpetuum Mobile: A Musical Joke* (orchestra)

Strauss, R. *Don Quixote* (orchestra and cello solo; symphonic poem in the form of variations depicting episodes, many of them of a humorous nature, in the life of Cervantes' medieval knight)

*———. *Till Eulenspiegel* (symphonic poem. Use of light, whimsical, and grotesque humor in a narrative symphonic poem.)

Stravinsky. *Circus Polka* ("Ballet for an Elephant," quotes theme from Schubert's *Marche Militaire*)

———. *Mavra* (comic opera)

Taylor. *Through the Looking Glass* (orchestral suite based on Lewis Carroll's humorous classic)

Weill. *Three–Penny Opera* (adapted from *The Beggar's Opera,* a parody opera)

Wolf–Ferrari. *The Secret of Suzanne* (one–act comic intermezzo)

PART SIX

Other Major Approaches to Appreciation

In Chapter 1, various approaches to music appreciation were mentioned (see pages 6 ff.). Parts Two, Three, Four, and Five have dealt with major approaches to music, with the object of enhancing your understanding of the study. Four more significant aspects remain to be discussed in Part Six: musical style, music history, biography, and interpretation. Each of these areas of musical knowledge can make an essential contribution to your total appreciation; each provides a different approach to the literature of music which you need in order to attain a well–rounded musical perception.

27. Musical Style

An awareness of musical style is a sure sign of the intelligent and experienced listener. To hear a composition for the first time and, on the basis of stylistic perception, to orient the composition in terms of a historical period, a specific composer, or some other frame of reference, is to attain one of the most gratifying bases for musical enjoyment.

Musical style is the aspect of music which is manifested by the synthesis of all musical elements and properties. When someone says: "That music sounds like Bach," or "This music has the romantic quality of the nineteenth century," he is revealing an awareness of the particular qualities of the music itself—the characteristics of its melody, rhythm, harmony, and so forth; in short, he has a grasp of this composition's total effect.

METHOD

There is no simple formula, no short–cut for developing stylistic perception. It comes inevitably with listening experience. If you listen perceptively to a quantity of music in any category of music literature, you will acquire a familiarity with the style of that particular category. If, for example, you hear a number of Beethoven's compositions, you will be able to distinguish his music from that of other composers. In the same way, after hearing a good deal of music of the late eighteenth century, you can distinguish that music from the literature of any other period.

The best way to develop an immediate perception of style is to hear and compare two compositions of strikingly different character (see suggestions at the end of this chapter). Astute comparison then brings to light various respects in which the two pieces are different. Effort in this direction is rewarding. The more you develop your powers of perception, the better position you will be in to gain the most from musical experience.

PERIOD STYLES

The broadest approach to musical style is through the study of music according to periods. This approach is related to the historical approach, to be discussed in the next chapter. By listening to music of a given period, you soon acquire a familiarity with the sound of the music, i.e., its style. The following paragraphs point out some of the prominent and distinctive style characteristics of six broad periods of music literature.

Medieval Style. The music of the twelfth, thirteenth, and fourteenth centuries is polyphonic, but makes little use of contrapuntal imitation. The monophonic troubadour and trouvère songs are exceptions. The music of the twelfth and thirteenth centuries favors triple meters and repetition of rhythmic patterns. Fourteenth–century music favors duple meter and more flexible rhythms. Three–voice polyphony prevails. Although instruments are employed, vocal music predominates over instrumental. The harmony sounds unorganized to our ears; it is often harsh and thin. The modes are the tonal basis of the music; the effect is modal.

Renaissance Style. The music of the fifteenth and sixteenth centuries, by comparison, has a much more refined sound. It is polyphonic in texture. Larger numbers of voice parts are used, and imitation is more extensive. The harmony sounds fuller. Rhythms are more diversified. The music has a smooth "flow" and produces an effect of continuity, especially in the melodic lines. The style is essentially vocal. Modes are still the tonal basis of the music, but major and minor effects are not uncommon, particularly in secular vocal music and instrumental music.

Baroque Style. The Baroque period (1600–1750) ushered in a new concept of dramatic expression which characterizes much of the music. Baroque music is on a larger scale, is more spectacular, has greater contrasts, and has a grandeur beyond that of the music of previous eras. Harmony becomes much more organized. The modern concept of major and minor tonalities emerges. New emphasis is placed on homophony, but it does not replace polyphony. Instrumental music comes into its own and develops an independent style. The *basso continuo* (a bass part with numerals below the notes to indicate harmony, played by basses and a keyboard instrument) is one of the most characteristic sounds of the period. It gives added emphasis to the bass part, which serves both as a melody and as a harmonic bass.

Classical Style. The half century from 1750 to 1800 witnessed a change of emphasis from polyphonic to homophonic textures. Thematic organization, phraseology, and larger sectional structures are simple and clear. Harmony and melody are more diatonic. The music in general is more restrained, impersonal, and objective. Dynamics were for the first time extensively employed in the second half of the eighteenth century. Perhaps the words *elegance, grace,* and *refinement* best describe the general style of the Classical period.

Romantic Style. Nineteenth–century music is dominated by a wider range of emotional expression, more personal and individual styles, and more subjectivity. Musical forms, such as the sonata and symphony, become longer and more involved, but short piano pieces are also numerous. Harmony and orchestration become much richer, as do sonorities in general. Homophonic texture still prevails.

Twentieth–Century Styles. Music since 1900 has produced such a wide diversity of styles and techniques that generalizations become more difficult than ever before. Nevertheless, some broad characteristics may be noted. Compared with previous styles, harmony is more complex and more dissonant. More music is atonal (or tonally obscure) than tonal. Meters are more obscured; rhythms are more complex and diversified. Textures are more contrapuntal and sonorities thinner. Timbres are more colorful and varied as a result of new mediums and combinations. Especially notable are the innovations in electronic mediums. Formal concepts have changed radically, and structure is often obscured or abandoned altogether (e.g., in aleatory music). In general, the twentieth century has more affinity to classical than to romantic principles.

STYLES OF GEOGRAPHIC AREAS

Indigenous styles from cultures throughout the world constitute a significant aspect of musical style. Styles distinctive to countries, races, or regions cut across period styles. (See Chapter 23 for a discussion of ethnic, folk, and national music.)

STYLES OF INDIVIDUAL COMPOSERS

A composer's style is largely the product of the time and place in which he lives. Even within such broad stylistic areas, however, composers have distinctive individual traits. This is especially true of music since the beginning of the nineteenth century. For example, there is far greater difference between the styles of Stravinsky and Schoenberg than between those of Haydn and Mozart or Bach and Handel. It is beyond the scope of this Outline to catalog the stylistic features of even principal composers. However, for the sake of illustration we shall point out the approaches and make a few comparisons.

Influences. In addition to chronological and geographical factors, the composer's early training is inevitably an influence. A composer naturally absorbs much of the style of his first teachers. He is also influenced by early musical impressions: the first music he hears and the musical models he studies. Famous examples of teacher–pupil influences are Rimsky–Korsakov's influence on Stravinsky, Giovanni Gabrieli's influence on Heinrich Schütz, César Franck's influence on Ernest Chausson, and Schoenberg's influence on Alban Berg and Anton Webern.

A composer's style may be influenced by numerous other factors, such as the type of music he writes (e.g., Handel wrote operas and oratorios; Bach wrote cantatas and other church music), the kind of posts he holds (e.g., choirmaster, conductor, organist), the way he responds to musical trends and to outstanding musical personalities of his time.

Distinctive Traits. In addition to characteristics caused by national, chronological, and other influences, a composer develops further individual traits of style, some more distinctive than others.

The distinctive style of a composer is manifested in the characteristic prominence he gives to certain elements (melody, rhythm, meter, harmony, texture, orchestration) and to his treatment of them. The prevailing contrapuntal textures in Hindemith's music; Stravinsky's strong irregular rhythms, complex metric schemes, and brilliant orchestration; Debussy's use of the whole–tone scale, modality, and harmonic parallelism; Wagner's chromaticism and continuous phraseology; Schoenberg's atonality, strong dissonance, and disjunct linear style—all these are examples of distinctive styles.

STYLES OF MEDIUMS, FORMS, AND OTHER CATEGORIES

Virtually every category of music has characteristic qualities of style which cut across such areas as historical period, geographical region, nationality, and individual composer traits.

Medium. Every musical medium has its own *idiom;* i.e., certain style characteristics which are determined by its special properties, capacities, and limitations.

In mediums, the broadest distinction of style is between instrumental and vocal music. Although stylistic differences between the two mediums are not always clearly defined, instrumental mediums are generally more disjunct melodically, have a wider melodic range, and may be more daring in harmony and rhythm. Vocal music is apt to be more restrained and technically less brilliant.

Solo mediums (both instrumental and vocal) tend to display greater flexibility in regard to ornamentation and improvisatory style than large ensembles.

The physical properties of instruments affect the style of music written for instrumental mediums. The style of harpsichord music is determined in part by its clearly defined tone and lack of sustaining power. The piano has greater sustaining power, more sonority, and more percussive qualities; the organ has even greater sustaining power and sonority and it cannot "collect" tones as the piano does with the damper pedal. Thus, all these physical properties have a definite effect upon the style of music written for the respective instruments.

Individual string instruments (violin, viola, cello) are harmonically limited, but they have greater variety and flexibility in the production of melody. Wind instruments are limited by human lung capacity (as is the human voice), but each wind instrument has its own capabilities and limits of manipulation. For example, the flute can play rapid scale passages and figuration; the trombone cannot.

Form. Certain musical forms are more characterized by their style than by their structural plans. The fugue and canon, for example, are based on a texture rather than on a sectional structure. The toccata and étude are characterized by virtuosity. The concerto usually displays more brilliance and virtuosity of style than the symphony or symphonic poem. An aria is more lyric than a recitative; the latter is more declamatory. An opera is more highly dramatic than a cantata or an oratorio.

Religious and Secular Music. The serious purpose of religious music in general and liturgical music in particular (see Chapter 24) makes it more restrained than secular music. There are, of course, many exceptions to this generalization.

Functional Music. The style of music written for a particular function is partly determined by that function. Funeral music is more sober than wedding music; dance music is more exuberant than processional music; and work songs correspond in mood and style to the nature of the task.

Virtuosity. A performer (singer or instrumentalist) who has exceptional technical ability and who is prone to display that skill is known as a *virtuoso musician*. Music which is composed primarily to display or exploit the technical dexterity of the performer is *virtuoso music*. Virtuosity in a performer and in a composition is not infrequently carried to such an extreme that artistic value and musical content are sacrificed for the sake of brilliant technical feats. Unfortunately, virtuosity is overemphasized by commercial concert managements, because uncritical audiences are impressed and entertained more by showmanship than by the aesthetic merits of a program.

Virtuoso composers and performers have nevertheless contributed to musical art insofar as they have advanced the technical resources of a particular medium. Mastery of technical difficulties in one period has often enabled a later composer to widen his horizons of expression.

Ethos and Pathos. These terms describe two opposite qualities of style which are applicable to all categories of music literature. The quality of *ethos* (objective style) is found in music in which considerations of form and technical construction predominate. The quality of *pathos* (subjective style) is found in music in which emotional content is more prominent than structural design. Ethos and pathos (objectivity and subjectivity) are best understood through the comparison of extremes, but all degrees of style ranging from extremely objective to extremely subjective are to be found in music literature, and the terms are always relative.

Ethos and pathos apply to certain periods in music history: the nineteenth century is an era of pathos, eighteenth–century classicism is predominantly an era of ethos, and so, too, is the twentieth century to a considerable extent.

Certain forms are more objective than others. For instance, the fugue and the canon are usually more objective than the rhapsody and the toccata. The secular madrigal is usually more subjective than the sacred motet.

Recommended Listening

The compositions listed here have been selected to illustrate the various aspects of style discussed in this chapter. This approach to music literature, through perception of styles, is perhaps the most challenging you have yet encountered. Whatever music you select for listening, seek the factors which in one way or another make the particular style distinctive. Keep in mind that this is only a beginning; familiarity with musical style in any category is based on extensive and perceptive experience.

Period Styles

Note: Two valuable anthologies of recorded music and scores (see Bibliography, page 221 f.) include representative music of the Middle Ages, Renaissance, and Baroque periods: *Masterpieces of Music before 1750* and *Treasury of Early Music*. Examples from the former anthology are listed here and indicated by the abbreviation MM.

Medieval:

Conductus: *De castitatis thalamo* (thirteenth century). MM, No. 11
Estampie (dance). MM, No. 12
Landino. Ballata: *Chi più le vuol sapere* (fourteenth century). MM, No. 14
Machaut. *Agnus Dei* from the *Notre Dame Mass* (fourteenth century). MM, No. 13
Motet: *En non Diu!* (thirteenth century). MM, No. 10
Perotin. *Alleluya* (organum, thirteenth century). MM, No. 9

Renaissance:

Bennet. Madrigal: *Thyrsis, Sleepest Thou* (sixteenth century). MM, No. 28
Byrd. *Ergo Sum Panis Vivus* (motet, sixteenth century). MM, No. 25
Dufay. "Kyrie" from the Mass, *Se la Face ay Pale* (fifteenth century). MM, No. 15
Josquin Des Prez. *Ave Maria* (motet, early sixteenth century). MM, No. 19
Lasso. *Tristis Est Anima Mea* (motet, sixteenth century). MM, No. 23
Marenzio. *S'io parto, i' moro* (madrigal, sixteenth century). MM, No. 27
Morley. *Now Is the Month of Maying* (madrigal, sixteenth century)
Obrecht. *Parce, Domine* (motet, fifteenth century). MM, No. 18
Okeghem. "Sanctus" from *Missa Prolationum* (fifteenth century). MM, No. 17
*Palestrina. "Kyrie" from *Missa Brevis* (sixteenth century)
———. "Agnus Dei" from *Missa Veni Sponsa Christi*. MM, No. 24
Victoria. *O Magnum Mysterium, O Quam Gloriosum* (motets, sixteenth century)

Baroque:

Bach. *Brandenburg Concerto No. 5 in D Major* (concerto grosso)

*————. *Cantata No. 140; Wachet auf, ruft uns die Stimme*

————. *Mass in B Minor*

————. *Partita No. 5 in G Major* (piano or harpsichord)

*————. *Passacaglia and Fugue in C Minor* (organ)

————. *Toccata and Fugue in D Minor* (organ)

Corelli. *Concerto Grosso No. 8 in G Minor* ("Christmas")

Frescobaldi. *Ricercar dopo il Credo* (organ; seventeenth century). MM, No. 34

Froberger. *Suite in E Minor* (harpsichord, seventeenth century). MM, No. 35

*Handel. *Messiah* (oratorio)

————. *Rinaldo:* recitative and aria. MM, No. 44

————. *Sonata No. 4 in D Major for Violin and Harpsichord*

————. *Trio Sonata in B Flat Major* (flute, oboe, continuo)

————. *Water Music* (suite for orchestra)

Lully. *Overture to Armide* (opera, seventeenth century). MM, No. 36

Monteverdi. Recitative: "Tu se' morta" from *Orfeo* (opera, seventeenth century). MM, No. 31

Pergolesi. *Stabat Mater* (seventeenth century)

Scarlatti, D. *Sonata in C Minor* (harpsichord). MM, No. 42

————. *Sonata in D Major* (harpsichord)

Classical:

Beethoven. *Quartet No. 2 in G Major* (strings)

Gluck. *Orfeo ed Euridice* (opera)

*Haydn. *Quartet in E Flat Major* (strings), Op. 33, No. 2

————. *Quartet in C Major* (strings), Op. 76, No. 3 ("Emperor")

————. *Symphony No. 94 in G Major* ("Surprise")

————. *Symphony No. 101 in D Major* ("Clock")

Mozart. *Concerto in E Flat Major for Piano and Orchestra,* K. 271

*————. *Don Giovanni* (opera)

————. *Eine Kleine Nachtmusik (Serenade,* for small orchestra), K. 525

————. *The Marriage of Figaro* (opera)

————. *Quartet No. 14 in G Major,* K. 387 (strings)

————. *Quintet in A Major for Clarinet and String Quartet,* K. 581

————. *Sonata in A Major,* K. 331 (piano)

*————. *Symphony No. 40 in G Minor,* K. 550

Romantic:

Beethoven. *Sonata No. 23 in F Minor* (piano; "Appassionata")

Berlioz. *Symphonie Fantastique (Fantastic Symphony)*

Brahms. *Dein blaues Auge (Thy Blue Eyes)*

*————. *Symphony No. 3 in F Major*

Chopin. *Nocturne in E Flat Major,* Op. 9, No. 2

*————. *Sonata No. 2 in B Flat Minor,* Op. 35

Fauré. *Après un Rêve (After a Dream;* song)

Franck. *Symphony in D Minor*

Liszt. *Étude de Concert No. 3 in D Flat Major* ("Un sospiro"; for piano)

————. *Les Préludes* (symphonic poem)

Mahler. *Symphony No. 2 in C Minor*

*Mendelssohn. *Concerto in E Minor for Violin and Orchestra*

————. *A Midsummer Night's Dream* (orchestra)

Mussorgski. *Night on Bald Mountain* (symphonic poem)

Offenbach. *Tales of Hoffmann* (opera): "Belle Nuit" (barcarolle)

*Puccini. *La Bohème* (opera)

Rachmaninoff. *Concerto No. 2 in C Minor for Piano and Orchestra*
———. *Isle of the Dead* (symphonic poem)
Rimsky–Korsakov. *Scheherazade* (suite for orchestra)
Saint–Saëns. *Danse Macabre* (symphonic poem)
Schumann. *Dichterliebe* (song cycle): No. 7, "Ich grolle nicht" ("I shall not complain")
*———. *Fantasiestücke* (*Fantasy Pieces;* piano)
Sibelius. *The Swan of Tuonela* (symphonic poem)
Tchaikovsky. *Concerto No. 1 in B Flat Minor for Piano and Orchestra*
———. *None but the Lonely Heart* (song)
———. *Nutcracker Suite* (orchestra)
———. *Romeo and Juliet* (orchestral fantasy)
———. *Symphony No. 6 in B Minor* ("Pathétique")
Verdi. *Requiem*
———. *La Traviata* (opera)
Wagner. *A Siegfried Idyll* (tone poem)
*———. *Tristan and Isolde* (opera)
Weber. *Oberon Overture*
Wolf. *Anakreons Grab* (*Anacreon's Grave;* song)

Twentieth Century:
Bartók. *Concerto No. 3 for Piano and Orchestra*
———. *Music for Strings, Percussion, and Celeste*
*———. *Quartet No. 5* (strings)
Berg. *Concerto for Violin and Orchestra* ("To the Memory of an Angel")
Bernstein. *Fancy Free* (ballet suite for orchestra)
Bloch. *Schelomo* (cello and orchestra)
Casella. *Five Pieces for String Quartet*
Chávez. *Sinfonia India*
*Copland. *Music for the Theatre* (orchestral suite, jazz style)
Cowell. *Toccata for Flute, Soprano, Cello, and Piano*
Debussy. *La Mer* (impressionistic symphonic poem)
*———. *Prélude à l'Après-midi d'un Faune* (*Prelude to the Afternoon of a Faun;* symphonic poem)
Gershwin. *Rhapsody in Blue* (piano and orchestra)
Hába. *Duo for Two Violins* (quarter-tone music; in *Columbia History of Music,* Vol. 5)
Harris. *Symphony No. 3* (in one movement)
Hindemith. *Das Marienleben* (*Life of the Virgin Mary;* song cycle)
———. *Mathis der Maler* (descriptive symphony in three movements)
———. *Quartet No. 4* (strings)
———. *Sonata for Two Flutes* (canonic)
*———. *Sonata No. 3 for Piano*
Honegger. *King David* (oratorio)
———. *Pacific 231* (tone poem for orchestra)
Ives. *Sixty-Seventh Psalm* (8-part chorus)
Kabalevsky. *Preludes* (24, for piano)
Křenek. *Pieces for Piano*
Martin. *Concerto for Harpsichord and Small Orchestra*
Martinu. *Sonata for Flute and Piano*
Menotti. *The Medium* (opera)
———. *The Telephone* (comic intermezzo)
Milhaud. *The Household Muse* (piano pieces)
———. *Sonatina for Clarinet and Piano*

Milhaud. *Suite Provençale* (orchestra)
Mossolov. *Iron Foundry* (tone poem for percussion)
Piston. *Suite from the Incredible Flutist* (ballet)
Prokofiev. *Concerto No. 2 in G Minor for Violin and Orchestra*
————. *Concerto No. 3 in C Major for Piano and Orchestra*
————. *Toccata in D Minor* (piano)
*Ravel. *Boléro* (orchestra)
————. *Concerto in G Major for Piano and Orchestra*
————. *Daphnis et Chloé Suite No. 2* (orchestra)
————. *Jeux d'Eau* (*Fountains;* for piano)
————. *La Valse* (orchestra)
Riegger. *New Dance* (orchestra)
Roussel. *Quartet in D Major* (strings)
Satie. *Three Pieces in the Form of a Pear* (piano)
Schoenberg. *Drei Klavierstücke* (*Three Piano Pieces*), Op. 11
————. *Pierrot Lunaire* (voice and chamber ensemble)
————. *Quartet No. 4* (strings; atonal)
Schuman. *Judith* (choreographic poem, orchestra)
Shostakovitch. *Preludes* (24, for piano)
————. *Symphony No. 5*
Stravinsky. *Capriccio for Piano and Orchestra*
————. *Card Game* (ballet suite)
————. *Dumbarton Oaks Concerto* (for 16 instruments)
————. *L'Histoire du Soldat* (*The Soldier's Tale;* ballet with chamber ensemble and narrator)
————. *Octet for Wind Instruments*
————. *Petrouchka* (ballet)
————. *Le Sacre du Printemps* (*The Rite of Spring,* a ballet)
————. *Symphony in Three Movements*
Thomson, V. *Filling Station* (ballet suite)
————. *Four Saints in Three Acts*
————. *Suite from the Plow that Broke the Plains*
Varèse. *Ionization* (percussion ensemble)
Vaughan Williams. *On Wenlock Edge* (song cycle for tenor, piano, and string quartet)
————. *Symphony No. 2* ("London")
Villa–Lobos. *Bachianas Brasileiras No. 5* (8 cellos and soprano)
Webern. *Concerto for Nine Instruments*

National Styles

American:
Bennett. *Suite of Old American Dances* (band)
Copland. *Billy the Kid* (ballet)
————. *Music for the Theatre* (orchestral suite, jazz style)
Gershwin. *Porgy and Bess* (folk opera)
————. *Rhapsody in Blue* (piano and orchestra)
Grofé. *Grand Canyon Suite* (orchestra)
Ives. *Sonata No. 2 for Piano* ("Concord, Mass.")
Piston. *Quintet for Piano and Strings*
Thomson, V. *Filling Station* (ballet)
————. *Louisiana Story* (film music)
Weill. *Down in the Valley* (folk opera)

Bohemian:
Dvořák. *Slavonic Dances* (8 pieces for orchestra)
Smetana. *The Moldau* (from the symphonie cycle, *My Fatherland*)

Brazilian:
Villa–Lobos. *Bachianas Brasileiras No. 5* (8 cellos and soprano)

English:
Vaughan Williams. *Symphony No. 2* ("London")

Finnish:
Sibelius. *Finlandia* (tone poem for orchestra)
————. *The Swan of Tuonela* (tone poem for orchestra)

French:
*Debussy. *Prélude à l'Après-midi d'un Faune* (*Prelude to the Afternoon of a Faun;* symphonic poem)
Milhaud. *Suite Française* (orchestra)

Hungarian:
Bartók. *Rondos and Folk Dances* (piano)

Jewish:
Bloch. *Schelomo* (cello and orchestra)
Bruch. *Kol Nidrei* (cello and orchestra)

Mexican:
Chávez. *Sinfonia India*

Norwegian:
Grieg. *Norwegian Dances* (orchestra)
————. *Peer Gynt Suite No. 1* (orchestra)

Polish:
Chopin. *Mazurka in A Flat Major,* Op. 59, No. 2 (piano)
————. *Polonaise No. 6 in A Flat Major,* Op. 53 (piano)

Rumanian:
Enesco. *Rumanian Rhapsody in A Major* (orchestra)

Russian:
Borodin. *Prince Igor* (opera)
Mussorgski. *Boris Godounov* (opera)
————. *Night on Bald Mountain* (symphonic poem)
Rimsky–Korsakov. *Russian Easter Overture*
Tchaikovsky. *Quartet No. 1 in D Major* (strings): II ("Andante Cantabile")

Spanish:
Albéniz. *Spanish Dances* (for orchestra)
————. *Tango in D Major* (piano)
Falla. *Nights in the Gardens of Spain* (symphonic suite for piano and orchestra)
Granados. *Spanish Dances* (orchestra)

Individual Styles

Note: Each of the following compositions is in some prominent way typical of the composer, although not necessarily a total picture of his style. One example is, of course, not enough music on which to gain familiarity with any composer's style, but you can accomplish this objective by repeated hearings of several pieces of the same composer. Keep in mind that familiarity with any style is a process of gradual growth.

Beethoven. *Sonata No. 8 in C Minor* ("Pathétique"; piano): I
(Forceful, dynamic quality, subjectivity, sudden changes of dynamic level)

*Brahms. *Symphony No. 3 in F Major:* I
(Rich, full orchestral sonority, wide melodic range of first theme, rhythmic changes)

Chopin. *Nocturne in E Flat Major,* Op. 9, No. 2 (piano)
(Lyric, cantabile style of melody, melismatic ornamentation, homophonic texture, romantic harmony, piano sonority)

*Debussy. *Prélude à l'Après-midi d'un Faune* (*Prelude to the Afternoon of a Faun;* symphonic poem)
(Orchestral color, flowing melody, rich harmony of the 9th chords, free rhythm and structure)

*Hindemith. *Sonata No. 3 for Piano:* IV
(Modern counterpoint, dissonance, obscured tonality)

Mozart. *Quartet No. 14 in G Major* (strings), K. 387: II (*Menuetto*)
(Clarity of form and phrasing, chromatic melody, delicacy of style)

Schoenberg. *Quartet No. 4* (strings)
(Atonality, dissonance, disjunct and angular melody, linear texture)

Stravinsky. *Le Sacre du Printemps* (*The Rite of Spring,* a ballet)
(Dynamic and complex rhythm, dissonance, color orchestration)

Tchaikovsky. *Symphony No. 5 in E Minor*
(Romantic subjectivity, rich harmony, orchestration, *cantabile* melody, somber mood)

*Wagner. *Tristan and Isolde* (opera): *Prelude to Act I*
(Harmonic and melodic chromaticism, continuous phraseology, rich orchestration)

Virtuosity

Balakirev. *Islamey* (piano)

Beethoven. *Sonata No. 23 in F Minor* (piano; "Appassionata")

Byrd. *The Carman's Whistle* (harpsichord variations)

Chopin. *Étude in C Major,* Op. 10, No. 1 (piano)

————. *Polonaise No. 6 in A Flat Major,* Op. 53 (piano)

*————. *Sonata No. 2 in B Flat Minor,* Op. 35 (piano): III

Delibes. *Lakmé* (opera): "Bell Song"

Franck. *Pièce Héroïque* (organ)

Hindemith. *Sonata for Trumpet and Piano*

*————. *Sonata No. 3 for Piano:* II, IV

Liszt. *La Campanella* (piano)

————. *Concerto No. 1 in E Flat Major for Piano and Orchestra*

————. *Étude de Concert No. 3 in D Flat Major* ("Un Sospiro," for piano)

————. *Hungarian Rhapsody No. 2 in C Sharp Minor* (piano)

Mendelssohn. *Capriccio Brillant* (piano)

Paganini. *Caprice No. 24* (violin solo)

Prokofiev. *Toccata in D Minor* (piano)

Rachmaninoff. *Rhapsody on a Theme of Paganini* (piano and orchestra)

Rossini. *La Danza* (*Tarantella Napolitana*)

Scarlatti, D. *Sonata in D Major* (harpsichord)

Schumann. *Symphonic Études* (piano)

————. *Toccata in C Major,* Op. 7 (piano)

Sibelius. *Concerto in D Minor for Violin and Orchestra: Finale*

Stravinsky. *Capriccio for Piano and Orchestra*

Tartini. *Sonata in G Minor* ("Devil's Trill"; violin and piano)

Widor. *Variations* from *Symphonie Gothique* (organ)

Ethos and Pathos

Note: Comparison of the pairs of compositions listed below will illustrate the difference between ethos and pathos, objectivity and subjectivity. The first composition in each pair illustrates ethos, objectivity; the second composition illustrates pathos, subjectivity.

Mozart. *Sonata in A Major,* K. 331 (piano)
Beethoven. *Sonata No. 23 in F Minor* ("Appassionata," piano)

Haydn. *Symphony No. 94 in G Major* ("Surprise")
Tchaikovsky. *Symphony No. 6 in B Minor* ("Pathétique")

Schubert. *Heidenröslein* (*Hedge Rose,* a song)
Schubert. *Der Erlkönig* (*The Erlking,* a song)

Bach. *Toccata and Fugue in D Minor* (organ). The fugue is more objective than the toccata.

Hindemith. *Sonata for Two Flutes* (canonic)
Hindemith. *Trauermusik* (*Funeral Music,* for viola and orchestra)

Rossini. *The Barber of Seville* (opera): *Overture*
*Wagner. *Tristan and Isolde* (opera): *Prelude to Act I*

Couperin. *La Galante* (harpsichord)
*Chopin. *Sonata No. 2 in B Flat Minor* (piano), Op. 35: III ("Funeral March")

Mozart. *Eine Kleine Nachtmusik* (*Serenade,* for small orchestra)
*Brahms. *Symphony No. 3 in F Major*

Beethoven. *Symphony No. 1 in C Major*
*Beethoven. *Symphony No. 5 in C Minor*

Stravinsky. *Octet for Wind Instruments*
Stravinsky. *Apollon Musagète* (ballet, string orchestra)

28. Music History

The value of studying music literature in terms of historical epochs, forms, trends, composers, and styles, can hardly be over-emphasized.* It is not our purpose here to outline the history of music but merely to indicate some of the ways in which the study of history may enhance appreciation.

GENERAL HISTORICAL BACKGROUND

Music history and music literature have more significance if viewed in the light of general history. Nonmusical events have frequently influenced musical development.

Other Arts. The art of music parallels other arts. Often the basic style trends in music can be seen existing side by side with the same trends in painting, sculpture, and architecture. Thus, the important developments in music in Paris and Chartres during the late Middle Ages were coexistent with the building of the great Gothic cathedrals in Europe. In the sixteenth century, while Andrea and Giovanni Gabrieli were composing impressive polychoral music in Venice, the school of Venetian painters (Titian, Veronese, etc.) was flourishing. Venetian art and music both reflect a spirit of richness and magnificence. The compositions of Debussy in the late nineteenth century were directly related to the ideas of Impressionist painters (Pissarro, Manet, Monet, Renoir, etc.) and poets (Mallarmé, Verlaine, and Baudelaire). In the twentieth century, the development of expression-

* See the author's *History of Music* in the Barnes & Noble Outline Series, 4th ed., 1972.

ism and of nonobjective painting seems to parallel the music of such composers as Stravinsky and Schoenberg.

Literature, Poetry, and Drama. Literature, poetry, and drama have a close kinship with music, and parallel developments are often to be seen. Elizabethan verse and the plays of Shakespeare are closely related to the English madrigals of the same period. The efforts of Florentine noblemen at the end of the sixteenth century to revive Greek drama led directly to the inception of opera. The works of French poets of the Pléiade (Ronsard and others) during the Renaissance were favorite sources in the setting of texts for polyphonic chansons. The literature of Dante, Boccaccio, and Chaucer was written at the same time as the music of the fourteenth–century composers De Vitry, Landino, and Machaut. The German poets of the late eighteenth and nineteenth centuries (Goethe, Heine, and Schiller) provided the superb romantic verse for the development of the nineteenth–century songs of Schubert, Schumann, Brahms, Wolf, and others. The French drama at the Court of Louis XIV in Versailles in the seventeenth century paralleled the excellence of French opera in the hands of Lully (court musician) and Quinault (librettist). An even more direct relationship between literature and music is discernible in the history of opera and its librettists: Rinuccini and Peri, Caccini and Monteverdi; Metastasio (in the eighteenth century), the librettist for Alessandro Scarlatti, Handel, and Mozart; Calzabigi for Gluck; da Ponte for Mozart; Boito for Verdi; and Gilbert for Sullivan. These are only a few of the celebrated collaborations between writers and composers. Also, literary works have often been the inspiration for program music: Liszt's *Les Préludes,* to which he appended a quotation from Lamartine; Debussy's *Prélude à l'Après-midi d'un Faune,* based on a poem by Mallarmé; and Richard Strauss's *Don Quixote* from the sixteenth–century work by Cervantes.

Church History. That the art of music in its early history was kept alive largely through the auspices of the Church is a significant fact. Religious history continued to have an important influence on music throughout the Baroque period. During the Renaissance the Church was responsible for the extensive polyphonic literature which was created (e.g., by Palestrina, Victoria, Byrd, and Lasso). The Reformation, too, had a tremendous impact on the course of music. It brought about the development of the chorale, organ literature, and church cantatas. The Calvinist and Huguenot movements had a marked influence on French religious music.

Economic and Political History. Cultural developments are always influenced by social and economic conditions and important political events. The feudal system engendered the troubadour movement in the Middle Ages. The nobility and the burgher and merchant classes in the Renaissance supplied patronage for the arts and provided the livelihood for such masters as Isaak, Des Prez, Okeghem, and Dufay. Wars often retarded musical development: the Hundred Years' War in the fourteenth and fifteenth centuries, the Thirty Years' War (1618–1648), and the Seven Years' War (1756–1763).

MAIN AREAS OF MUSIC HISTORY

A review of the following subjects, which are included in any study of the history of music, should contribute to a better insight into music literature.

Forms. The history of music is in part a history of musical forms. Most musical forms are typical of a period; some of them are distinctive to a period. We think of the motet and madrigal as belonging primarily to the Renaissance, although the terms appeared before and after that era. Dramatic forms (opera, oratorio, cantata) were unknown before the seventeenth century. The sonata had its inception in the seventeenth century, but it changed considerably in subsequent periods. Dance forms (see Chapter 20) are especially representative of their respective periods. The symphony was the product of the Classical period; the symphonic poem was the product of the nineteenth century. Ballet music (a type rather than a form) has a long history, but as an independent creation it belongs to the late nineteenth and twentieth centuries. All forms can be studied in terms of their historical background and developments.

Styles. The preceding chapter summarized period styles. Each period has its distinctive style characteristics. The study of music literature, as previously indicated, is perhaps best understood through a familiarity with the prevailing characteristics of style in each major epoch.

Composers. The study of music history involves knowledge about the principal composers in each period and the special contributions which each made to the literature of music. For our purposes we shall list only a few of the most outstanding names in each century. You are undoubtedly already familiar with many of these names.

Twelfth and thirteenth centuries (Middle Ages): Leoninus, Perotinus

Fourteenth century (late Middle Ages): Machaut, Landino

Fifteenth century (early Renaissance): Dunstable, Dufay, Okeghem, Obrecht, Des Prez

Sixteenth century (late Renaissance): Palestrina, Lasso, Victoria, Byrd

Seventeenth century (early and middle Baroque): Monteverdi, Schütz, Purcell, Lully

Eighteenth century (to 1750, late Baroque): Bach, Handel, Domenico Scarlatti, Rameau

Eighteenth century (from 1750, Classical): Haydn, Mozart, Gluck

Nineteenth century (Romantic):

German: Beethoven, Schubert, Schumann, Wagner, Mendelssohn, Brahms

French: Berlioz, Chopin (Polish), Fauré, Franck, Bizet, Gounod, Saint–Saëns, Debussy

Italian: Rossini, Donizetti, Bellini, Verdi, Puccini (d. 1924)

Russian: Glinka, Mussorgski, Rimsky–Korsakov, Tchaikovsky, Borodin

Spanish: Albéniz, Granados

Hungarian: Liszt

Bohemian: Smetana, Dvořák

Norwegian: Grieg

Finnish: Sibelius

English: Elgar

United States: MacDowell

Twentieth century (Modern):

Bartók, Hindemith, Prokofiev, Schoenberg, Shostakovitch, and Stravinsky. In the United States: Copland, Piston, Harris, Menotti, Ives, Thomson, Cowell, Schuman, Bernstein, Hanson, Barber

Trends and Developments. Certain aspects of music history do not pertain to forms, styles, or composers. Important factors in music history include the development of musical notation from ancient Greece to the seventeenth century, when our present system was established. The beginning of music printing in the early sixteenth century had a far–reaching effect upon musical art. The changes in musical mediums, especially the innovations and mechanical improvements in instruments, affected musical developments in all periods. In any given period, the contemporary literature about music reveals much concerning the musical thinking of the time. Music employed as a means of dramatic expression in the seventeenth century began an important trend in music history. Finally, broad movements such as humanism, classicism, romanticism, impressionism, neoclassicism, and expressionism are clearly reflected in the literature of music.

Recommended Listening

See lists for period styles, pages 201–204.

29. Biography

The life story of an important person almost always makes fascinating reading, and biographies of the great composers contribute much to the appreciation of music literature.

Biographical Factors. Biographical information which may illuminate a composer's creative work includes geographical influences, professional activities, circumstances of musical creation, and other personal factors such as economic status and health.

GEOGRAPHICAL INFLUENCES. Appreciation is enhanced by geographical information about the composer—where he was born, where he received his musical training and experience, and in what countries he traveled. An interesting comparison in this respect between the lives of Bach (1685–1750) and Handel (1685–1759) illustrates this point. Bach spent his entire life within the radius of about thirty miles; Handel traveled widely and lived in Germany, Italy, and England. The fact that the English composer, Frederick Delius, studied in Germany, lived in Florida and France, and traveled in Norway gives some insight into the style of his music. Rimsky–Korsakov's Russian heritage, his extensive travels in the navy, and his obvious fondness for Oriental exoticism, are geographical influences on his style.

PROFESSIONAL ACTIVITIES. What composers have done for a living is pertinent biographical information. Few composers have earned their livelihood solely from composition. Liszt was a concert pianist; Mozart was a concert master, pianist, and organist; Robert Schumann was a music critic and essayist, in addition to his other music occupations; Mendelssohn was a conductor as well as a pianist and an organist; Bach was an organist, a court composer, and a director of church music; Haydn spent a large part of his life in the service of the Esterhazy princes as music director. Many famous composers have been teachers. Beethoven was the first great master whose income was derived more often from commissions and the proceeds of his published compositions than from service to the nobility.

CIRCUMSTANCES OF MUSICAL CREATION. The circumstances under which a composer wrote a particular masterpiece constitute enlightening biographical information. The circumstances may be directly related to the music itself, as in the case of a commissioned work. Thus, Hindemith's *Trauermusik (Funeral Music)* was composed for broadcasting at the time of the death of King George V of England. Menotti's *Amahl and the Night Visitors* was written for television performance (the first television opera). *Euridice,* by Rinuccini and Peri, was composed for the wedding of Maria de' Medici and Henry IV of France. Ravel's *Piano Concerto for Left Hand Alone* was written for his friend Paul Wittgenstein, a one–armed pianist. Bach's *Musical Offering* was composed as a gift to Frederick II of Prussia, and his *Goldberg Variations* was commissioned by a Russian, Count Kayserling. Mozart's *Requiem Mass,* anonymously commissioned, was his last work, incomplete at the time of his death. Verdi's *Aida,* set in Egypt, was composed in celebration of the opening of the Suez Canal. His last opera, *Falstaff,* is a masterpiece composed at the age of eighty. Biographical facts such as these give added interest to the compositions themselves.

OTHER BIOGRAPHICAL FACTORS. The kinds of biographical information are too numerous to classify. The vicissitudes of a composer's life include such facts as his economic status (whether he was well–to–do, like Mendelssohn, or poor, like Schubert); illness and infirmities (e.g., Schumann's injury to his hand which turned him from a career as pianist to that of composer and critic, Bach's and Handel's blindness in their late years, Beethoven's deafness, and Lully's death from an infection caused by inadvertently striking his foot with a heavy cane which he used as a baton); love affairs, marriage, family, and circle of friends and associates.

Musical Factors. A biographical work on an important composer generally assesses his musical contributions and discusses the characteristics of his style as well as giving a biographical account of his life. Often these factors are integrated to show cause and effect; i.e., biographical circumstances are shown to affect the composer's music.

30. Interpretation

Our final approach to the appreciation of music literature consists of the comparative study of interpretation. Here we are dealing with the art of the performer. The performing artist is the second among the three main agents of musical art mentioned in Chapter 1; i.e., between the composer and the listener.

LATITUDE OF EXPRESSION

A music score indicates the four properties of tone (pitch, duration, intensity, and quality) which are employed by the composer to form a musical composition. But the score does not indicate these properties precisely. Much is left to the discretion of the performer. This is the realm of expression or interpretation.

VARIABLE FACTORS IN INTERPRETATION

The performing artist has no right to alter the notes of the printed page. But he has three important prerogatives in his interpretation of the score. These relate to tempo, dynamics, and phrasing.

Tempo. The rhythm and meter of a composition are indicated in the score, but the tempo is usually indicated only in a general way, especially in the matter of *ritardando* and *accelerando*. Two artists will perform a given composition in different tempos. One will play the composition generally faster than the other, and the nuances of *ritardando* and *accelerando* are likely to be quite different. One performance is not necessarily better than the other.

Dynamics. Even less exact than tempo is the matter of dynamics (see Chapter 7). Dynamic markings in the score (sometimes called "expression marks") are only relative. How loud is *forte,* how soft is *piano,* how strong is an accent, how quickly does loudness increase in a *crescendo*—all these questions are individually answered by the artistic judgment of the performer. And no two performers completely agree.

Phrasing. The phrase is indicated in performance by a slight shortening of the last note and the interpolation of an almost imperceptible rest. Phrasing is indicated in the score by means of curved lines above or below the group of notes included in the phrase. Here again, much latitude is allowed the performer, and artists differ in their phrasing techniques.

There are also subtle differences in the playing of *staccato* (short and separated notes of a melody) and *legato* (connected notes).

MUSIC CRITICISM

It is the job of the professional music critic who writes reviews of concerts to make an assessment of the artistic value of a performance in terms of two main factors: (1) the music of the program, especially when a new composition is performed, and (2) the manner in which it was performed, i.e., the technique and interpretation of the artist. In either case you should not rely upon the opinions of a single critic as the sole basis of your own judgment. In reading the reviews of several critics you will quickly observe that their judgments are rarely uniform, and consequently that there is no absolute right or wrong, no fixed standard of good or bad, in musical interpretation. You should retain an open mind and avoid dogmatic judgments. You should cultivate your own perceptive listening powers with the object of being able to detect differences of interpretation.

COMPARATIVE STUDY

Observing different interpretations of the same composition by different artists can be a highly interesting experience. By means of phonograph recordings you can hear one composition (or corresponding passage) right after the other, thus making an immediate comparison. In orchestral music you can compare interpretations of the same composition by different conductors leading the same orchestra, or by the same conductor leading different orchestras. There are also recordings of the same concerto by the same and by different soloists, conductors, and orchestras. Such comparisons clearly demonstrate the fact that the world's great performers and conductors differ considerably in such matters as tempo, dynamics, and phrasing, and that there is no absolute standard of aesthetic quality in interpretation.

Recommended Listening

There are multiple recordings of these masterpieces by different performing artists. Record catalogs or record jackets will supply the information you need regarding the performing artists, conductors, and ensembles. Any two recordings of one of these compositions will serve as a basis for the study of interpretation.

Compositions recorded by different artists:

Bach. *Brandenberg Concerto No. 5 in D Major* (concerto grosso)
*———. *Cantata No. 140; Wachet auf, ruft uns die Stimme*
*———. *Passacaglia and Fugue in C Minor* (organ)
*———. *Suite No. 3 in D Major for Orchestra*
———. *Toccata and Fugue in D Minor* (organ)
Beethoven. *Concerto No. 5 in E Flat Major for Piano and Orchestra* ("Emperor")
———. *Quartet No. 2 in G Major* (strings)
———. *Sonata No. 23 in F Minor* (piano; "Appassionata")
*———. *Symphony No. 5 in C Minor*
*Bizet. *Carmen* (opera)
*Brahms. *Symphony No. 3 in F Major*
*Chopin. *Sonata No. 2 in B Flat Minor,* Op. 35 (piano)
Copland. *El Salón México* (orchestra)
*Debussy. *Prélude à l'Après-midi d'un Faune* (*Prelude to the Afternoon of a Faun;* symphonic poem)
Franck. *Symphony in D Minor*
Gershwin. *Rhapsody in Blue* (piano and orchestra)
*Handel. *Messiah* (oratorio)
Lalo. *Symphonie Espagnole* (violin and orchestra)
*Mendelssohn. *Concerto in E Minor for Violin and Orchestra*
Mozart. *Cosi fan' tutte,* K. 588 (opera)
———. *Eine Kleine Nachtmusik* (*Serenade,* for small orchestra), K. 525
———. *Quartet No. 14 in G Major,* K. 387 (strings)
———. *Quintet in A Major,* K. 581 (clarinet and string quartet)
*———. *Symphony No. 40 in G Minor,* K. 550
Prokofiev. *Classical Symphony in D Major*
*Puccini. *La Bohème* (opera)
Rachmaninoff. *Concerto No. 2 in C Minor for Piano and Orchestra*
Ravel. *Daphnis et Chloé Suite No. 2* (ballet suite for orchestra)
Rimsky–Korsakov. *Scheherazade* (orchestra)
Schubert. Songs (see collections by different artists)
*———. *Die Winterreise* (*The Winter Journey,* a song cycle)
Schumann. *Carnaval* (piano)
———. *Dichterliebe* (song cycle)
———. *Frauenliebe und Leben* (song cycle)
Shostakovitch. *Symphony No. 5*
Sibelius. *Symphony No. 5 in E Flat Major*
Strauss, R. *Ein Heldenleben* (*A Hero's Life,* symphonic poem)
*———. *Till Eulenspiegel* (orchestra)

*Stravinsky. *Petrouchka* (ballet suite)

———. *Le Sacre du Printemps* (*The Rite of Spring,* a ballet)

Tchaikovsky. *Concerto No. 1 in B Flat Minor for Piano and Orchestra*

*———. *Nutcracker Suite* (orchestra)

———. *Romeo and Juliet* (overture fantasy for orchestra)

———. *Symphony No. 5 in E Minor*

Wagner. *Die Meistersinger* (opera)

Wolf. Songs (collections by different artists)

Compositions recorded more than once by the same artist and/or conductor:

Beethoven. *Concerto in D Major for Violin and Orchestra* (Oistrakh)

Bruch. *Concerto in G Minor for Violin and Orchestra* (Milstein)

Khachaturian. *Concerto for Violin and Orchestra* (Oistrakh)

Mozart. *Eine Kleine Nachtmusik* (*Serenade,* for small orchestra; Von Karajan)

Prokofiev. *Concerto No. 1 in D Major for Violin and Orchestra* (Oistrakh)

Rimsky–Korsakov. *Scheherazade* (orchestra; Dorati)

Schubert. *Symphony No. 8 in B Minor* ("Unfinished"; Furtwängler)

Schumann. *Concerto in A Minor for Piano and Orchestra* (Novaes)

Shostakovitch. *Symphony No. 5* (Rodzinski)

Tchaikovsky. *Concerto in D Major for Violin and Orchestra* (Milstein, Oistrakh)

———. *Concerto No. 1 in B Flat Minor for Piano and Orchestra* (Gilels)

*———. *Nutcracker Suite* (orchestra; Woss)

———. *Symphony No. 6 in B Minor* ("Pathétique"; Rodzinski)

Wagner. *Die Meistersinger; Preludes* (Furtwängler)

BIBLIOGRAPHY

A Guide to Various Types of
Information about Music

BIBLIOGRAPHY

This bibliography is designed to help you find further information about music. The books listed here are arranged according to various categories of musical information, and are selected on the basis of their usefulness to the amateur listener. In no category does the bibliography attempt to be complete or definitive. These are books likely to be found in any public or college library. You may want to acquire some of them for your personal library.

Music Dictionaries and Encyclopedias

When you want a definition of, or information concerning, a musical term, or information about a composer, consult one of the following dictionaries.

Ammer, Christine. *Harper's Dictionary of Music:* Harper & Row, New York, 1972. Terms and names.

Apel, Willi. *The Harvard Dictionary of Music:* Harvard, Cambridge, Mass., 2nd ed., 1969. (Biographical entries are not included.)

Baker, Theodore. *Baker's Biographical Dictionary of Musicians:* G. Schirmer, New York, 5th ed., rev. by Nicholas Slonimsky, 1958. Supplement, 1965.

Blom, Eric. *Everyman's Dictionary of Music:* Dutton, New York, Rev. ed., 1954. A concise one-volume dictionary of terms and names.

Grove's Dictionary of Music and Musicians: St. Martin's, New York, 5th ed., 1954. Nine volumes; encyclopedic information about music and musicians. Supplement, 1961.

Scholes, Percy. *The Oxford Companion to Music:* Oxford, New York, 10th ed., ed. by John O. Ward, 1970.

Thompson, Oscar. *The International Cyclopedia of Music and Musicians:* Dodd, Mead, New York, 10th ed., ed. by Bruce Bohle, 1975. An extensive one-volume reference.

Watson, J. M. and Corinne. *Concise Dictionary of Music:* Dodd, Mead, New York, 1965.

Westrup, J. A., and F. L. Harrison. *New College Encyclopedia of Music:* Norton, New York, 1960.

Thematic Dictionaries

If you wish to find the principal themes of a given composition, or if you know a theme and are unable to identify it, consult one of the following works.

Barlow, Harold, and Sam Morgenstern. *A Dictionary of Musical Themes* (instrumental music): Crown, New York, 1948.

————. *A Dictionary of Opera and Song Themes:* Crown, New York, Rev. ed., 1976.

Burrows, Raymond, and Bessie Redmond. *Concerto Themes:* Simon & Schuster, New York, 1951.

————. *Symphony Themes:* Simon & Schuster, New York, 1942.

Concert Guides

When you seek information about a particular composition, consult one of the following books.

Ewen, David. *The World of 20th Century Music:* Prentice-Hall, New York, 1968.

Ferguson, Donald. *Masterworks of the Orchestral Repertoire:* Univ. of Minnesota Press. Minneapolis, 1954. Analytical notes on over 260 symphonic compositions by 53 composers.

Frankenstein, Alfred. *A Modern Guide to Symphonic Music:* Meredith Press, 1966. 246 compositions by 62 composers; includes themes in score.

Opera Guides

For information about an opera (composer, librettist, characters, synopsis of plot, and so on), consult one of the following books. Brief synopses are also given in *Grove's Dictionary,* Scholes' *Oxford Companion,* and Oscar Thompson's *Cyclopedia.* (See above under "Dictionaries.")

Biancolli, Louis. *The Opera Reader:* McGraw-Hill, New York, 1953. Contains 90 operas by 40 composers.

Cross, Milton. *The New Milton Cross Complete Stories of the Great Operas:* Doubleday, New York, 1955.

Howard, John Tasker. *The World's Great Operas:* Grosset & Dunlap, New York, 1950. Over 200 operas by 95 composers. Includes an index of operatic characters.

Kobbe, Gustave. *Kobbe's Complete Opera Book.* Putnam's, New York. 4th ed. by the Earl of Harewood, 1976. 1 volume, complete summaries, commentary, list of characters, principal themes in score of over 300 operas by over 100 composers.

Milligan, Harold Vincent. *Stories of the Famous Operas:* Permabooks, New York, 1950. Brief summaries of 70 popular operas.

Moore, Frank L. *Crowell's Handbook of World Opera:* T. Y. Crowell, New York, 1961.

Simon, Henry W. *Victor Book of the Opera:* Simon & Schuster, New York, 13th ed., 1968.

Record Catalogs

For guidance in the selection and purchase of recorded music, the following catalogs will be the most helpful. They can be obtained in most music stores, record libraries, and by subscription.

Schwann Record & Tape Guide. A monthly publication listing about 45,000 LP records. In addition to classical music, listed alphabetically by composer, the catalog contains listings of jazz, jazz anthologies, electronic music, classical collections, musicals, movies, and TV shows.

Folkways Records. Current catalogs contain complete lists of folk and ethnic music, listed alphabetically by continents, subdivided alphabetically by country and/or tribe. Also, they contain new album releases in jazz, gospel, blues roots, square dances, and other categories.

Music Appreciation

For supplementary reading, the following music appreciation textbooks will be helpful. They usually give biographical information and full discussions of specific compositions.

Bamberger, Jeanne Shapiro, and Howard Brofsky. *The Art of Listening,* 3rd ed.: Harper & Row, New York, 1975.

Daniels, Arthur, and Lavern Wagner. *Music:* Holt, Rinehart and Winston, New York, 1975.

Hoffer, Charles. *The Understanding of Music,* 3rd ed.: Wadsworth Publishing, Belmont, California, 1976.

Machlis, Joseph. *The Enjoyment of Music,* 3rd ed.: Norton, New York, 1970.

General Histories of Music

The following books will help you obtain general and specific information about music history. Consult the table of contents of a music history book to locate information about general topics; consult the index for specific names and terms.

Bauer, Marion, and E. R. Peyser. *Music Through the Ages:* Putnam's, New York, 3rd ed., rev. by Elizabeth E. Rogers, 1967.

Ferguson, Donald. *A History of Musical Thought:* Appleton-Century-Crofts, New York, 3rd ed., 1959.

Grout, Donald Jay. *A History of Western Music,* rev. ed.: Norton, New York, 1973.

Lang, Paul Henry. *Music in Western Civilization:* Norton, New York, 1941.

Leichtentritt, Hugo. *Music, History, and Ideas:* Harvard, Cambridge, Mass., 1938.

Miller, Hugh M. *History of Music:* Barnes & Noble, New York, 4th ed., 1973. A title in the *Barnes & Noble Outline Series.*

Sachs, Curt. *Our Musical Heritage:* Prentice-Hall, New York, 2nd ed., 1955.

Ulrich, Homer, and Paul Pisk. *A History of Music and Musical Styles:* Harcourt, Brace & World, 1963.

Historical Anthologies of Music

Historical anthologies in score listed here are indicated by (S) following the title; record anthologies are indicated by (R) following the title; combined score and record anthologies are indicated by (SR).

Davison, Archibald T., and Willi Apel. *Historical Anthology of Music* (S): 2 vols. Harvard University Press, 1950. Vol. 1, Oriental, Medieval, and

Renaissance Music; Vol. 2, Baroque, Rococo, and Pre-Classical Music. Each volume has commentaries and text translations in the back.

History of European Music (R): The Musical Heritage Society. Orpheus Series. Three LP discs (OR349/351), which are recordings of numbers 9 through 41 of the *Historical Anthology of Music,* above.

Historical Anthology of Music (R): Pleiades Records. Seven LP discs (P250/256), which are recordings of numbers 42 through late Renaissance of the Davison & Apel *Anthology* (S) listed above.

Lerner, Edward. *Study Scores of Musical Styles* (S): McGraw-Hill, 1968. Eighty-six complete examples of music from plainsong to Bach; descriptive commentaries and translations of texts.

Parrish, Carl, and John Ohl. *Masterpieces of Music Before 1750* (SR): Norton, 1951. A concise anthology of 50 representative examples of music from plainsong through the Baroque, with commentaries and text translations. Recordings of this music issued by Haydn Society HSE 9038/9040.

Parrish, Carl. *A Treasury of Early Music* (SR): Norton, 1958. A companion anthology to the above work. Recording by Haydn Society HSE 9100/9103.

Wennerstrom, Mary. *Anthology of Twentieth-Century Music* (S): Appleton-Century-Crofts, 1969. Twenty-three compositions representing various styles, media, and composers of the 20th century. Brief biographical and analytical commentaries.

Biography

For biographical information about composers, conductors, and performers, you will often find "thumbnail" sketches in the textbooks on music appreciation (consult their tables of contents or indexes). More extensive biographies are to be found in the music dictionaries (those of Grove, Thompson, and others). For book-length biographies, consult (1) *Schirmer's Guide to Books on Music and Musicians* (refer to the name of the musician), (2) the bibliographies at the ends of articles on musicians in some of the dictionaries listed above, or (3) biographies suggested in the bibliographies of music appreciation textbooks. In addition to these sources, the list below contains a few recent books about important composers and their music.

Bach: Karl Geiringer's *The Bach Family:* Oxford, New York, 1955.

Barber: Nathan Broder's *Samuel Barber:* G. Schirmer, New York, 1954.

Bartók: Halsey Stevens' *The Life and Music of Bela Bartók:* Oxford, New York, Rev. ed., 1964.

Copland: Julia Smith. *Aaron Copland:* Dutton, New York, 1955. Arthur Berger. *Aaron Copland:* Oxford, New York, 1953.

Corelli: Marc Pincherle. *Corelli: His Life, His Music:* Norton, New York, 1956.

Gershwin: Isaac Goldberg. *George Gershwin: A Study in American Music:* Ungar, New York, 1958. David Ewen. *George Gershwin: His Journey to Greatness:* Prentice-Hall, Englewood Cliffs, N. J., Rev. ed., 1970.

Grieg: Gerald Abraham, ed. *Grieg: A Symposium:* Univ. of Pennsylvania, Philadelphia, 1950.

Ives: Henry and Sidney Cowell. *Charles Ives and His Music:* Oxford, New York, 1955.

Liszt: Humphrey Searle. *The Music of Liszt:* De Graff, New York, 1954.

Milhaud: Darius Milhaud. *Notes without Music; An Autobiography:* Knopf, New York, 1953.

Mozart: Alfred Einstein. *Mozart: His Character, His Work:* Oxford, New York,

1945. Also, W. J. Turner's *Mozart: The Man and His Works:* Barnes & Noble, New York, Rev. ed., 1966.

Rachmaninoff: Victor I. Seroff. *Rachmaninoff:* Simon & Schuster, New York, 1952.

Ravel: Victor I. Seroff, *Maurice Ravel:* Holt, New York, 1953.

Schubert: Alfred Einstein. *Schubert: A Musical Portrait:* Oxford, New York, 1951.

Schumann: Gerald Abraham. (Robert) *Schumann: A Symposium:* Oxford, New York, 1951. Alan Walker, ed. *Robert Schumann: The Man and His Music:* Barnes & Noble, New York, 1974.

Sibelius: Robert Layton. *Sibelius and His World:* Viking, New York, 1970. Nils–Eric Ringbom. *Jean Sibelius:* Univ. of Oklahoma, Norman, 1954.

Vaughan Williams: E. T. Hurd. *Vaughn Williams:* T. Y. Crowell, New York, 1970.

Verdi: George Martin. *Verdi: His Music, Life and Times:* Dodd, Mead, New York, 1963. Joseph Wechsberg. *Verdi:* Putnams, New York, 1974.

Wagner: Robert Jacobs. *Wagner; In The Master Musicians Series:* Farrar, Straus, New York, 1949.

Miscellaneous Areas

The books listed below under various headings are suggested for further profitable reading and study.

American Music:

Barzun, Jacjues. *Music in American Life:* Doubleday, New York, 1956.

Chase, Gilbert. *America's Music:* McGraw-Hill, New York, 2nd ed., 1966.

Sablosky, Irving L. *American Music:* University of Chicago Press, Chicago, 1969.

Ballet:

Clarke, Mary, and Clement Crisp. *Making a Ballet:* Macmillan, New York, 1975.

Martin, John. *World Book of Modern Ballet:* World, Cleveland, 1952.

Terry, Walter. *Ballet Companion:* Dodd, Mead, New York, 1968.

Baroque Music:

Bukofzer, Manfred. *Music in the Baroque Era:* Norton, New York, 1947.

Chamber Music:

Ulrich, Homer. *Chamber Music:* Columbia Univ., New York, 2nd ed., 1966.

Concerto:

Hill, Ralph. *The Concerto:* Penguin, London, 1952.

Lang, Paul, ed. *The Concerto, 1800–1900:* Norton, New York, 1970.

Veinus, Abraham. *The Victor Book of Concertos:* Simon & Schuster, New York, 1948.

Dance:

Nettl, Paul. *The Story of Dance Music:* Philosophical Library, New York, 1947.

Sachs, Curt. *World History of the Dance:* Norton, New York, 1937.

Form:

Erickson, Robert. *The Structure of Music: A Listener's Guide:* Noonday, New York, 1963.

Leichtentritt, Hugo. *Musical Form:* Harvard, Cambridge, Mass., 1951.

Moore, R. O. *The Structure of Music: An Outine for Students:* Oxford, New York, 1935.

Gregorian Chant:
> Apel, Willi. *Gregorian Chant:* Indiana University Press, Bloomington, 1958.

Keyboard Music:
> Apel, Willi. *Masters of the Keyboard:* Harvard, Cambridge, Mass., 1947.

Medieval Music:
> Hughes, Dom Anselm. *Early Medieval Music:* Oxford, New York, 1954. Volume II of *The New Oxford History of Music.*
>
> Reese, Gustave. *Music in the Middle Ages:* Norton, New York, 1940.

Modern Music (The Twentieth Century):
> Austin, William. *Music in the 20th Century:* Norton, New York, 1966.
>
> Copland, Aaron. *Our New Music:* Norton, New York, Rev. ed., 1969.
>
> Deri, Otto. *Exploring Twentieth-Century Music:* Holt, Rinehart & Winston, New York, 1968.
>
> Hansen, Peter. *Twentieth Century Music,* 2nd ed.: Allyn & Bacon, Boston, 1967.
>
> Machlis, Joseph. *Introduction to Contemporary Music:* Norton, New York, 1961.
>
> Salzman, Eric. *Twentieth-Century Music: An Introduction:* Prentice-Hall, Englewood Cliffs, N.J., 1967.
>
> Wilder, Robert. *Twentieth-Century Music:* Wm. C. Brown, Dubuque, 1969.
>
> Yates, Peter. *Twentieth Century Music:* Pantheon Books, New York, 1966.

Opera (History):
> Grout, Donald J. *A Short History of Opera:* Columbia Univ., New York, 2nd ed., 2 vols., 1965.
>
> Knapp, J. Merrill. *The Magic of Opera:* Harper & Row, New York, 1972.

Psychology of Music:
> Lundin, Robert W. *The Objective Psychology of Music:* Ronald, New York, 2nd ed., 1967.
>
> Revesz, G. *Introduction to the Psychology of Music:* Oklahoma Univ., Norman, 1954.

Renaissance Music:
> Reese, Gustave. *Music in the Renaissance:* Norton, New York, Rev. ed., 1959.

Romantic Period:
> Einstein, Alfred. *Music in the Romantic Era:* Norton, New York, 1947.

Song:
> Hall, James Husst. *The Art Song:* Oklahoma Univ., Norman, 1953.

Theory (Elementary):
> Boatwright, Howard. *Introduction to the Theory of Music:* Norton, New York, 1956.
>
> Cole, William. *The Rudiments of Music:* Novello, London, 1951.
>
> Harder, Paul. *Basic Materials in Music Theory:* Allyn & Bacon, Boston, 3rd ed., 1975.
>
> Hill, Frank W., and Roland Searight. *Study Outline in the Elements of Music:* Wm. C. Brown, Dubuque, 6th ed., 1976.
>
> Jones, George T. *Music Theory:* Barnes & Noble, New York, 1974. A title in the *Barnes & Noble Outline Series.*

Appendix I.
Musical Notation

Musical notation serves mainly to indicate two properties of tone: pitch and duration (see Chapter 2).

Notation of Pitch. Musical notation is written on five horizontal lines called a *staff* (plural, *staves*):

The pitch range of a staff is indicated by a sign called a *clef*. There are three clef signs used in musical notation: G clef, C clef, and F clef. The G clef (or treble clef) locates the tone G by circling the "G line" above Middle C*:

The C clef indicates "Middle C"*:

This clef, usually pointing to the middle line of the staff, is also called the "viola clef" or the "alto clef" because that instrument

---

* Middle C can be located near the center of the piano keyboard, about 21 inches from the left end.

and that voice usually read music in the register around Middle C. The F clef (or bass clef) has two dots which locate the "F line" below Middle C:

F

The following chart shows you the pitch symbols on three staves, and above each staff are the corresponding white keys on a piano with their letter names.

Middle C

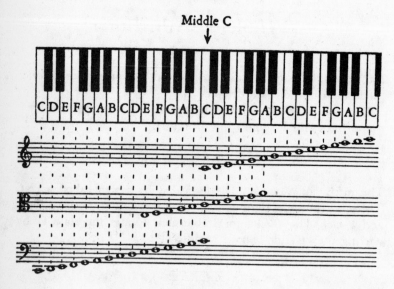

When a note on the staff is preceded by a sharp sign (♯) the tone is one half step higher and played on the piano one key to the right. Thus, the tone C♯ may be written: and played on the black key between C and D:

When a note on the staff is preceded by a flat sign (♭) the tone is one half step lower and played on the piano one key to the

left. Thus, the tone D♭ may be written: and played

on the black key between C and D (the same black key and the same sound as C♯):

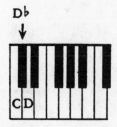

The pitch distance between any note and the next note of the *same* letter, either to the right or left on the keyboard, is called an octave. There are four octaves on the chart on the preceding page from the "low C" to the "high C."

Notes on the staff which are arranged in vertical position are played simultaneously:

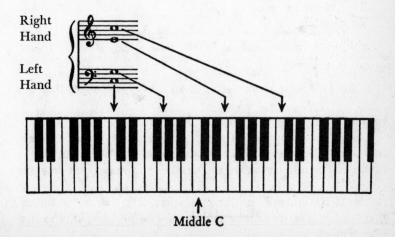

Such vertical groups of notes are called *chords*.

Notation of Duration (Note Values). To read music you need to know not only where a note is (its pitch position) but also how long a time it is held (its duration). The shape of a note indicates its time value. Duration of silence between notes is indicated by a *rest*. The following kinds of notes and the equivalent rest signs in parentheses are most commonly used in musical notation.

Whole note   𝅝   (▬)

Half note   𝅗𝅥   (▬)

Quarter note   𝅘𝅥   (𝄽)

Eighth note   𝅘𝅥𝅮   (𝄾)

Several eighth notes together:

Sixteenth note   𝅘𝅥𝅯   (𝄿)

Several sixteenth notes together:

Each kind of note is relatively twice as long as the next smaller value. Or, putting it another way, it takes two notes of one kind to make the same time value of the next larger kind of note: two half notes make one whole note, two sixteenth notes make one eighth note, etc.

Sometimes note values are divided by three's instead of two's. These are called triplet groups and are indicated by the sign
⌣̳³ . For example:

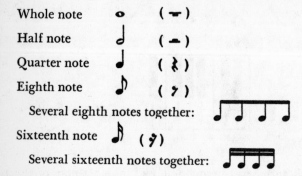

A dot following a note gives it an additional one-half of its regular value. Hence, 𝅘𝅥. = 𝅘𝅥 + 𝅘𝅥𝅮 and 𝅗𝅥. = 𝅗𝅥 + 𝅘𝅥 .

The *actual* time value of a note is determined by metronome indications, consisting of a note value, an equation sign, and a number. The number means the number of notes of that denomination to a minute. Thus, the indication 𝅘𝅥 = 60 means there are 60 quarter notes a minute, or one per second (a rather slow tempo).

Most music is written in meter (see pages 19 f). The measuring of music is indicated by a *time signature* appearing on the staff or staves at the beginning of the score. A time signature consists of two numbers: (1) the upper number indicates the number of beats to a measure (vertical lines drawn through the staff), and (2) the lower number indicates the kind of note that gets a beat. Thus, the time signature   means that there are three quarter notes to a measure (or any combination of note values that add up to the total value of three quarter notes):

Other Signs in Musical Notation. The principal signs used in musical notation have been explained. There are a few more signs which you will need to know in order to read music accurately.

The *fermata* (⌒) means to hold a note or chord longer than its normal value.

The *accent mark* above a note (> or ∧) gives extra stress to the note it accompanies; it means to play it louder.

The *crescendo mark* (———◁) indicates a gradual increase in loudness. The *decrescendo mark,* also called *diminuendo mark* (▷———), gradually decreases the loudness.

A dot over or under a note indicates *staccato,* i.e., detached, shortening the sound. Thus, ♩̣ or ♩̣ would be the approximate equivalent of ♪ ⅞ ⅞ ⅞.

A curved line above or below two or more notes means *legato,* i.e., connected, no silence between notes:

A passage or section of music between the signs 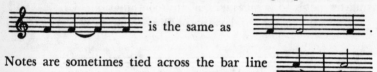 and is to be repeated.

When two notes are "tied" by a curved line, the tone is sounded for the duration of both values without being repeated. Thus,

is the same as .

Notes are sometimes tied across the bar line

so that, in this case, the quarter note is held over into the next measure without being repeated.

The principal signs for musical ornamentation are:

The *trill*, written , played .

The *mordent*, written , played .

The *inverted mordent*, written , played .

The *turn*, written , played .

The *appoggiatura*, written , played .

Certain abbreviations occur rather frequently in music. Dynamic indications (see page 44) are abbreviated as follows: p (piano), pp (pianissimo), mp (mezzo piano), f (forte), ff (fortissimo), mf (mezzo forte), sfz (sforzando), cresc. (crescendo), dim. (diminuendo). Other abbreviations are rit. (ritardando), accel. (accelerando), a tempo (return to the original tempo after a ritardando or accelerando), da capo (return to the beginning of the piece), dal segno (play from the sign 𝄋), al fine (to the end).

Tempo terms are usually written out (see page 18). Full definitions for them can be found in any good musical dictionary.

Key Signatures. A group of sharps or flat appearing immediately to the right of a clef sign at the beginning of every staff is called a *key signature*. Each sharp or flat, appearing on a line or a space of the staff, means that that tone (and all others of the same letter name) is to be raised (sharps) or lowered (flats) throughout the piece unless it is temporarily cancelled for the duration of the measure by the use of a natural sign (   ) appearing immediately to the left of a note.

A key signature also indicates the key in which a piece is written. Every key signature may indicate either a major or a minor key. Here is a chart of key signatures and the keys, major and minor, which each indicates.

No sharps, no flats: C major, A minor

One sharp: G major, E minor

Two sharps: D major, B minor

Three sharps: A major, F♯ minor

Four sharps: E major, C♯ minor

Five sharps: B major, G♯ minor

Six sharps: F♯ major, D♯ minor

Seven sharps: C♯ major, A♯ minor

One flat: F major, D minor

Two flats: B♭ major, G minor

Three flats: E♭ major, C minor

Four flats: A♭ major, F minor

Five flats: Db major, Bb minor

Six flats: Gb major, Eb minor

Scales. The melodic and harmonic construction of most music is based upon a series of consecutive tones called a *scale*. Although there are many different scale patterns to be found in music, the most commonly used are the major scale and the minor scale. Every major and minor scale is a pattern of whole steps (alternate keys on the piano, including the black keys) and half steps (adjacent keys on the piano). For example, C to C♯ or Db is a half step; C to D is a whole step. The major scale has a half step between the third and fourth scale degrees and again between the seventh and eighth scale degrees. For example, the C major scale has half steps between E and F and between B and the upper C; and all other scale degrees are a whole step apart:

(– indicates whole steps; ∪ indicates half steps). This scale is played entirely on the white keys of the piano.

The minor scale in its natural form has the following pattern of half steps between the second and third scale degrees and between the fifth and sixth scale degrees:

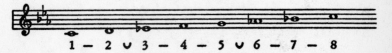

Notice that the C minor scale has three flats and, correspond-ingly, three black keys on the piano.

You can construct all the scales, major and minor, by using the key signature chart above, or by beginning with any tone and applying the pattern of half and whole steps.

Appendix II.
Index-Guide to Music

The following index, arranged alphabetically by composer (with a few exceptions), includes all the compositions listed at the end of every chapter. Arabic numbers after each title entry (also arranged alphabetically) indicate the *chapters* in which that particular composition is listed. Roman numerals after a title indicate movements.

Twenty-five Basic Compositions. This index lists in bold-faced type twenty-five basic compositions which can be used as the core of your study of music literature; collectively they represent almost all mediums, forms, periods, and nationalities, as well as other important categories of music literature. You can find them by looking under the names of the following composers: Bach (3), Bartók, Beethoven, Bizet, Brahms, Chopin, Copland, Debussy, Handel, Haydn, Hindemith, Mendelssohn, Mozart (2), Palestrina, Puccini, Ravel, Schubert, Schumann, Strauss (R.), Stravinsky, Tchaikovsky, and Wagner. (See also page xvii.)

235

Jolivet, André (1905–   )
  Concerto for Trumpet, Piano, and Strings: 10
Joplin, Scott (1868–1917)
  Maple Leaf Rag: 21
  Gladiolus Rag: 21
Josquin Des Prez (1450?–1521)
  Ave Maria (motet for *a cappella* choir; No. 19 in *Masterpieces of Music before 1750*): 15, 24, 27

K

Kabalevsky, Dmitri (1904–   )
  Concerto for Violin and Orchestra, Op. 48: 10
  Concerto for Cello and Orchestra, Op. 49: 10
  Preludes (24, piano): 16, 27
Kaufman, Armin (1902–   )
  Music for Trumpet and Strings: 10
Khachaturian, Aram (1903–1978)
  Concerto for Piano and Orchestra: 10
  Concerto for Violin and Orchestra: 30
  Saber Dance (from the ballet *Gayaneh;* orchestra, also arranged for piano): 18, 20
Kodály, Zoltán (1882–1967)
  Duo for Violin and Cello: 10
  Galanta Dances (orchestra): 20
  Háry János Suite (orchestra): 18, 23
  Missa Brevis in Tempore Belli (chorus, vocal solos, and organ): 24
Kreisler, Fritz (1875–1962)
  Rondino on a Theme by Beethoven (violin and piano): 2, 14, 25
Křenek, Ernst (1900–   )
  Bagatelles (4, piano): 16
  Pieces for Piano: 5, 10, 16, 27

L

Lalo, Édouard (1823–1892)
  Symphonie Espagnole (violin and orchestra): 10, 18, 23, 30
Landino, Francesco (c. 1325–1397)
  Chi più le vuol sapere (Who wishes to know them more,

ballata; No. 14 in *Masterpieces of Music before 1750*): 6, 22, 27
Lasso, Orlando di (c. 1530–1594)
  Tristis Est Anima Mea (Sad Is My Soul, motet for *a cappella* choir; No. 23 in *Masterpieces of Music before 1750*): 6, 9, 15, 24, 27
Leclair, Jean (1697–1764)
  Concerto in A Minor for Violin and Orchestra: 10
  Sonatas (8, for flute and continuo): 10
Leoncavallo, Ruggiero (1858–1919)
  I Pagliacci (opera): 19
  "Vesti la giubba": 9
Liszt, Franz (1811–1886)
  La Campanella (piano): 10, 13, 16, 25, 27
  Concerto No. 1 in E Flat Major for Piano and Orchestra: 10, 17, 27
  Étude de Concert No. 3 in D Flat Major ("Un Sospiro," for piano): 16, 27
  A Faust Symphony (orchestra, tenor solo, and male chorus): 10, 18
  Finale: 9
  Hungarian Rhapsody No. 2 in C Sharp Minor (piano or orchestra): 8, 10, 16, 23, 27
  Mephisto Waltz (piano or orchestra): 18, 20
  Les Préludes (symphonic poem based on Lamartine's *Méditations Poétiques*): 10, 11, 16, 18, 25, 27
  Variations on the Bach Prelude, "Weinen, klagen" (piano): 13
Locke, Matthew (1620?–1677)
  Consort of Four Parts (contrapuntal fantasies for small string ensembles): 10, 16
Lockwood, Normand (1906–   )
  Concerto for Organ and Brasses: 10
Loeffler, Charles (1861–1935)
  Memories of My Childhood (symphonic poem): 18
Loeillet, Jean-Baptiste (1680–1730)
  Sonata for Flute, Oboe, and Continuo: 10

Index of Subjects